STYLE FOLLOWS FUNCTION

ARCHITECTURE OF
Marcus T. Reynolds

Eugene J. Johnson

WITH PHOTOGRAPHS BY
Ralph Lieberman

D1279091

Washington Park Press, Ltd.   Mount Ida Press

ALBANY, NEW YORK

Printed in the United States of America.

Library of Congress Cataloging-in-Publication Data
Johnson, Eugene J., 1937-
        Style follows function: architecture of Marcus T. Reynolds / Eugene J. Johnson with photographs by Ralph Lieberman.
        128 p. 28 cm.
        Includes bibliographical references and index.
        ISBN 1-881324-01-X
        1. Reynolds, Marcus T. (Marcus Tullius), 1869-1937. – Criticism and interpretation.
        2. Eclecticism in architecture – United States. I. Lieberman, Ralph. II. Title.
        NA737.R48J65   1993   93-24456
        720'.92–dc20   CIP

Copublished by:

Washington Park Press Ltd.
7 Englewood Place
Albany, New York 12203
518-465-0169 • 518-438-5391

Mount Ida Press
4 Central Avenue
Albany, New York 12210
518-426-5935

Book design: Kristina Almquist Design
Cover design: Karelis & Timm
Printing: Thomson–Shore Inc.
Photography credits: All photographs of buildings are by Ralph Lieberman, and all photographs of Marcus Reynolds drawings, which are in a private collection, are by Nick Whitman, except for the following: Albany Institute of History and Art Collection, Fig. 35; Albany Institute of History and Art, McKinney Library Architectural Drawing Collection, Figs. 108, 111; Albany Institute of History and Art, McKinney Library Photograph Collection, figs. 49, 93, 96, 109, 119, 133; Amsterdam Savings Bank, Figs. 47, 48; author, Figs. 34, 66; Arnold Brunner, *Studies for Albany*, Figs. 104, 105, 106; Robert Cohn Collection, Fig. 42; Morris Gerber Collection, Figs. 15, 16, 17, 19, 22, 23, 25, 26; Mr. and Mrs. C. H. Grose Collection, Fig. 64; Historic Albany Foundation, Fig. 118; New York Historical Association, Figs. 12, 13, 124 and p. 6; private collection, Figs. 3, 4, 5, 6, 8, 94, 129, 130 and p. 92; Norman Rice Collection, Fig. 9; Margaret Satterthwaite, Fig. 11; Schenectady County Historical Society, Fig. 29; Betsy van Ostenbrugge Collection, Fig. 65; Williams College Archives and Special Collections, Fig. 7; Harry Yates, Fig. 2 and opp. p. 1.

CONTENTS

for Eugene and Nick
who make me happy to be a father

PREFACE

This book has been written to accompany an exhibition of the work of the architect Marcus T. Reynolds (1869-1937) at the Williams College Museum of Art (October 7, 1993, to February 6, 1994) and at the Albany Institute of History and Art (March 19, 1994, to June 5, 1994). Because almost nothing has been written on Reynolds since his lifetime, this book will have to serve both as an exhibition catalogue and as an introductory study of his work. For that reason, the standard catalogue format of a general essay followed by separate entries for each work displayed has been abandoned in favor of a text that we hope will prove more useful after the exhibition has closed.

In the text, rather than give a strictly chronological account of Reynolds's career, I have ordered his buildings according to type, because that seemed a more fruitful way to study them. His most important work, the Delaware & Hudson and Albany Evening Journal Buildings, has been given its own chapter, while other chapters are devoted to banks, houses, funerary monuments and, finally, a diverse group of commercial and public structures. No attempt has been made to produce a complete list of designs by a man who practiced architecture for some forty busy years. Instead, what is offered here is a selective group of buildings that seemed particularly important, or admirable, or typical, or some combination of those qualities.

The foundation of this study is the set of thirty-eight diaries, or day books, that Reynolds kept in his office from 1899 to 1937. From a reading of these diaries came a list of commissions and clients, which then had to be checked against other evidence. The second major source of information about Reynolds's career is the very large number of drawings from his office that have been preserved. The drawings form the backbone, visually, of the exhibition, and they also document many of his works, including some that no longer stand. The drawings are not all preserved, however. The main set of ink drawings on linen for the D & H Building, for instance, has disappeared. The drawings for the Clark gardens at Cooperstown, another major work, are also gone, as are those for the Van Rensselaer Houses in Albany. Early sketches for buildings are notably lacking. It seems that someone systematically eliminated such drawings from Reynolds's files. That is too bad, because we are left with almost no visual record of how his final designs were reached.

In college and graduate school I was trained to loathe precisely the kind of architecture Marcus Reynolds practiced. The apologists for the modern movement in architecture were so successful in their polemics against any twentieth-century building that used historical architectural sources or ornament that the minds of generations of students were poisoned against the work of people like Reynolds. Only in the last twenty years or so have attitudes begun to shift toward something more balanced. If this study makes nothing else clear, it should demonstrate that architects like Reynolds used their historical sources with intelligence and sensitivity, and with considerable attention to local history and custom. Reynolds understood how historical architectural styles, which for him carried certain associations, could be used to make political and social points.

In the fifties and sixties, we were also trained to ignore the work of architects who were not great innovating geniuses (we knew who those were, because they were assiduous self-publicists). Now, one can see this attitude breaking down, and the work of architects like Reynolds studied, not just because the buildings themselves can be wonderful, but also because looking at the work of A- and B+ architects enormously enriches our sense of what has happened in American architecture. There are advantages, moreover, to studying a geographically concentrated set of clients such as Reynolds's, because it is essential to understand the clients and the milieu in which they operated before one can understand the buildings. The reader should be aware that something of the zeal of the reformed reprobate lurks in these pages.

ACKNOWLEDGEMENTS

Norman Rice. That is the name that heads the list of the many people I want to thank for helping to make this book and exhibition possible. It all started a few years ago at a lunch organized by my cherished colleague, Sheafe Satterthwaite, with whom I was teaching a course on cities. We wanted our students to experience a city firsthand, and Albany recommended itself for convenience. Since we knew little about Albany, Sheafe thought we might learn something by having lunch with Norman, but little did we realize that we were about to experience the man who knows almost everything about Albany. Norman slyly suggested that it might be interesting to do something on Marcus Reynolds. After initially dismissing the idea, I started to look at Reynolds's buildings and to realize that they were worth studying. Now, many lunches later, Norman is my teacher and friend. His contributions to this book are so many that his name should be on the title page as co-author. But I would not want him blamed for its mistakes; he has saved me from too many of those already.

The second gray eminence to enter the picture was Kenneth G. Reynolds, Jr., great-nephew of Marcus and an architect in his own right. He has been extraordinarily generous with his time and in making available the large number of Reynolds drawings that have made the exhibition and the book possible. Without his cooperation, all this would not have happened. We have also received generous support from Mr. and Mrs. Marcus T. Reynolds; he too is a great-nephew.

The exhibition has been assisted by generous grants from the Graham Foundation and from the Mellon Foundation, for which I am particularly grateful. Most of the writing of this volume was done while I was Lehman Fellow at the Center for the Humanities and Social Sciences, Williams College, during the spring semester of 1992. There, Jean-Bernard Bucky and Rosemary Lane were marvelously helpful.

In carrying out the research and assembling the material for the book, I have been blessed with three remarkable student assistants: Greg Woods, Damon Hemmerdinger and Heather Bensko. Greg and I spent a whole summer combing through the Reynolds diaries. Such picky archival work, I am glad to say, did not dissuade him from entering graduate school in art history. Damon actually volunteered to help — in my experience, a unique offer. Heather's hard work got the manuscript together, and, as an independent study project, she has designed the exhibition, for which she and Jill Bernheimer executed a model.

Much of the research on Reynolds has been carried out in the McKinney Library of the Albany Institute of History and Art, where I have had unstinting assistance from the head of the library, Prudence Backman, and two superb librarians, Susan Safford and Mary Schifferli. Another miracle worker of information retrieval has been Betty Allen of the Union College library. I would like to thank the helpful staffs at the New York State Library in Albany, and the public libraries in Albany, Amsterdam, Catskill, Glens Falls, Hudson and Troy. I have received much appreciated assistance from the staffs of the Williams College Library and the Williamsiana Collection.

A remarkable number of people, from a remarkable number of places, have been helpful. I would like to thank, deeply and in alphabetical order, Mimi Danzig Arnold, Raymond Beecher, Bruce Cole, David P. Currey, Jr., Catherine Huyck Elmore, Rebecca Evans, Ruth Anne Evans, Violet Fallone, Morris Gerber, Mr. and Mrs. C. H. Grose, James Gwynn, S. Garrett Haefner, Betty Hallenstein, Marshall Hannock, Patricia A. Hayner, Caroline Keck, James Kettlewell, Roger F. Lane, Mr. and Mrs. Arthur Lord, Kate and Bill McLaughlin, Kenneth W. Parker, Francis A. Poulin, Meile Rockefeller, Douglas G. Roque, Caroline Peltz Schultze, Earle G. Shettleworth, Jr., Douglas Sinclair, Betsy Van Oostenbrugge, Gilbert Vincent, Diana Waite, Wally Wheeler and Harry Yates.

Colleagues have also been extremely generous with time and support. I have been lucky enough to have a number of stimulating and informative talks with one of the great figures in the field of American architecture, William H. Pierson. Mark Hewitt and William Morgan were kind enough to read portions of the manuscript and make useful comments. As a neophyte in the field, I needed all the help I could get from such experts. My thanks also to Zirka Filipczak, who gave the text a very thoughtful reading, and to Matthew Rohn and Sheafe Satterthwaite. And, in the colleague category, to my wife, Leslie Nicholson Johnson, who over the years it took to do this work has not only been unstinting in her support but has also consistently prodded me to ask hard questions about what I was doing. Whenever the trees and shrubs and flowers I was finding got too fascinating, she always insisted that they made up a forest. A colleague and old friend, who has made a most substantial contribution to the book and the exhibition, is Ralph Lieberman, whose photographs adorn these pages. Ralph's pictures supply the architectural historian with something that is rare — views of buildings that are handsome objects in themselves, but that do not achieve their own beauty by telling lies about the structures they depict. Many of Ralph's observations on Reynolds's work have found their way into the text.

The staff of the Williams College Museum of Art has been wonderful to work with on this exhibition. I want to thank them all, particularly Linda Shearer, Rod Faulds, Deborah Menaker Rothschild, Vivian Patterson, Marion Goethals and Zelda Stern. The staff at the Albany Institute has also been wonderful, and I would single out for thanks Christine Miles and Tammis Groft.

Anne Older of Washington Park Press and Diana Waite of Mount Ida Press graciously agreed to publish this book as a joint effort. They have made it by far the happiest experience I have had with a publication. For his support of the publication I offer my sincere thanks to President Francis Oakley of Williams College.

Unconventional,

yet law abiding;

spontaneous,

yet cultivated.

INTRODUCTION

In Edith Wharton's *The Age of Innocence*, Dallas Archer, a New Yorker from an old family, chose a profession that had recently become acceptable for a free-spirited young man of his class. He became an architect.

The young men nowadays were emancipating themselves from the law and business and taking up all sorts of new things. If they were not absorbed in state politics or municipal reform, the chances were that they were going in for Central American archaeology, for architecture or landscape-engineering....[1]

In Albany, Marcus T. Reynolds, a young man who was descended from the old families about which Wharton wrote, embarked on an architectural career in the 1890s, a decade before the fictitious Dallas Archer.[2]

Reynolds (Fig. 1) was a social creature, a bachelor who dined abroad in Albany's best houses, who lunched with his buddies at the Fort Orange Club, who played a lot of poker, who spent his weekends golfing at the Albany Country Club or traveling around to visit friends at their country places. Tailored in a slightly old-fashioned way, he was "a tall man with watery eyes and the smell of someone who ate and drank well," according to Caroline Peltz Schultze, a younger cousin.[3] When you were with him, she added, you felt you were in the presence of someone important.

This well-fed, well-dressed, prepossessing personage had a sardonic sense of humor. On New Year's Day, 1930, he gave a luncheon party for the younger set. Among the guests were the captain of the Yale football team, a son of Franklin and Eleanor Roosevelt and his fiancee, and Erastus Corning, eventually to be mayor of Albany for an inordinately long time. The menu included "Lobster Chops," the specialty of a local caterer, and vast quantities of wine, even though Prohibition was the law of the land. Knowing that his young guests were unused to liquid luncheons, Reynolds amused himself by seeing how they handled themselves while getting soused at midday.[4] He could play with clients in similar ways.

In his office Reynolds kept a diary, or day book, from 1899 until his death in 1937.[5] These diaries are useful because they tell us what every-

one in his office worked on every day for thirty-eight years, and that information allows us to construct a list of his clients and commissions. But the diaries also contain a lot of material extraneous to the practice of architecture. Deaths of people he knew or people in public life were set down, often with a note about how they died or an assessment of their contributions to humanity. The comments can be acerbic: "Charles Gibson died in bed (his own)" or "William Jennings Bryan died in bed (too good for him)." Of his chief architectural rival in Albany, Albert Fuller, Reynolds noted: "A W Fuller died in his office of heart disease while listening to the ball game over his radio. St. Louis 8 — Detroit 3 (5 errors)."[6] The diaries also contain comments on Reynolds's health, his frequent trips abroad, current events (on July 1, 1934, "Hell of a revolution in Germany"), the weather, the income tax, Prohibition, clients[7] and even friends. From time to time he would draw on the edge of a page a little amoeba-like form with a dot in the center. Those marks were explained with great gentility by a helpful librarian: "He made those when he had been out with a lady and *had a good time*." Often Reynolds wrote down exclamations of dismay — "A Damned Black Day" — but he almost never entered comments on architecture. From the diaries, it would be impossible to know Marcus Reynolds's deepest thoughts about what he spent

Facing page. Detail, desk of Marcus T. Reynolds, 98 Columbia Street, Albany, photograph c. 1935

Fig. 1. Kenneth G. Reynolds, Portrait of Marcus T. Reynolds, 1919

1

his life doing. He had, nonetheless, a clear sense of good and bad, of who in the profession was admirable and who was not. His restrained enthusiasm for his fellow architects appeared in an entry of November 22, 1925: "J. Stewart Barney died — a better architect than many & that is not saying much."

He received people in the building trades with a mixture of fear and contempt. A white glove was kept in the office to put on when he had to shake hands with a contractor or workman. "You never know where that hand has been," he reportedly said. In correspondence, he could be courtly and complimentary to firms that supplied materials for his buildings, as long as the work came up to his exacting standards. The Atlantic Terra Cotta Company made the mistake of sending him a sample with a smooth finish, when he wanted rough. Reynolds suggested that they try to produce something more interesting than a chocolate eclair. They, in turn, offered to make a gargoyle of Reynolds's head for the Albany Evening Journal Building. "May we ask," purred a representative of Atlantic Terra Cotta, "if you want this caricature of yourself to reflect benevolence, or an architect's professional expression?"[8]

The Albany in which Reynolds grew up and in which he chose to practice was a significant place in the America of his day. As the capital of the most populous state in the union, Albany was important politically. During Reynolds's professional lifetime, two governors, Theodore and Franklin D. Roosevelt, became president, and Charles Evans Hughes and Al Smith ran unsuccessfully for that office. These men were not unknown to Reynolds. On December 22, 1928, Reynolds "Dined at the Executive Mansion. The Al Smiths good bye dinner of 30." He returned to the governor's mansion for the New Year's Eve dance that Eleanor and Franklin Roosevelt gave in 1929, and the next day he had one of their sons to lunch.[9]

Albany was not just a political town. It had its own society, made up of well-educated and well-connected members of the old Dutch and Yankee families that dominated life in the Hudson Valley. Tied through marriage and kinship to most of the major clans of New York and Boston, these Albanians rightly saw themselves as no less cosmopolitan than their relatives who lived on the coast. Reynolds was born into this society, and from it he drew many of his clients. He was also

heir to both Dutch and Yankee cultures, a dual heritage that informed his life and his art. Albany had, as well, its share of "self-made men," some of whom came to Reynolds for buildings, perhaps because using a society architect enhanced their own status. His clients were part of a national managerial class — the ones who ran the country by serving in the national or state governments or by directing major banks and corporations. On the side, they were also writers, students of history, and collectors of art or objects of rarity and historical importance. One Reynolds client, Seymour Van Santvoord, a banker and lawyer, devoted almost as much time to writing about history and archaeology as he devoted to his business affairs. Reynolds's architecture clearly reflected the political, financial and intellectual interests of these clients.

Like his clients, Marcus Reynolds took history seriously, particularly the history of Albany and its early Dutch settlers. A writer on architecture in his early years, he published a learned article that lamented the passing of the Dutch houses of the Albany area.[10] As a writer, Reynolds also contributed significantly to a compendious volume on the genealogy of his own family. His first architectural work, from 1893, involved removing the old Van Rensselaer Manor House, which belonged to his cousins, from its site north of Albany and re-erecting it in Williamstown, Massachusetts, as the Sigma Phi fraternity house. In 1923 he purchased and donated to the city of Albany the full-length portrait of the city's first mayor, Pieter Schuyler, and he designed the frame in which the portrait still hangs in the mayor's office.

Reynolds's interest in history was shared not only by many of his clients but also to a remarkable degree by his brother, Cuyler, who might fairly be characterized as a history nut. For many years the director of what is now the Albany Institute of History and Art, Cuyler published three works that are essential to the study of the Albany area — one an eight-hundred-page chronological list of events in Albany from its founding to 1906,[11] and a four-volume and a three-volume genealogical history of the Hudson and Mohawk Valleys.[12] The four-volume work opens with an account of the life of Kiliaen Van Rensselaer, the Amsterdam diamond merchant given a vast tract of land around the site of Albany in the seventeenth century. It closes, some two thousand pages later, with the ongoing story of the

life of Marcus T. Reynolds, architect. In all seven volumes one finds a vast reservoir of information about many of Marcus Reynolds's clients and their families. The preoccupation with origins that these volumes demonstrate should alert us to the fact that the past was a dominant force in Reynolds's life. Making the past serve the present was a major theme in his architecture. On Reynolds's desk in his house at 98 Columbia Street stood a bust of the Emperor Augustus (Fig. 2), and behind Augustus hung a view of Rome around 1600.[13] History presided even over the paying of his personal bills

Much of Albany's historic architecture has been so badly treated in the post-World War II period that it now takes a leap of the imagination to realize that the city had a vital architectural life in the nineteenth and early twentieth centuries. As a child, Reynolds grew up amidst works by Philip Hooker, Richard Upjohn, Leopold Eidlitz, Henry Hobson Richardson, Robert W. Gibson and Russell Sturgis. During Reynolds's career those buildings were joined by designs of McKim, Mead & White; Shepley, Rutan & Coolidge; York &

Sawyer; Henry Ives Cobb; and Palmer & Hornbostel. Few, if any, cities its size could display such a bouquet of the flower of the American architectural profession. The city had good architecture because its citizens hired good architects. Reynolds played a large part in constructing or reconstructing the visual world of Albany. His own buildings made a setting for his life; the clubs and houses he frequented were often his own designs, as was the skyscraper in which he kept his office.

Reynolds became aware of the American architectural scene when he was a student in the 1880s. For him that world had two centers, Boston and New York, the big cities to which Albany was most directly connected. In Boston H.H. Richardson reigned supreme, even after his death in 1886. The architectural king of New York was Richard Morris Hunt. Educated at the École des Beaux-Arts in Paris, both men brought to this country the rational training they had received in France. Richardson produced the most coherent group of buildings of the age, while Hunt almost singlehandedly raised the social status of the profession to something which a young gentleman of Reynolds's class might aspire to join.

The architecture of the entire nineteenth century had been obsessed by history, either in terms of how to use it or how to create a new architectural style for the nineteenth century by avoiding its use. In Germany Heinrich Hübsch had posed what turned out to be the architectural question of the century: "In what style should we build?" There were, of course, no easy answers. Historical styles, architects and clients discovered, could be remarkably flexible in meaning. Clever minds could put one style to the service of quite opposing functions or ideas. Throughout the century, architects fought endlessly over the appropriateness of one style to different uses or meanings. Frequently an architect chose a style because of the associations which that style was understood to bring with it. One of the brightest American observers of the architectural scene at the end of the century, Mariana Griswold Van Rensselaer, put the situation very clearly. Her carefully chosen words express a generally held assessment of the history of nineteenth-century architecture at the moment that Reynolds's architectural consciousness was being formed:

Fig. 2. Desk of Marcus T. Reynolds, 98 Columbia Street, photograph c. 1935

in our architecture we have largely followed England... [which] has been through a varied and perplexing architectural experience since the beginning of the century. First, there dawned the Greek revival.... Then came the Gothic revival, bringing about the famous 'battle of the styles' between classicism in general and mediaevalism in general, and the faction fights (almost as bitter) of the mediaevalists among themselves. Every phase of English Gothic had its exclusive advocates, and there were others, almost as exclusive, who enforced in stone as well as in speech and print the claims of French or Tuscan or Venetian builders as the best models for the modern architect to follow. Then, just when the main battle seemed to have decided itself in favor of mediaevalism...began an unexpected reaction among the younger men into a love for...'Queen Anne'...which most rarely counts among its qualities those of discretion, sobriety, and dignity.[14]

For most of the nineteenth century, architects worked in one, or at most a few, historic styles. The great Richardson, for instance, had devoted himself to his own highly original version of the Romanesque. During the course of the 1880s, however, a shift toward a more inclusive use of historical styles took place, particularly in the work of the New York firm of McKim, Mead & White. They cast a wide net in terms of time, place and building type to find styles appropriate to the great variety of their commissions.[15] The closer the present use of a building was to an old function, the more likely McKim, Mead & White were to make it look like its historic prototype. The farther the new building strayed from an old function, the less they made it resemble an old source.[16] Within a flexible building type like houses, they could simultaneously make designs that looked back to the Italian Renaissance, to the American Colonial period or to the Middle Ages, while also developing a native domestic architecture we now know as the Shingle Style.[17] By 1896, when Reynolds first began to practice architecture, McKim, Mead & White, by exploring numerous styles, had established a way of thinking about the use of historical prototypes into which Reynolds readily fell.

McKim, Mead & White's work was based on a wide scholarly knowledge of architectural history, fostered at century's end by the publication of a plethora of books and by the founding of several magazines devoted to architecture. The good fortune of late nineteenth-century architects in having history more widely open to them than it had been to earlier generations was seen as a "vast advantage" by Mariana Van Rensselaer.[18] Her sentiments were shared by A. D. F. Hamlin, a

Paris-trained architect who would become Reynolds's teacher: "Let us be catholic in our criticism and study of architecture, and we shall find our resources of design wonderfully enlarged and enriched."[19]

The purpose of studying history, according to these writers, was to learn how problems had been solved by great architects. Van Rensselaer and Hamlin thought architects should have a broad base of knowledge of architectural precedents to help them find solutions for contemporary problems. Rightly used, great knowledge of the past would lend authority to an architect's work, without compromising the architect's own chance for personal growth and change.[20] But Hamlin, an architect himself, recognized that the storehouse of knowledge available to architects could be dangerous as well as helpful.[21] Ideally, through study of the work of great designers, architects of the present would learn the laws of architectural composition. According to Hamlin, these laws were like the rules of grammar — "less detailed and specific...but none the less binding."[22] As a theoretician, Hamlin was quite pragmatic. He was more interested that the building come out a strongly unified expression of plan, structure, function, form and meaning than it be a clearly articulated statement of theory.[23] From the lack of architectural statements in Reynolds's diaries, it may be fair to conclude that he was no theoretician at all.

Almost all Americans in the architectural community at the turn of the century felt they were living in an age in which technology, industry and democratic politics had created a new way of living. The times required a novel architecture, and America needed to establish its own architectural traditions, independent of Europe. Naturally, not every American agreed on the best method for arriving at this goal. Writers like Van Rensselaer and Hamlin believed that change could come only through an evolutionary process. An American architecture would eventually appear by adapting established architectural grammar to the problems of modern times in a new land. Although others of their countrymen were arguing for wholly novel forms, they felt no need to invent a new architectural language. That, according to Van Rensselaer, made as little sense as writing "something else than English ere we can have a literature essentially our own."[24]

Perhaps the most outspoken proponent of a new architectural language was Frank Lloyd

Wright, who hardly shared the faith of Van Rensselaer and Hamlin in a Darwinian arrival at something new and appropriate for American conditions. (Wright and Reynolds were almost exact contemporaries, the former born two years before the latter.) Wright consciously sought an architecture no longer bound to that of the past,[25] an architecture that expressed the democratic spirit of the New World and a unity of building and landscape. His first clear expression of his architectural intentions, an article in *Architectural Record* entitled "In the Cause of Architecture," bore a preface by the editors that put Wright's remarks in the context of the debate about how to create an American architectural style. They noted that the proponents of the new consistently espoused turning away from the study of historical architecture to the study of nature.[26] Indeed, Wright's essay is a plea to use the direct study of nature as a means to achieve simplicity and an organic connection of architecture to the land. All great architecture of the past, according to Wright, had grown directly from the observation of nature. In the twentieth century, he argued, an understanding of nature had to be accompanied by a profound understanding of the possibilities of the new industrial materials for architectural design.

Wright felt the need for an architecture that expressed the individuality of each client in a democratic society. Wright found his ideal client "chiefly among American men of business with unspoiled instincts and untainted ideas....the 'common sense' of the thing appeals to him. While the 'cultured' are still content with their small château, Colonial wedding cakes, English affectations or French millinery, he prefers a poor thing but his own."[27] An accomplished polemicist, Wright pronounced American aesthetics "dyspeptic from incontinent indulgence in 'Frenchite' pastry." He exulted in the "democratic character" of his exteriors, singling out their "lack, wholly, of what the professional critic would deem architecture; in fact, most of the critic's architecture has been left out."[28] That is, references to historical styles had been (mostly) omitted.

It was exactly this kind of polemical language, skillfully employed by Wright and others, that drove the brand of architecture practiced by Reynolds into the oblivion from which it has only begun to escape in the last twenty years. Together with a few other major figures of twentieth-century architecture, Wright cultivated the idea of the architect as solitary genius, as the great creative master whose work alone is worthy of admiration and emulation. Architecture that did not bear the mark of genius was to be ignored by the truly cultivated. Most writers on architecture earlier in this century bought this marvelously self-promoting line and focused their attention on "heroic" figures like Wright, Mies van der Rohe and Le Corbusier. Not for those writers the point of view of the conservative Van Rensselaer, who expressed an antithetical notion of what was worthy of the attention of the studious. Writing on English cathedrals, which she admired even though she found them inferior to French examples, she remarked sharply: "There is no more stupid mood for student or traveler than one which refuses to delight itself in anything but the very best. The second best — yes, the twentieth best — produced in the noble days of art is good enough to give a wise man pleasure, and the wiser he is the more pleasure he will be able to take in it."[29]

Wright saw American architecture, as he practiced it, becoming simpler, closer to nature, more attuned to the expression of the individuality of the client, more in tune with modern processes.[30] By implication, it would distance itself farther and farther from historical sources. In contrast, Mariana Van Rensselaer proposed a course more closely tied to the architectural past: "We should be independent in a scholarly way — unconventional, yet law abiding; spontaneous, yet cultivated; free to do new things, yet bound not to do them in crude and blundering and illiterate fashion."[31] When Van Rensselaer wrote these words, Marcus T. Reynolds was about to enter college. His architecture would be a fulfillment of her hopes.

*I am
more in love
with
my profession
than anything else.*

CHAPTER 1

AN ARCHITECT'S BEGINNINGS

How Marcus Tullius Reynolds came to architecture is not at all clear. Little in his family background — for whatever that may be worth — would suggest an interest in things artistic. Around 1830 his maternal grandfather, Colonel William Tremper Cuyler (1802-64), had purchased a handsome house with a classical portico, built in 1813-14 in western New York. That house, which had a splendid view of the Genesee Valley and the village of Cuylerville, which Reynolds's grandfather had laid out, burned in 1857, before Reynolds was born. The memory of the house was still strong in the family in the early years of the twentieth century, however. Colonel Cuyler, before becoming a gentleman farmer, had been a manufacturer of carriages in Rochester, where he had moved from Albany to seek his fortune shortly after the opening of the Erie Canal.[1]

Reynolds bore the good neoclassical name Marcus Tullius (as in Cicero) of his paternal grandfather, who had been born in 1788 in Montgomery County, New York, and graduated in 1808, second in his class, from Union College.[2] In 1811 he was admitted to the bar, and he practiced law in Johnstown, New York, for seventeen

years before removing to Albany, where he lived out the rest of his days. He also interested himself in railroads, becoming president of three small lines, one of which, prophetically, became part of the Delaware & Hudson system, for which our Marcus Tullius designed his most important building. The elder Marcus Tullius Reynolds died in 1864.

Marcus Tullius Reynolds and his second wife, Elizabeth Ann Dexter, had a son, Dexter Reynolds (1828-1906), who graduated in 1848 from Union College, where he belonged to Sigma Phi, the same fraternity his son would join at Williams. He attended Harvard Law School and was admitted to the bar in 1851, after which he practiced with at least three different firms. Dexter was an inventor who held twenty or so patents, none of which seems to have brought him particular fame or remuneration.

Dexter Reynolds married Catherine Maley Cuyler (1845-75) in 1864. Reynolds referred to his parents' wedding in his diary on April 19, 1934: "Seventieth anniversary of marriage of D.R. and C.M.C. in Rochester The church being draped in black because of Lincoln's assassination, the wedding had to be in the Cuyler house."

Facing page. Fernleigh, Stephen and Susan Clark House, Cooperstown, New York, view of bridge across Susquehanna River, 1927-28

Fig. 3. Marcus T. Reynolds (far right) and friends, Lake Luzerne, New York, photograph, summer, 1889

The marriage, begun under lugubrious circumstances, produced two sons: Cuyler, born in 1866, and Marcus Tullius, born in 1869 in Great Barrington, Massachusetts. (What Catherine Cuyler Reynolds was doing in Great Barrington when it came time to give birth to her second child no one seems to know.) In 1906 Marcus Reynolds designed a slate slab for Dexter's grave in Albany Rural Cemetery that memorialized both parents. Decorated with the Reynolds arms at the top and the Cuyler arms below, and surrounded

Fig. 4. Marcus T. Reynolds's room, Morgan Hall, Williams College, Williamstown, Massachusetts, photograph, 1888-89

with a band of laurel signifying eternal life, the slab also records Reynolds's grandparents.[3] The monument speaks volumes about the obsession with family history that Reynolds and Cuyler shared.[4] It vividly illustrates Reynolds's Dutch (Cuyler) and Yankee (Reynolds) heritage, a duality that dominated his entire career, just as it dominated the cultural and social life of the Albany in which he worked. After his death on March 18, 1937, from appendicitis, Reynolds joined his father in the family plot, which contains a number of slabs he designed. He lies under a similar block of slate that must have been drawn up by his nephew and partner, Kenneth G. Reynolds.

After Catherine Cuyler Reynolds died in 1875, Dexter and his two sons moved into the house at 98 Columbia Street owned by his younger sister, Laura, the widow of Bayard Van Rensselaer. Marcus was raised by his aunt in the company of her two sons, William Bayard, (born 1856) and

Howard (born 1858). Reynolds never lived in another house. When his aunt died in 1912, he stayed on in the house, which he finally bought from Howard in 1923. Laura had married very well indeed; her husband had been the reigning head of the great Van Rensselaer clan, the grandson of the last patroon and the man to whom that title would have descended, had it survived into the latter part of the nineteenth century. Laura's marriage allied Reynolds to all of the great Dutch families of the Hudson Valley to whom he was not already related through his Cuyler ancestry, as well as to large segments of the New England and New York upper crust. He remained very close to William Bayard and Howard, who became his clients and who helped him in acquiring a number of commissions. This family relationship, which placed him firmly atop the social heap in Albany, must have played a large role in his decision to practice architecture in his native city. One also suspects that the early death of his mother and the apparent aimlessness of his father's career led him to value the security of 98 Columbia Street.

Marcus Reynolds's early years followed the pattern established for his cousins: Miss Gaylord's Boarding School for very young gentlemen in Catskill, New York, followed by study at the Albany Academy, followed by four years at St. Paul's School in Concord, New Hampshire, from which he graduated in 1886, just a few months before construction began on Henry Vaughan's Gothic chapel in September, 1886.[5] As a senior, Reynolds perhaps heard or saw something of the design, but he never had the opportunity to inhabit on a daily basis one of the great spaces built by an educational institution in New England in the late nineteenth century.

For college Reynolds chose not to follow his father to Union nor his cousins to Harvard and Yale. Rather, he went east over the mountains to Williams. From his Williams days Reynolds preserved a fairly large group of photographs, which reveal some of his collegiate interests. One was sports, for he had pictures of baseball, football and tug-of-war teams, even though he played on none of them. There are individual portrait photographs of a dozen or so of his classmates, including the second black student to enter Williams, Livingsworth Wilson Bolin, as well as photos of his class and of his fraternity brothers. There are portraits of faculty he admired, including one of the black-bearded Prof. S. F. Clarke, biologist, who would become Reynolds's client twice over. The tenor of his life is suggested by a group portrait from the summer of 1889 (Fig. 3), in which well-dressed young ladies and gentlemen, some with tennis rackets in hand, recline on a porch at Lake Luzerne, a favorite upstate New York watering spot for well-heeled Albanians.[6] It was from this social class, his own, that Reynolds would draw the bulk of his clients. Reynolds is the nattily dressed figure in the striped suit and matching cap at the right. One wonders if it is entirely accidental that he seems slightly removed from the rest.

Reynolds owned several views of the Sigma Phi House, a not completely undistinguished work of 1883 by James G. Cutler of Rochester, New York. More revealing personally are snapshots, from his junior year, of his rooms in Morgan Hall (Fig. 6), a newly constructed dormitory which had the highest rents at the college. Reynolds decorated his digs (Fig. 4) with framed reproductions of pre-Raphaelite paintings (two rather rakishly draped), a small plaster cast of the Venus de Milo, a photograph of the Sigma Phi House, and some unidentifiable plaster reliefs. We may take these objects as a fair representation of Reynolds's interest in art as a college student. No one taught art at Williams in the 1880s, and so his taste must have been formed largely on his own. One hesitates to claim that there was anything remarkable about it.

Reynolds's photo collection contained views of a carefully chosen group of college buildings. In his day, the history of Williams architecture could be divided into two distinct periods, roughly dating from before and after the Civil War. From the first period were brick structures of classical derivation, while the later period was characterized by stone buildings of a picturesque bent. He had only one photo of the early buildings, the Bulfinch-like Griffin Hall of 1828 (Fig. 5). All the others were shots of the most recent buildings on campus, such as the gymnasium of 1886 and Morgan Hall of 1882 (Fig. 6), both by the very successful New York architect J. C. Cady. These buildings, designed to form an entrance to the main shopping street of the town, sported scrolled gables of Flemish or Jacobean origin, something fairly novel for the day. Reynolds also owned what must be one of the earliest photographs of Hopkins Hall, a Richardsonian design of 1888 by the young Boston architect Francis Allen, who had just returned from studying in Paris at the École des Beaux-Arts. Although these buildings had no

specific influence on Reynolds's work, they do show his interest in the latest developments in the profession, as he could know them from the isolated vantage point of Williamstown. One new building of which he did not possess a photograph was the Shingle Style fraternity house designed by McKim, Mead & White for Delta Psi (St. Anthony).[7] This building (Fig. 7) had just been completed when Reynolds entered Williams, and it may have played a role in his design of a country house (Fig. 67) for a Williams alumnus, Edmund Niles Huyck, a member of the fraternity.

Fig. 5. Griffin Hall, Williams College, 1828

Fig. 6. J. C. Cady, Morgan Hall, Williams College, 1882

After graduating from Williams in June, 1890, Reynolds entered Columbia University in the fall of the same year. His report to his Williams classmates, dated April 24, 1892, gives us a sense of the excitement he felt about his new professional life and of the ambition that drove him to excel:

Fig. 7. McKim, Mead & White, St. Anthony Hall, Williams College, 1884-86

I started my architectural studies the week after I left college, and by hard work during the summer and cheek in the fall I managed to enter the second year in the Architectural School of the (Columbia) School of Mines, though pretty well handicapped with conditions. By doing extra work during the year and working all Christmas and summer vacations I did all of the architectural work of the first and second years.

As you know, mathematics was never my forte, so that when I had to study Calculus, with no knowledge of algebra or trigonometry, I found myself rather beyond my depth, and this, with my other work, brought my study hours up to twelve a day many a time. The course is a four-year one, with a postgraduate course of one year, so that when we meet at our triennial I will be a full-fledged Ph. B.

During last summer I spent nearly every evening on an essay, which I entered last November for the competition offered by the American Economic Association for the best essay on 'The Housing of the Poor in American Cities.' Much to my surprise, I received word three days ago that my essay had received the first prize of $300.

As to my matrimonial prospects, I am glad to state they they are *nil*, as I am more in love with my profession than with anything else. My love and interest in that increases daily, and I am thankful that I have found it so.

You will probably gather from all this that I have turned over a new leaf and become a 'grub'; and so indeed I have, but I am encouraged, especially at this season of the year, by the thought that the grub is a creeping grub for a short time only, and that he then leads a life all the brighter by contrast.[8]

By skipping the first year of architecture school at Columbia, Reynolds escaped a host of courses — including trigonometry, conic sections, algebra, analytical geometry and physics — that probably were not much to his taste. But he also lost out on a whole year's history of ancient architecture and something called "Archaeology (French)." Probably the most crucial course he skipped was "Drawing: Freehand and Architectural." There is little evidence that he ever learned to draw particularly well, even though all architecture students at Columbia were required to participate in a drawing laboratory every year.

His professors included William R. Ware, the founder of the architecture school at Columbia, who had previously established the first school of architecture in the country at the Massachusetts Institute of Technology. Reynolds compiled a notebook, outlining the basic elements of classical architecture, that follows very closely the layout of Ware's famous classroom text, *The American Vignola*.[9] The dog-eared character of the notebook suggests that Reynolds kept it at his side throughout his career. Another major member of the Columbia faculty was A. D. F. Hamlin, who taught courses on architectural history and ornament. Throughout his career, Reynolds took very seriously Hamlin's theories on the appropriate use of historical styles in modern times.

In addition to calculus, Reynolds took a number of technical courses: hygiene, chemistry, mechanics, engineering, geology, stereotomy, sanitary engineering, economic geology and a practice course in specifications. Some of this technology must have appealed to him, for throughout his career he reserved for himself the job of writing the specifications for every important design that came from his office. He also got a good dose of the history of architecture— Modern Architectural History, Archaeology (German), Medieval Architectural History, History of Ornament (two years), History of Construction, and the Decorative Arts. There were also courses in theory of design and in historical design, as well as in both freehand and historical drawing. It was a very busy schedule.

What in the Columbia curriculum or in his own life that may have inspired Reynolds to take on the task of writing an essay on housing for the poor after his first year of architecture school is not clear. Perhaps he was simply ambitious to make a name for himself quickly. That he did, by winning the essay prize of the American Economic Association for 1892 and having it published in the association's journal in 1893.[10] It is not without irony that Reynolds, who spent substantial portions of his career designing houses for the rich, first achieved national recognition through an essay on this subject.

Founded in 1885, the American Economic Association (which remains the leading professional organization for economists) was composed of a distinguished group of scholars and of lay people like Andrew Carnegie. According to Richard T. Ely of Johns Hopkins University, the first secretary of the association, the society: "should seek truth from all sources, should be ready to give a respectful hearing to every new idea, and should shun no revelation of facts, but on the contrary, should make the collection, classification and interpretation of facts its chief task."[11]

By 1888 the association had embarked on a program of awarding prizes for essays by neophytes on topics that focused on pressing social issues such as immigtration, child labor, women wage earners, and state and local taxation. Of the winners of these contests, only the two writers who shared the prize for essays on child labor had been doubly rewarded by having their efforts published in the association's journal.[12] In 1891 a group of donors, including Carnegie, offered a first prize of $300 and a second prize of $200 for a fifth subject, "The Housing of the Poor in American Cities."

This choice of subject was surely stimulated by the publication in 1890 of Jacob A. Riis's *How the Other Half Lives*, a gut-wrenching account of slum life in New York City that outraged a good part of the nation. Reynolds wrote vivid descriptions of real life in the slums, based on his own personal observations, as well as on his reading of Riis. Reynolds subscribed to the widely held notions that tenement life was bad for society because it encouraged immoral behavior, because it bred disease, and because the shocking contrasts it created between the rich and poor might lead to political upheaval. One finds in Reynolds, however, a genuine sympathy for the plight of those forced to live

Fig. 8. Marcus T. Reynolds in 1895

in slums, as well as a touchingly naive belief that the absentee landlords of his own class would never allow such conditions to persist if they really knew what was going on. Happily, Reynolds did not share another widely held view of the time, that poverty was largely the result of heredity.[13] Reynolds's essay displays considerable learning, acquired from a lengthy bibliography of titles in English, French and German, and includes a knowledgeable discussion of important developments in housing for the poor in England.[14]

Reynolds's essay moved beyond Riis's work in at least two ways, through a deeper economic analysis of the lives of the poor and through a wide-ranging discussion of the architectural problems encountered in designing shelters for those lives. In particular, Reynolds confronted the architectural issues of arranging rooms so that they might provide privacy as well as healthful amounts of light and air. Even though Reynolds ultimately agreed with Riis that it was impossible to build decent, multiple-family housing on a standard 25' x 100' city lot, he illustrated his article with plans of permutations on that restricted rectangle, because he realized that those lots were a reality builders had to face. Reynolds found the large tenement building a far better solution. He particularly praised the Riverside Building of 1890, erected by Alfred T. White in Brooklyn just in time to be lauded in the last chapter of the Riis book. To such a large tenement Reynolds proposed adding a new wrinkle: a common kitchen. From his studies of the expenditures of the average

poor family, he concluded that a disproportionate part of its income was spent on subsistence items, such as food and fuel. His common kitchen would supply well-prepared food to all the families living in the building. The savings afforded by buying food and fuel in bulk, instead of in the tiny amounts individual families bought daily at inflated prices, would considerably improve each family's financial lot. Reynolds also felt that the common kitchen would offer opportunities for employment to some of the women living in the complex, who would be freed from cooking in their own apartments. Reynolds claimed the common kitchen as an original idea; it seems a surprisingly radical proposition to come from a young man of his background.[15]

Reynolds's suggestions for low-cost housing seem never to have been taken up. Although there is no evidence in his office diaries that he thought about housing for the poor again, his obituary states that it remained a lifelong interest.[16] Certainly, the essay itself was a promising performance from a young man who had had only one year of graduate study in architecture. It was recognized as such by Williams, which gave him an honorary Master of Arts in 1893 at the college's centennial commencement.

We know little of Reynolds's life in New York outside the classroom. For all three years he lived at 34 West 51st Street. Nearby, at Fifth Avenue and 51st Street, was William H. Vanderbilt's mansion, built in 1881 to designs of John B. Snook and the Herter Brothers. Reynolds must have

passed this great Renaissance pile daily, as well as Richard Morris Hunt's French Renaissance chateau for William K. Vanderbilt, located just a block north on Fifth. More radical than the work of Hunt were the new palazzi of McKim, Mead & White, such as the Villard Houses, completed between 1886 and 1888 on Madison Avenue between 51st and 50th streets. These were a far more severe and satisfying essay in the Renaissance mode than the William H. Vanderbilt House. Every time Reynolds walked to Columbia, which then stood on the east side of Madison between 50th and 49th streets, he must have passed the Villard Houses.[17]

Through his cousins Reynolds could certainly have gained an introduction in New York to Mariana Griswold Van Rensselaer, a leading writer on architecture and the author of a splendid biography of H. H. Richardson, but we do not know if he did so.[18] On February 8, 1892, he must have been at the wedding in New York of his cousin and lifelong friend, William Henry Bradford, to Mary Kingsland Jones.[19] There he could have encountered a member of the bride's family, Edith Jones Wharton. Within a few years, both Wharton and Reynolds would write about Italian Renaissance villas and gardens. Might they have talked about that subject, if they met in the winter of 1892?[20]

As soon as he received his Ph. B. from Columbia in June, 1893, Reynolds returned to Albany and began to practice architecture on his own. It took courage, and even a certain arrogance, to start out alone, without the experience of first working in an established architectural office. Certainly others of his social standing who had studied architecture at roughly the same time entered offices like that of McKim, Mead & White to gain experience and to meet clients before striking out on their own.[21] By returning to Albany, where he would have the advantage of social connections over any other local architect, Reynolds avoided the need to cultivate clients but hardly the need for experience. How his decision not to apprentice himself to an established firm may have affected his subsequent career is not clear. What is clear is that he had the self confidence to start out alone, a confidence that looks out at us from a photograph, taken in 1895, of the young architect at the beginning of his professional life (Fig.8).

Some of Reynolds's first independent works as an architect involved the Van Rensselaer Manor House property that belonged to his cousins. The manor house had been built in 1765 on a large tract of land then north of the city near the river. It had been enlarged by Philip Hooker in the early nineteenth century and then remodelled by Richard Upjohn between 1840 and 1843.[22] From this house, his cousins's forebearers had ruled over a vast feudal territory that stretched from the Massachusetts border to the Hudson and then a like distance west from the river.

The last occupant of the house (Fig. 9) was Harriet Elizabeth Bayard Van Rensselaer, the widow of Stephen, who had ordered the Upjohn renovation. When she died in 1875, the house was abandoned because its surroundings had been seriously compromised four decades earlier by the construction of the Erie Canal, which passed through the estate to join the Hudson just south of house, thereby separating the house and its extensive gardens from the river. The Van Rensselaers developed the land between the canal and the Hudson into the great Albany lumber district, where several generations of timber barons stored logs that had come down the canal before shipping them to other points. Eventually a railroad (which in later years became part of the Delaware & Hudson system) was constructed between the west side of the canal and the house. By the 1870s the Van Rensselaers had subdivided much of the manor house land adjacent to the railroad and canal into industrial properties.[23] In the 1890s W. B. Van Rensselaer ran a railroad spur

right through the middle of the garden into a wing of the old house. On the southeast corner of the property he erected a brick warehouse, designed in 1893 by Reynolds, to house the Albany Terminal Storage Warehouse Company, of which Van Rensselaer was president. That structure still stands, at least in part, at the east end of Tivoli Street.[24] Reynolds advised his cousin to tear the manor house down rather leave it standing in such an ignominious setting.[25]

Razing the house provided an opportunity to move it to some more hospitable site. Serious consideration had been given to making it the New York Pavilion at the World's Columbian Exposition in Chicago, where it would have remained after the fair.[26] That idea was killed by Charles Follen McKim, one of the principal figures in the architectural layout of the fair, who designed his own version of the Villa Medici in Rome for New York State. Then in January, 1893, Reynolds's old fraternity house burned

down. The derelict Van Rensselaer Manor House offered itself as a splendid replacement. Reynolds tried to persuade the trustees of Signa Phi fraternity to move the whole house to Williamstown, but the man who was donating the money for the replacement balked at a house with so many large room to be used as lounges by fraternity members.[27] The interior of the center hall went to the Metropolitan Museum in New York,[28] and a truncated version of the house arrived in

Fig. 10. Project for Sigma Phi House, Williams College, perspective, 1893

Fig. 11. Sigma Phi House, Williams College, 1893-94, south facade, demolished

Williamstown. During October, 1893, Reynolds supervised the demolition of the old house (Fig. 9) and the numbering of every part. During the winter of 1894 Reynolds drew up the plans for the new Sigma Phi House in Williamstown, and in the spring he supervised its construction in the center of the campus, where the previous Sigma Phi house had stood. The bricks of the old house crumbled as it came down, so that in the end all that Reynolds was able to move were Upjohn's Renaissance Revival trim and the timber frame. Reynolds had wanted to keep the stone cornice under the pediment (Fig. 10), but the pedimented window frame he transferred from the side of the old to the front of the new was too tall to allow the old cornice to persist. The loss of the cornice was a serious blow to the facade (Fig. 11). The plan of the new house, although it recalled the center-hall layout of the old, was entirely Reynolds's doing, and it suited the life of the fraternity well . He gave the second floor over to well-planned suites and included on the third floor, for the secret meetings of the brothers, a square room articulated by eight columns supporting a circular dome.[29] On July 2, 1973, the reincarnated Van Rensselaer Manor House was razed again, to make way for the Sawyer Library. Some of the Upjohn orna-

ment was removed to Albany, where there was hope (unrealized) of using it in a Bicentennial structure of 1976.

The work on the Van Rensselaer Manor House stands behind Reynolds's second important published work, "The Colonial Buildings of Rensselaerwyck."[30] In this essay Reynolds briefly lamented the passing of the old, gable-ended, Dutch houses of Albany, a few of which had stood into his day, but he neither illustrated them nor discussed them in any detail. He concentrated instead on the country houses surrounding the city: Schuyler Flatts, the Schuyler Mansion, the Ten Broeck Mansion, Crailo, the Vlie House (built by an ancestor, Hendrick Cuyler) and Beverwyck Manor, but his descriptions are disappointingly terse. For the Van Rensselaer House, however, he gave ample details of its history and descriptions of the ground-floor rooms, plus several photographs of the interior and a plan of the first floor that he drew himself. Reynolds's article emphasized the importance of knowing the history of the area in order to understand its architecture, a stance that reflected the emphasis Reynolds's teacher, A. D. F. Hamlin, placed on understanding the historical and social background of architecture. Reynolds's article joined several other essays on colonial architecture published in *Architectural Record* since its founding in 1891 and thus took its place in the history of the interest in colonial buildings that had begun in the late 1870s and flowered in the 1890s.

With work on the Sigma Phi House well along, Reynolds sailed for Europe on July 2, 1894, to study the architecture of the past firsthand.[31] He travelled slowly through Holland, Belgium, France and northern Italy and spent the winter in Rome. "In the spring," he wrote, "I may go to Spain for the month of March, returning to spend the rest of the spring in northern Italy, Venice and Florence, my object being to obtain a thorough knowledge of the architecture of the Italian Renaissance."[32] By October, 1895, he was back at work in Albany, his plans for a two-year stay in Europe having been cut short, for what reason we do not know.

Reynolds's considerable firsthand knowledge of Renaissance architecture found its way into print in Reynolds's third important article, "The Villas of Rome,"[33] a more extensive and important piece than the one on the colonial architecture of Albany. In *Harper's New Monthly Magazine* for July and August, 1893, Charles A. Platt, a painter soon to become an important architect, had published two articles on Italian gardens that seem to have been the first writings in English on Renaissance villas.[34] In 1894 these articles, with more illustrations and a slightly revised text, appeared as a very handsome book, *Italian Gardens*.[35] Reynolds could well have read the articles during the summer after his graduation from Columbia, or he could have acquired the book before his departure for Europe in 1894, or both. Platt concentrated on the gardens, particularly their flowers, rather than on the architecture of Italian villas. He did make the crucial point, however, that these buildings and their gardens went together: "the architect proceeded with the idea that not only was the house to be lived in, but that one still wished to be at home while out-of-doors; so the garden was designed as another apartment."[36]

Platt's writing, like his paintings, was impressionistic. He intended his photographs to carry more of the burden than his words, and he deliberately eschewed any attempt at scholarship. Platt had two aims: to convey a sense of how the gardens appeared at the moment he wrote and to make understandable the principles of Renaissance

gardens. He hoped his book might: "be of value towards a more thorough understanding and appreciation of the reasons which led to a formal treatment of the garden; and as there is a great similarity in the character of the landscape in many parts of our country with that of Italy, that it might lead to a revival of the same method."[37]

Although Reynolds, like Platt, saw Italian villas and their gardens as appropriate prototypes for contemporary American houses, his purpose in writing about Roman villas was somewhat different. For Reynolds, Italian villas demonstrated how to integrate classical buildings with the landscape. He believed that in colonial days clipped boxwood gardens had worked to unify the classical

Fig. 12. Fernleigh, Stephen and Susan Clark House, Cooperstown, New York, view from southeast across the Susquehanna River with bridge, 1927-28, in foreground

houses of the era with nature, while in the later Victorian Gothic and Romanesque periods architecture had been made subservient to nature. He was relieved that the "unbridled license of shingled turrets and creosote stains" of the Queen Anne style, suitable as it may have been for suburban houses, was "giving place in popular favor to the revived Colonial," but he lamented that American architects had not figured out how to make the revived Colonial seem a part of the land. In the new, classical, American country seat, Reynolds wrote, there should be no abrupt transition from house to nature; rather "there must be a middle ground where nature is indeed present, but restrained by architectural lines."[38] Reynolds's article seems to have provided the first opportunity for an English-reading audience to put the buildings of Renaissance villas together with the plans of their gardens, which he reproduced from Percier and Fontaine. He took a scholarly approach, making a valiant effort to separate out hands of architects and to characterize their styles.

Late in his career, Reynolds had a splendid chance to use his knowledge of Roman villas. In 1923 the art collector Stephen Clark, an heir to the Singer Sewing Machine fortune, asked Reynolds to draw up a plan for the gardens of his country house at Cooperstown, New York,[39] at the same time Clark was buying paintings by Henri Matisse. This was an unusual commission for Reynolds, who usually relied on landscape architects if his clients wanted elaborate gardens around their houses. Clark was married to Reynolds's cousin, Susan Hun, whose brother Thomas Hun had been a friend of Clark at Harvard Law School.[40] During the six years that

Reynolds worked on the Clark gardens, he and the younger couple became close friends, to the point that Clark was a pallbearer at Reynolds's funeral. When the gardens were finally completed in August, 1929, Reynolds, then sixty, had such a good time at the opening party that he did not go to bed until six a.m.

At Cooperstown, the Clarks lived in a large Second Empire house designed in 1868 by James Van Dyke, a little-known architect from New Jersey. That house, with the rather pretentious name of Fernleigh, faced west. To the east a bluff dropped sharply to the headwaters of the Susquehanna River; a wooden footbridge connected Fernleigh to Fernleigh Over, land on the east bank that the Clarks also owned. South of the house was what Reynolds called the "old garden," flanked on the east by a servants house and on the west by the Turkish Bath, a small two-story structure designed by Henry Hardenbergh in the 1870s.[41] In his garden plan Reynolds sought to anchor the ungainly, top-heavy house to the land and to provide outdoor spaces in which the family

Fig. 13. Fernleigh, view south over upper terrace, swimming pool and tennis courts, 1923-29

could enjoy nature and entertain guests during the brief summers of upstate New York. In short, he did what both he and Platt had advocated.

At the south end of the west, or main, facade of the house, there was a one story conservatory with an attached porte-cochère at its southern end. Reynolds made the porte-cochère the node of his entire design. Around the porte-cochère he placed a rectangular terrace, which he called the upper terrace, that joined the driveway on the west, the house on the north, the old garden on the south and a new terrace, called the lower terrace, on the east. From the porte-cochère Reynolds developed an axis that led east toward the lower terrace and, ultimately, the river. The lower terrace offered a sweeping view of the river below, and from the north edge of the terrace a steep path led down the bluff to the water, the bridge and Fernleigh Over (Fig. 12). In 1927 Clark decided to replace the wooden bridge with a new one, designed by Reynolds, with a steel frame covered by a stone veneer.[42] To fuse the bridge with the landcape, Reynolds placed planters at each end and on the parapets over the piers.

From the porte-cochère Reynolds laid out a second axis, at right angles to the first, that led south across the upper terrace to the old garden. About a year into the commission, however, plans changed, and the old garden was replaced by a swimming pool, a wrought-iron casino with flanking pavilions, and a pair of tennis courts[43] (Fig. 13). To the east of the swimming pool, on its cross axis, he developed a rose garden enclosed by a segmental curve of segmentally arched trellises, while to the west of the pool he converted the old servants' wing into a guest house with nine bedrooms and nine baths. Across the swimming pool, the new guest house faced the Turkish Bath, which stood between the main house and the rose garden. Reynolds cleverly used his gardens to unify the main house, the guest house and the Turkish Bath into a new whole centered on the swimming pool and its surrounding terraces.

On the terrace at the south end of the pool, a tall fountain with three basins marked the north-south axis of the garden and stood in front of the wrought-iron arches of the vaulted casino. That casino was connnected by iron trellises to terminal pavilions whose open, curved roofs supported iron bird cages articulated by little twisted columns. The casino, whose vault was frescoed by Agnes Tate with rinceaux and monkeys,[44] offered a shady spot that overlooked either the pool or the tennis courts. The delicate iron arches created a diaphanous visual break between the two spaces.[45]

Although Reynolds cribbed a few details directly from Roman villas, the Clark gardens by and large show him working with principles of Roman villa design rather than with direct quotations. He had learned from Roman villas the idea of the garden as an architectural, rather than a horticultural, experience that depended greatly on axes and cross axes. The wrought-iron casino at the Clark Gardens divides the pool from the tennis courts much as the masonry loggia at the Villa Giulia in Rome separates the courtyard from the nymphaeum, while allowing the visitor to look into either from the same spot. We know Reynolds had the Villa Giulia in mind, because he gave photos of it to Vera Leeper, an artist who was asked to come up with a decorative scheme for the vault of the casino.[46] Reynolds's casino and the loggia at Villa Giulia, however, are about as far apart visually as Rome and Cooperstown are geographically. In the Clark garden, the pavilions at either side of the casino reflect pairs of buildings that Reynolds knew from Rome, such as the aviaries of the Orti Farnesiani on the Palatine Hill or the casinos at the Villa Lante. But Reynolds used the concept of paired structures flanking the main axis rather than actual Renaissance forms. The Clark gardens show Reynolds as an architect who used his knowledge of history creatively.

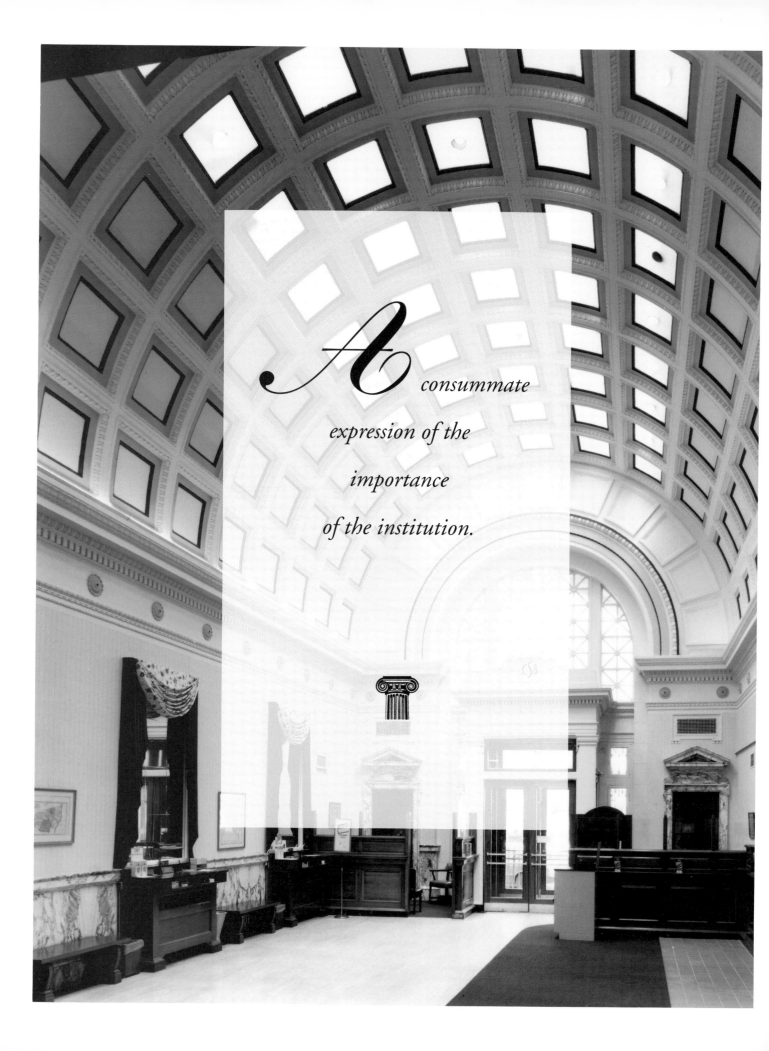

A consummate expression of the importance of the institution.

CHAPTER 2

BANKS

Marcus Reynolds considered himself a specialist in bank architecture, and indeed his banks form the most stylistically coherent group of buildings of his career.[1] Of all his buildings, the banks were the best published.

His banks were mostly built between 1901 and 1912, during or following one of the greatest periods of economic expansion in the nation's history. After the boom of the 1880s, the panic of 1893 had caused a serious setback in economic growth. Once recovery began in 1897, however, greenbacks grew like kudzu. Between 1897 and 1907 the number of banks in the country increased from 7,718 to 17,190, their deposits from $2.2 billion to $9.5 billion, and their investments from a mere $767 million to $2.7 billion.[2] Banks played a crucial role in financing an economic expansion from which they in turn profited. In the midst of this boom, new bank buildings sprang up everywhere. After 1907 the country went through a "dispiriting retrogression" which lasted until World War I brought its own brand of prosperity.[3] Even so, the expansion of the previous decade had formed a deep pool of financial resources from which commissions continued to flow to Reynolds.

Reynolds designed banks for both larger and smaller cities. Around the larger cities — Albany, Schenectady and Troy — the smaller centers form an irregular ring that stretches east as far as Greenfield and Taunton, Massachusetts. Albany once held the largest concentration of Reynolds's banks, five on lower State Street. Of these, only two remain. The Union National Bank in Schenectady has also disappeared. The banks in the smaller cities have by and large survived, although many have been altered in unhappy ways.

Reynolds's banks can be distinguished according to their location within their towns and cities — those that occupy corner lots and those that have mid-block locations. On corner lots the architectural problems, and the expense, were increased by the fact that the bank had to have two facades, coherently related to each other. But the gains were great in terms of publicity. A noted architect of bank buildings, Albert Hopkins, had a revealing discussion with a banker about the pros and cons of buying an expensive corner lot for a new building. The banker hesitated to pay the price, but Hopkins convinced him that the carrying charges on the property would require only a modest part of his annual advertising budget.

Asked Hopkins: "Is not a bank on this corner worth $3000 a year to you?"

The banker replied instantly, "It seems to me $3000 a year is very little to pay to have a billboard on the best corner is town. A bank is only a billboard, isn't it?"

"That's just what it is," Hopkins answered. "A bank building is advertising; the best kind of advertising."[4]

Facing page. Catskill Savings Bank, Catskill, New York, 1907-8, interior

Fig. 14. Project for a bank interior, 1897

Fig. 15. Albany City Savings Institution, 100 State Street, 1901-2, view from northeast

tem of vaults. The side windows tell us that the building would have stood on a street corner, and the skylight makes clear that there would have been no rental space above. These details accord with the site at the southwest corner of North Pearl Street and Maiden Lane where the new Albany Savings Bank, a handsome, domed structure designed by Henry Ives Cobb, opened in 1899.[6] Its construction seems to have set off a frenzy of bank building; Reynolds was the architectural shark that gobbled up most of the clients.

The drawing shows the strong impression that the Bowery Savings Bank in New York by McKim, Mead & White — one of the most important bank designs of the late nineteenth and early twentieth centuries — had made on Reynolds.[7] Stanford White's sumptuous classical interior was lit by two rows of windows and encircled by rows of Corinthian columns bearing a coffered, coved vault pierced at its center by a skylight of amber glass. While Reynolds did not copy these details, the rich feeling of his brightly lit space must have resulted from his encounter with White's bank, which had opened in 1895, the year Reynolds returned to this country after his *Wanderjahre* in Europe. The complexities of Reynolds's vault suggest that while he was in London he fell under the influence of the buildings of Sir John Soane, such as Soane's magnificent vaulted spaces in the Bank of England. On the other hand, the Italianate lunettes with their polychromed decorations were very up to date for America, predating the similar vault of the east library of McKim, Mead & White's Morgan Library in New York of 1902-7.

Reynolds's first completed bank building is the Albany City Savings Institution (Fig. 15), the competition for which he won on April 16, 1901.[8] The building, which opened on May 1, 1902,[9] was the first skyscraper in Albany. The ten-story bank was set on a narrow, north-facing, mid-block lot on the south side of State Street. To get the maximum amount of light into the banking room, Reynolds devoted almost the entire width of the building to a single, round-arched opening. Above a balcony, the shaft of the tower rises in six clean stories, topped by round arches that suggest more than a passing acquaintance with buildings by Louis Sullivan. Above the arcade, however, Sullivanesque rationality gives way to a Second Empire exuberance in which Reynolds indulged his taste for rich display.

Reynolds would have understood this conversation; he probably had several like it.

No matter what the location, a major issue was interior lighting. Banks on corners could be lit by large windows at the front and side and by a large skylight over the main space. Those at mid-block had to rely on skylights and whatever light could be admitted through the facade. Rental property on upper floors ruled out a skylight; natural light had to come through the outside walls.

The earliest of Reynolds's bank designs to survive is a watercolor, signed and dated 1897, of an elaborate but unidentified interior (Fig. 14). Given the grandeur and the early date of the design in Reynolds's career, it seems reasonable to suppose it to be a project for the Albany Savings Bank, of which his cousin, William Bayard Van Rensselaer (for whom he had just done a palazzo on State Street) was vice president.[5] The drawing shows a tall interior lit by high, round-arched windows and by a large skylight supported on an elaborate sys-

Fig. 16. View of State Street, Albany, from east, photograph c. 1918-20

Fig. 17. Albany Trust Company, State Street and Broadway, 1902-4, view from southeast

The Reynolds design seems to depend on at least two prototypes in New York, the Tower Building by Bradford L. Gilbert and the Washington Life Building by Cyrus L. W. Eidlitz. Completed in 1889, a year before Reynolds entered architecture school, the Tower Building coped with the same design problem that faced Reynolds: a tall structure on a narrow city lot.[10] Gilbert had solved the problem by uniting the lower three floors under a round arch. Above the arch rose a five-story shaft topped by a two-story attic and a pyramidal roof. Reynolds's green-tiled Mansard roof with dormers, on the other hand, seems to depend on the top of Eidlitz's building, which had been praised by Montgomery Schuyler in 1899.[11] Reynolds's roof is over-scaled, but with reason. Readable from a distance by visitors arriving by boat or train from New York, the roof made the bank an important visual part of Albany by connecting it to the Capitol at the top of State Street and the Federal Building at the bottom (Fig. 16). State Street gained a certain visual coherence from Reynolds's design. On July 18, 1902, Reynolds moved his offices into his skyscraper[12] and kept them there for the rest of his life.

In 1902 three more bank commissions on State Street came his way. In addition, he lost the com-

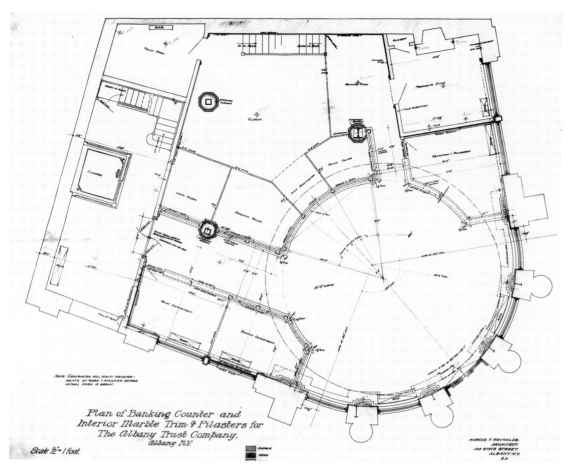

Plan of Banking Counter and
Interior Marble Trim & Pilasters for
The Albany Trust Company.
Albany N.Y.

Scale ½"= 1 foot.

MARCUS T. REYNOLDS.
ARCHITECT.
100 STATE STREET
ALBANY N.Y.
E.A.

Fig. 18. Albany Trust Company, plan of first floor

Fig. 19. National Savings Bank, Albany, 1902, facade, demolished

petition for the new National Commercial Bank building at 60 State Street to York & Sawyer;[13] his design for the Union Trust Company was put aside,[14] never to be built; and he was asked to design the Security Safe Deposit in Troy. The banks of 1902 are remarkably different, and their differences illuminate some important aspects of the way Reynolds operated as an architect.

For the Albany Trust Company, at the northwest corner of Broadway and State (Fig. 17), Reynolds designed a seven-story building topped by a round dome in a style that one might characterize as Beaux-Arts Northern Renaissance.[15] Here, too, he was much concerned with the effect of the building on the cityscape. The Albany Trust mediates among three diverse and strong architectural forces — the French Renaissance Federal Building that stands across Broadway, the Romanesque National Commercial Bank by Robert W. Gibson at 40 State, and Russell Sturgis's Mechanics' National Bank just to the west on State. The limestone trim of the Albany Trust picks up the color of the first; the dark red brick and orange dome, the earth tones of the latter two. The roof details belong to the same family as those of the Federal Building, while the surface ornament plays three-dimensional variations on the rich two-dimensional patterning of the Gibson design. The contrast of buff trim against warm brick walls and the general sense of the origin of the design in northern European architecture recalls Sturgis's bank of 1876. Admired even by H. H. Richardson, the Sturgis bank[16] includes a corbelled tower with a conical roof at the James Street corner (Fig. 26, right edge). Reynolds's corner dome, in part, is a variation on this idea.

Reynolds was highly conscious both of how his building would be viewed on a diagonal from the south and how it would act as a monumental form on one of the most important corners in town. To make his building perform this double duty, he used something of a cliché in Beaux-Arts design: a rounded, domed corner, an urban exclamation point that both acts as focus and allows the streets to slip away to either side. The physical presence of the banking room at ground level was originally stressed by banded columns that were later replaced by rather self-effacing pilasters.

Reynolds's corner recalled the architectural history of the site. The previous building, known as the Museum, was a Greek Revival structure with two-story columns set in a curve on the street corner. After the Civil War, an incongruous Second Empire dome was placed over this facade. Reynolds's dome and columns maintained a memory of the old building. Eventually, the slender proportions of the Albany Trust building were modified by additions at the sides which gave the bank more rental space. The addition on the State Street side covered up a later Reynolds building, the First National Bank.

Inside the Albany Trust was a circular banking room, which the *Albany Evening Journal* lavishly praised, especially for the concave ring of tellers'-cages (Fig. 18) which allowed the customer to see, instantly, which teller he or she wanted to use.[17] The vault of the banking room was decorated by a fresco with "exquisitely blended colors" by an Italian artist, Antonio Bassi, that contained personifications of energy and thrift.[18]

A second Reynolds bank of 1902 was the National Savings Bank, a now demolished mid-block structure devoted to the banking facility alone.[19] The triumphal arch facade on State Street (Fig.19) was dominated by a two-story arch flanked by pairs of free-standing Ionic columns raised on tall pedestals. From the pedestals projected bronze lanterns, whose curved crowns echoed the curvature of the arch and thrust its form onto the space of the sidewalk. The whole was so richly (perhaps too richly) decorated that it would have been hard to walk down State Street and not notice it. Banks at mid-block had to try harder. Here Reynolds was seeking not so much to start a conversation among new and old buildings as to make a singular and rather insistent statement.

Although the building no longer stands, we can still get an idea of its complex spatial sequence from the longitudinal section that shows the progression from the street to the interior (Fig. 20). The lanterns, columns, arch and marble door screen of the facade provided a four-plane

Fig. 20. National Savings Bank, longitudinal and cross sections

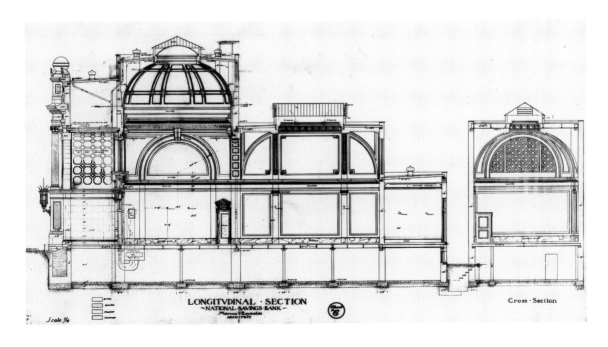

LONGITUDINAL · SECTION
~NATIONAL·SAVINGS·BANK~
Marcus T. Reynolds
ARCHITECT

Cross·Section

Scale ¼

sequence through which the customer passed before entering the banking room, which was capped by a hemispherical dome concealed behind the tall attic story of the facade. Beyond the domed space was a second room with a ceiling as high as the top of the arch of the facade. Domed banking rooms were hardly uncommon in American banks, but usually

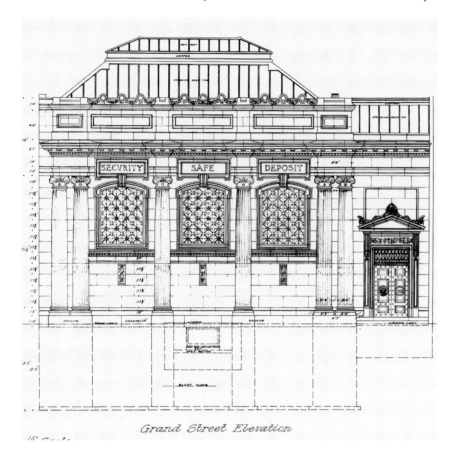

Fig. 21. Security Safe Deposit, Troy, New York, 1902-4, Grand Street elevation

the domes were revealed on the exterior.[20] Reynolds saved the dome as a surprise to make entering the building all the more exciting. Reynolds used this combination of arched facade and vaulted banking room only once again, in the Catskill Savings Bank of 1907.[21]

The president of the bank when Reynolds designed the new building was a remarkable figure in the Albany of his day, Simon W. Rosendale. Born in 1842 in Albany and educated in Barre, Vermont, Rosendale was a lawyer whose first partner, Rufus W. Peckham, became a United States Supreme Court justice. Rosendale then went into partnership with Albert Hessberg, whose brother Samuel was to build a large country house designed by Reynolds. At age fifty, Rosendale became Attorney General of New York, and in 1899 Theodore Roosevelt appointed him State

Commissioner of Charities, even though Rosendale was a Democrat.[22] In 1880, he was the only Jew to be a founding member of the Fort Orange Club, whose membership was to be "composed of gentlemen...born at the top, as well as those who possessed the qualities which make good men and had risen to the top."[23] Rosendale's education in Vermont may have given him a taste for marble. In the fall of 1902, he spent considerable time with one of Reynolds's assistants considering Vermont marbles before settling on a white from Proctor. Rosendale was willing to spend extra money to get a richly detailed building.[24] His bank was certainly a "billboard" and probably a proclamation of his social status.

Before the building opened, Rosendale was succeeded as president by James H. Manning, who as vice president of the bank had been in on the planning of its new structure. Like many of Reynolds's clients, Manning belonged to that class of people who ran the country; his father, Daniel, had been Secretary of the Treasury under Grover Cleveland. Also like many Reynolds's clients, Manning could point to diverse accomplishments. He was managing editor of Albany's Democratic newspaper, the *Argus*, and president of the Argus Corporation, and he had served two terms as mayor of Albany. For our purposes, his most interesting accomplishment was the writing of a two-volume history of savings banks in the United States,[25] published in 1917 for the centennial of the founding of savings banks in America.[26] By 1917 Manning had completed two terms as president of the Savings Bank Association of the State of New York. Manning the historian described his own National Savings Bank in glowing terms:

beautiful in design, harmonious in proportions, combining utility with beauty in the hope that it might prove in every way suited to the requirements of a growing business. The site on which the building stands is historic, dating back to and beyond 1660. At that time, Albany ... had but three streets. Its south gate, at what is now South Pearl and State streets, ... was located at only a stone's throw west of the present bank.[27]

For Reynolds, the National Savings Bank represented his arrival nationally as a designer of banks. The facade was published in *The American Architect* in 1907, on the same page as the neighboring National Commercial Bank, designed by the well-known New York firm of York & Sawyer.[28]

The robust relief and rich decoration of the National Savings Bank reappeared, but to different

Fig. 22. *Philip Hooker,
New York State National Bank,
Albany, 1801, facade*

Fig. 23. *Philip Hooker and
Marcus T. Reynolds, New York
State National Bank, facade
after 1904*

ends, in Troy in a bank that turned out to be one
of Reynolds's very best (Fig. 21). Actually, it was
not a free-standing bank, but a side-street addition
to the cast-iron Troy City Bank building, erected
in 1862 by D. D. Badger's Architectural Iron
Works of New York, a month after a great fire had
swept Troy.[29] In 1901 the Troy City Bank was
succeeded by the Security Trust Company, whose
president, Seymour Van Santvoord,[30] asked
Reynolds to design a structure to house a new
enterprise, the Security Safe Deposit Company.[31]

Van Santvoord was one of Reynolds's most
interesting clients, "one of the type of men who
make cities and keep them in the van of civilization," as an editorial in the Troy *Times Record* put
it on the occasion of his death.[32] Law, banking
and business were only three of Van Santvoord's
occupations. He was active in Democratic state
politics and ran unsuccessfully for mayor of Troy
in 1901. For our purposes, however, his interest in
archaeology and Roman history are most perti-
nent. A member of the Archaeological Institute of
America, Van Santvoord published in 1902 *The
House of Caesar and the Imperial Disease,*[33] a nearly
four-hundred-page history of the Roman emper-
ors, illustrated with photographs of imperial busts,
some of which Van Santvoord and his mother had
taken by their own photographer in Rome. By
imperial disease, he meant "death by violent
means."[34] Not content with this excursion into
ancient history, Van Santvoord subsequently published *Octavia, A Tale of Ancient Rome,* a novel
that had as its heroine Nero's wife, whom the
moralizing author celebrated for her close-to-
Christian purity. "If Octavia was never baptized by

the Apostle," he wrote, "I am sure she was embat-
hed in the spirit of Christ and enrolled among the
pure in heart who shall see God."[35] These writings
were informed by a remarkable command, for an
amateur, of the monuments of and the contemporary archaeological literature on the Roman
Forum, which was also the subject of a learned
address he delivered at the Albany Institute
Historical and Art Society in 1906.[36]

For Van Santvoord, ardent Romanist, Reynolds
produced his most Roman design. The old bank
stood on the southeast corner of Fourth and
Grand streets. Grand was a narrow street on which
the new safe deposit building would rise behind
the old bank. Reynolds gave this facade a particularly bold articulation, a row of free-standing
Corinthian columns that moved aggressively
toward the street. The effect is like that of the
Forum of Nerva, a long, narrow space whose most
salient architectural feature was a set of large, free-
standing columns projecting from its enclosing
walls. At Troy (which Van Santvoord and
Reynolds, of course, would have understood as the
namesake of the putative progenitor of Rome,
through Aeneas), the columns served to attract the
attention of passers-by on busy Fourth Street,
while their strength bespoke the security a safe
deposit building had to offer.

The great columns frame large windows, covered with elaborate metal grilles that permit the
entrance of light but not the larcenous. Over the
windows Reynolds inscribed the name of the new
company in such large letters that it is impossible
to miss either the words or the protection they
promise. This wall owes no inconsiderable debt to

the street facade of another treasure house, Richard Morris Hunt's Metropolitan Museum of Art in New York. The tall, narrow interior has gravely bare walls that contrast splendidly with the

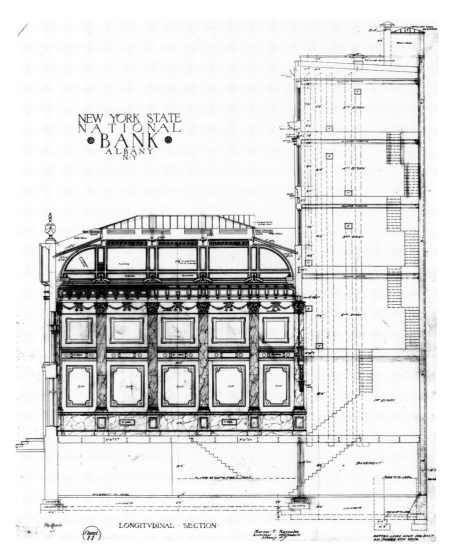

Fig. 24. New York State National Bank, 1902-4, longitudinal section, demolished

robust relief of the exterior. The interpenetrations and lunettes of the coved vault recall those in the bank project of 1897 (Fig. 14). A sizeable vault crowds the interior at ground level.

The commission for the New York State National Bank in Albany confronted Reynolds with a question of historic preservation that was hardly as commonly raised in 1902 as it is today. Here Reynolds for the first, but not the last, time consciously preserved a work by the earlier Albany architect he most admired, Philip Hooker.[37] Hooker's bank of 1804 had an elegant facade, based on Robert Adam's Royal Society of the Arts in London (Fig. 22). Behind the facade were typi-

cal early nineteenth-century banking rooms and offices, all of little architectural interest and all inadequate to the needs of a modern bank. On the second floor were lawyers' offices.[38] Reynolds preserved the Hooker facade intact, with the exception of new glazing and the addition of an attic above the pediment (Fig. 23). The attic, like that of the National Savings Bank, concealed a vault, this one coved and opening into a large skylight (Fig. 24). The interior was articulated by a giant order of slender pilasters that continued the elegant proportions of the early nineteenth-century facade. If the large scale of the new banking room was entirely modern, to serve present needs, the detailing was late eighteenth century to present the customer with the myth that interior and exterior belonged to the same historical moment.

The bank required not just a new banking room, but also new office space, which Reynolds provided in a six-story, brick-faced tower set far enough behind the banking room that it seemed disconnected from the bank itself (Fig. 23). The tower, in turn, was joined to James Street by a narrow wing, barely more than the width of a passageway. At the lobby level, a lavish directors' room was constructed, its walls lined in stamped leather.[39] The room was dominated by a sixteenth-century French mantelpiece that Reynolds believed to be the work of the sculptor Jean Goujon (Fig. 25). After the bank was torn down in the 1920s, Reynolds acquired the mantelpiece and attempted to donate it to the Metropolitan Museum.[40]

Extending at the rear to James Street, the new bank building enclosed the corner lot, which the bank acquired a decade later to build an addition, designed by Reynolds, that opened in 1916. The addition (Fig. 26) showed Reynolds's remarkable sensitivity to the Hooker facade. He extended the rusticated, arched openings of the ground floor across both street fronts. Above rose two-story brick walls that continued the second floor of the Hooker building and the attic Reynolds had added to it. He raised the rectangular windows of the second floor, however, to elevate the light sources for the addition to the banking room. Under them he added rectangular panels with swags. The center of the James Street facade projected slightly to echo the main motif of the Hooker facade without detracting either from the three-dimensional relief of Hooker's half columns or from the focal point of his Palladian window. The Reynolds addition

was surely one of the most successful Colonial
Revival extensions of a genuine Federal building
created during the early part of this century.

Both building campaigns at the New York
State National Bank occurred during the presidency of Ledyard Cogswell, who must have made the
initial decision to preserve the Hooker facade and
to continue its style in the addition. In 1902
Cogswell and Reynolds spent several hours discussing the project before Reynolds put much
down on paper.[41] For Cogswell, Hooker's facade
of 1804 was a potent symbol of the bank's ancient
lineage that signalled the enduring character of
the institution.

Unfortunately for Reynolds's design, the bank
became too successful in the following decade. In
1927 the bank commissioned Henry Ives Cobb to
design the skyscraper that now occupies the whole
block between North Pearl and James streets.[42]
While the Hooker facade still stands, it was moved
to the center of Cobb's design, where it is dwarfed
by the new office tower. Cobb did, however, allow
the Hooker building to suggest details of his skyscraper. Reynolds tried to get this commission, but
he failed, for reasons which are not clear.[43]

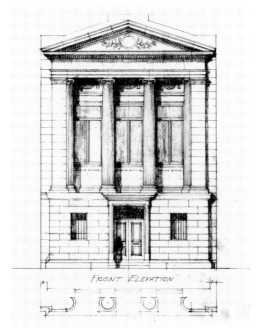

FRONT ELEVATION

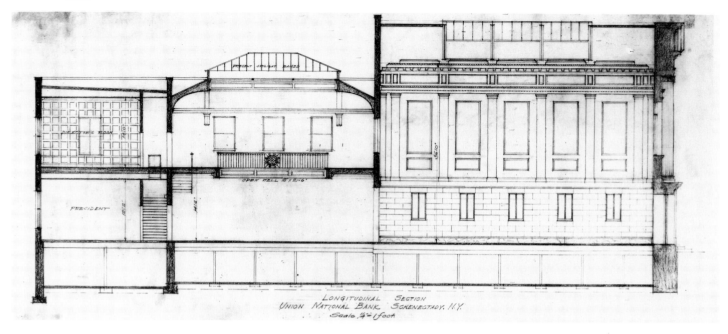

Fig. 28. Union National Bank, longitudinal section, project, 1908

Fig. 29. Union National Bank, 1908, exterior, demolished

In 1905 Reynolds was approached by the First National Bank of Albany to enter a competition to replace their quarters on the north side of State Street, immediately west of the Albany Trust Company (the old building appears in Fig. 17, while Reynolds's facade can be seen on angle in Fig. 105). He was named winner of the competition in the *Albany Evening Journal* on June 11, 1907, with completion of the new structure projected for May, 1908. The building matched the seven-story height of the Albany Trust, but the exterior was to contrast in material, marble or granite, and in its purer classical style. The facade of the banking room was treated like a store-front, with pairs of Ionic columns framing a two-story glass wall broken by the elaborate frame of the main portal. The second floor would hold bank

offices, and the directors' room would be in the front on the third floor. Other spaces on the upper floors would be rented to tenants who would gain entrance through the elevator in the Albany Trust Company next door. Later, the interlocking circulation with the Albany Trust building caused the facade of the First National to be replaced by a wall that attempted to continue, somewhat ineptly, the architecture of the latter.[44] Probably at the same time Reynolds's bold columns on the ground floor of the Albany Trust were replaced by the present reticent pilasters.

The Union National Bank of Schenectady owned a narrow, deep lot at 334 State Street, occupied by a commercial building with a three-bay, glass store-front articulated by slender pilasters that supported oversized Corinthian capitals.[45] This Reynolds replaced in 1907 with a four-bay store front, with three Ionic columns set *in antis* (Fig. 29). Reynolds's design clearly referred to the previous building on the site. The rather modest design for Schenectady was not what Reynolds really wanted; he had something grander in mind for a bank that had prospered mightily since its founding in 1892.[46] Reynolds's office experimented with facades for a building that would have housed only the bank and presented a monumental stone facade to the street. In one of these designs (Fig. 27) a rusticated wall surmounted by an Ionic temple front formed a facade for a skylit, two-story banking room, which was surrounded by walls articulated by pilasters

supports the tower, crowned by a 9-foot replica of Giovanni da Bologna's Mercury, a fitting symbol of commerce (and a challenge to Augustus St. Gaudens's Diana on the tower of Madison Square Garden) to fly over the business district of a prosperous city (Fig. 31). Even if the building does not quite hang together visually, one cannot help but admire the way Reynolds knit the old into the new

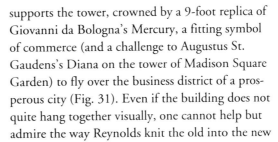

Fig. 30. Albany City Savings Institution, 100 State Street, 1922-24, view from northwest

Fig. 31. Albany City Savings Institution, plans, section and elevation of tower

and shallow rustication and which preceded a two-story space centered on an open well (Fig. 28).[47] As built, the banking room was one-story tall, and there was little spatial play to the rear.

Reynolds's last large bank design was for his first bank client, the Albany City Savings Institution. In 1922 City Savings acquired the theater immediately to the west of its tower (Fig. 15), and the president, William S. Hackett, who was also the newly elected mayor of Albany, called on Reynolds to design an addition.[48] Reynolds turned the original structure into the eastern third of a tripartite composition, which, like that of the Woolworth Building in New York, had a tall tower over the center (Fig. 30). At ground level Reynolds added two round arches, filled with glass to light the expanded banking room. At the right he duplicated his old building to form two elements that flank a rather plain central section that

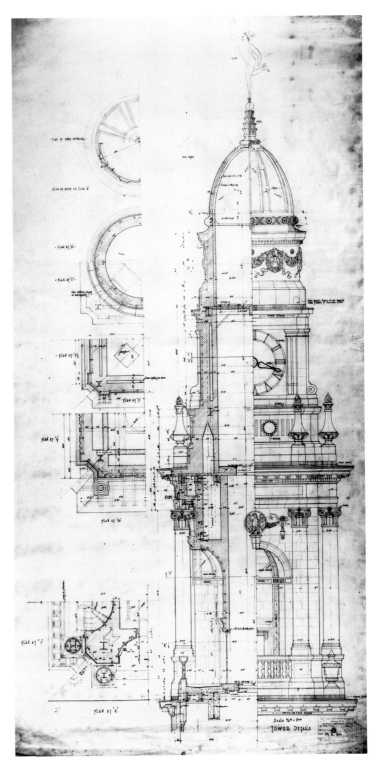

29

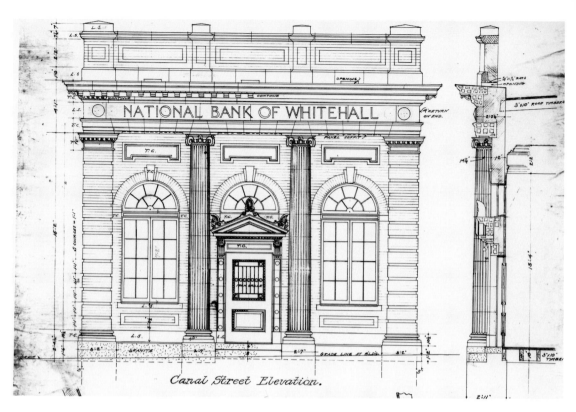

Canal Street Elevation.

Fig. 32. National Bank of Whitehall, Whitehall, New York, 1906, front elevation

Fig. 33. National Bank of Whitehall, first floor plan

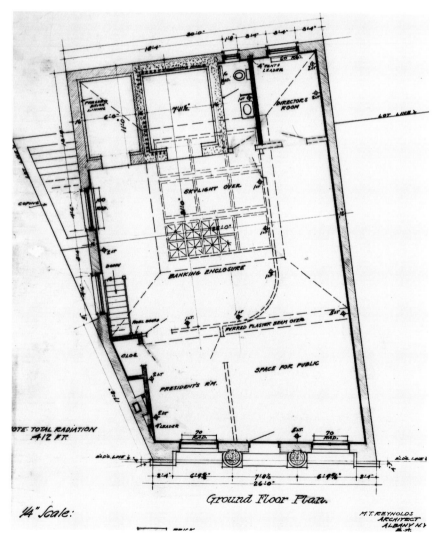

Ground Floor Plan.

¼" Scale:

M.T. REYNOLDS
ARCHITECT
ALBANY N.Y.

whole. This was achieved after a considerable haggling with the client, who at first wanted a court carved out of the center of the facade.[49]

The tower belongs to the visual world of classical public buildings that Reynolds in the 1920s systematically gave Albany's Democratic machine, of which Mayor Hackett was the elected standard-bearer. Born in 1866 in the South End of Albany of Scottish and Scotch-Irish heritage, Hackett was a self-made man who rose from near poverty to be president of the second largest savings bank in the city. Between 1917, when he became president of the bank, and his death in 1926, its deposits rose from almost $12 million to well over $26 million.[50] Small wonder that Hackett decided to turn the bank's headquarters into a much larger building. Reynolds's new tower for the bank quoted rather literally from Philip Hooker's cupola on Albany Academy (Fig. 132), a fine detail from the Anglicizing architecture of Albany's past.[51] Although the Adamesque character of the bank tower has nothing to do stylistically with the building beneath it, it surely has much to do with Hackett's origins.[52] By going back through Hooker to the work of Robert Adam, Reynolds went back to one of the greatest architects of Scottish descent.

Reynolds's tower also allowed the bank to restate its importance architecturally in the cityscape, after its first, eleven-story building had been eclipsed by the thirteen-story tower of the

recently completed Delaware & Hudson Building at the foot of State Street. But the bank's ascendency was short lived. At the end of the decade, Reynolds's former client, the National Savings Bank, built a bulky new tower immediately east of City Savings[53] that blocked the view of most of his building from the river. Reynolds was furious.

On the City Savings interior, Reynolds developed a two-story banking room marked by square columns, clad in polished pink granite, from whose gilded, composite capitals spring flat vaults decorated with the kinds of grotesque designs Reynolds knew from Roman villas. The room combines a clear expression of the structure of the skyscraper with antique elegance to suggest an ancient subterranean sanctuary. From each bay of the vault, an electrified chandelier provides a substitute for daylight in this mock grotto.

In each of his banks in smaller communities, Reynolds faced the question of whether to make the bank fit its environment or stand up and proclaim its differences. On the main street of Whitehall, New York, overlooking the upper reaches of the Champlain Canal, stands the Whitehall National Bank (Fig. 32). Set into a row of older brick commercial buildings, this Reynolds design of 1906 seems simultaneously of its place and from another world. Its brick walls belong with the brick of the neighboring structures, but its white Ionic columns set between banded brick antae, its carefully proportioned entablature and its pedimented door frame introduce notes of classical correctness foreign to the surroundings. At

Whitehall, as he did elsewhere, Reynolds walked a middle line between display and context.

Whitehall has the only preserved interior of all the Reynolds banks outside Albany, thanks to the fact that the town, which took it over for town offices, has not remodelled it. The irregular plan (Fig. 33) fits the irregularities of the lot, which is narrow on the street and wide at the rear. As he did in a number of later banks, Reynolds cleverly fudged the shift in axis between the front wall and and the interior space. The banking room, with its coved vault of plain plaster, is lit by windows on the south wall, behind the mahogany tellers'-screen. The subdivision of the interior into a lobby on one side and work space behind the screen on the the other approaches the status of being unique in Reynolds's work, even though such a division of space was much recommended by other bank architects, because it gave the customer a clear view of the tellers and the bank a conveniently unified work space.[54] The use of the screen at the side at Whitehall may well be related to the fact that the adjoining buildings blocked all sources of light save for a stretch of wall on the south side. The drawings for the bank include a skylight, but that apparently was not executed.

In almost all his other banks, Reynolds preferred the spatially more striking solution of a tellers'-screen that advanced into the center of the banking hall from the rear, somewhat in the manner of an Early Christian *schola cantorum*, a space enclosed by a wall that filled part of the nave of a church. For Albert Hopkins, the architect who wrote a book on bank design, this type of plan,

Fig. 34. Glens Falls Trust Company, Glens Falls, New York, 1907, facade (bay windows added later)

Fig. 35. Cohoes Savings Institution, Cohoes, New York, competition entry, 1904, rendering by Hughson Hawley

Fig. 36. Catskill Savings Bank, Catskill, New York, 1907-8 , facade

Fig. 37. Catskill Savings Bank, interior

which he called the island, was designed more for the convenience of the bank than the customer: "Customers are obliged to wander around a semi-circle looking for various holes in the screen through which they may do business. ...we are told that when the human mind has lost the sense of direction, it causes the body to travel in circles. Why start the body on a circuit which, if persisted in, may very soon affect the mind?"[55]

Like the Whitehall bank, the Glens Falls Trust Company, designed in 1907,[56] also has walls that echo those of the brick commercial structures of the center of the city (Fig. 34). The client here was one of Reynolds's most colorful, Addison Beecher Colvin, for whom Reynolds had designed a house in 1899. An entrepreneur who was engaged in printing, newspapers, banking, railroads and real estate, Colvin latched onto the profit-making possibilities of trust companies in 1898, when he founded the Glens Falls Trust. Within a few years the burgeoning enterprise needed a home that bespoke its success.[57] That Reynolds gave him in a handsome building with pairs of Ionic columns that support a pediment and frame a round-arched doorway.[58] A vaulted vestibule, flanked by offices, leads to the banking room, where pilasters rise to support an entablature and a coved vault with a skylight set in its center. The tellers'-screen with a semicircular front on the island plan has disappeared, but otherwise the interior retains much of its original character.

In the competition of 1904 for the Cohoes Savings Institution[59] Reynolds entered another design that combined brick walls and stone articulation (Fig. 35). Again, the brick referred to an existing urban context, while the stone would have made the bank stand out from its environment. Although the main facade of the Cohoes bank had projecting columns reminiscent of those on the Security Safe Deposit in Troy (Fig. 21), the arched windows between the columns gave the facade an entirely less-forbidding aspect.[60] Indeed, there were so many windows that the interior would have been one of Reynolds's most light-filled. Probably it would have looked something like the the water-color of 1897 (Fig. 14). Even though Reynolds's design was splendidly presented by a great master of architectural renderings, Hughson Hawley, the commission went to a local architect.[61]

Catskill, New York, boasts a pair of Reynolds's finest banks, standing side by side, that go out of their way to disassociate themselves from the context of the main street on which they rise. The Catskill Savings Bank was designed in 1907,[62] and the Tanners Bank followed in 1908.[63] The two institutions had a symbiotic relationship. Founded in 1868, the savings bank, like many of its ilk, operated at first out of the offices of an older institution, in this case the Tanners Bank, founded in 1831. As chartered in New York State, savings banks existed to encourage thrift on the part of those at the lower levels of the economic strata. The directors and officers, with a few exceptions, were not allowed to draw salaries, and the banks' profits from depositors' savings were returned to the depositors as interest. Cutting down on operating expenses by using the premises of another institution (with which a savings bank generally shared directors, as well as office space) allowed savings banks to pay higher returns on deposits.

Most savings banks eventually outgrew their borrowed nests. When that happened, the directors usually opted to erect an impressive building. Reynolds's Catskill Savings Bank (Fig. 36) did this in spades, with a stone facade that combined aspects of the temple front and the triumphal arch. Engaged Ionic columns shoot up from the sidewalk to bear an entablature that proclaims the bank's name and to frame a round arch that shelters the door. That door opens into one of Reynolds's most noble spaces, a barrel-vaulted hall lit from the top by the five rows of glazed coffers (Fig. 37). The arch of the facade foretells the shape of the interior, but not its size and not its dramatic lighting. Although Reynolds was working at a small scale, he achieved here something of the effect of going through the round-arched door of the Pantheon into its vast, vaulted interior. Into this banking hall once projected a marble and bronze tellers'-screen, ending in a semicircle that repeated the shape of the vault above (Fig. 38).[64] Looking back at the entrance wall, one can see the square of the coffers repeated in the bronze grille over the door.

Reynolds had used an aedicular facade with a round-arched opening in front of a vaulted interior five years earlier, in the National Savings Bank (Fig. 19). There, however, the facade lacked the directness and clarity of the Catskill facade. Clearly, by 1907 Reynolds had grown as a designer; he had learned to do more by doing less, perhaps from the example of the National Commercial Bank facade by York & Sawyer that had risen almost next door

to his National Savings Bank.[65]

As soon as the new savings bank in Catskill was finished, the parasitic relationship between it and the Tanners Bank was reversed. The latter temporarily moved its offices into the former, while a new Reynolds building was constructed on its old

Fig. 38. Catskill Savings Bank, first floor plan

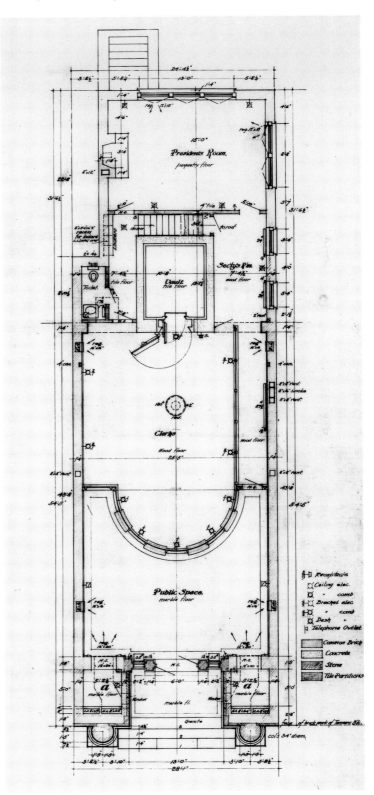

Fig. 39. *Tanners National Bank, Catskill, New York, 1908-9, facade*

Fig. 40. *Tanners National Bank, first floor plan*

site next door. This second Catskill bank is remarkably different from the first: its facade as insistently about shallow relief as the other is about the development of forms in depth (Fig. 39). The only depth is provided by the arch of the doorway, and by the bold projections of the cornice and the console-keystone that supports a large bull's head — one of Reynolds's engagingly quirky but appo-

site animal details. (The bank takes its name from the industry that made Catskill prosperous in the early nineteenth century: tanning. The shores of Catskill Creek were blessed with abundant stands of hemlock, whose bark of was essential to the process of turning cowhide into leather.) Because the bank sits on a corner, the rusticated, white marble masonry is continued around the angle to cover the full depth of the banking room.[66] The great round-arched window, centered in the center of the side and flanked by two rectangular windows, replays the theme stated on the main facade.

The rectangular space of the interior continues the game of flatness (Figs. 40 and 41). The screen formed a low wall across the space, its center bulging only slightly to maintain even here the theme of low relief that characterizes the whole building. The ceiling was ivory and grey-buff, the walls a stronger grey, the pilasters, entablature and beams gilded; the screen was white marble and the tellers'-cages mahogany with bronze grates, possibly gilded.[67] All this related harmoniously to the white stone and grey shadows of the outside, but the more intense colors were saved for the dimmer light of the interior.[68] The elaborate clock over the vault door came from the old New York State Capitol by Philip Hooker.

In Catskill Reynolds once again kept visually alive a memory of the old buildings that his designs replaced. The Tanners Bank had occupied a structure from the 1830s with a flat facade articulated by four shallow pilasters that recalled Italian Renaissance buildings. The facade of the Greek Revival commercial building which the savings bank replaced had two freestanding Ionic columns that supported a pediment. Its simplicity may well

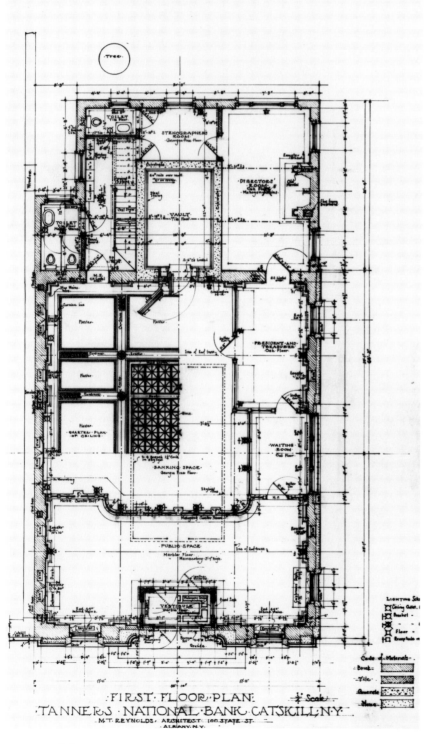

FIRST·FLOOR·PLAN·
·TANNERS·NATIONAL·BANK·CATSKILL·N·Y·
·M·T·REYNOLDS·ARCHITECT·100·STATE·ST·
·ALBANY·N·Y·

have helped Reynolds achieve the strength of his own design. Here one sees embodied in stone Reynolds's belief that progress is built on tradition. He probably also satisfied the nostalgia of the savings bank's president, Washington Irving Jennings, for the old Greek Revival structure in which he had kept his law offices for many years

Some of the banks that followed failed to come up to the high quality of the Catskill designs. Reynolds's competition design of 1909 for the Hudson City Savings Institution[69] lost out to a design with a dome.[70] The rather dry Manufacturers Bank in Mechanicville, New York, of 1911-12, has Tuscan columns on the front and pilasters flanking round arched windows along the side. Its interior has been sliced in half by a dropped ceiling, behind which the pilasters of the side walls now ignominiously disappear.

The Franklin Savings Institution (Fig. 42) in Greenfield, Massachusetts,[71] is a powerful "billboard" on a street dominated by dark red brick commercial structures of the nineteenth century. Reynolds made a particularly strong contrast between his design and the Venetian Gothic facade of the adjoining Franklin County National Bank. In 1911, when the new offices opened, there could have been little doubt which bank was the more "progressive."[72]

Arches, not Reynolds's more typical columns and pilasters, dominate the exterior. The three on the flank, sprung from broad piers and separated by roundels, ultimately recall the flanks of Alberti's Tempio Malatestiano in Rimini, perhaps as that design had been filtered through the facade of McKim, Mead & White's Boston Public Library, both buildings of great civic importance. On the front the central arch springs from two Ionic columns, set into the depth of the wall to provide some modest three-dimensional activity on a rather tight corner. The spandrels bear reliefs of

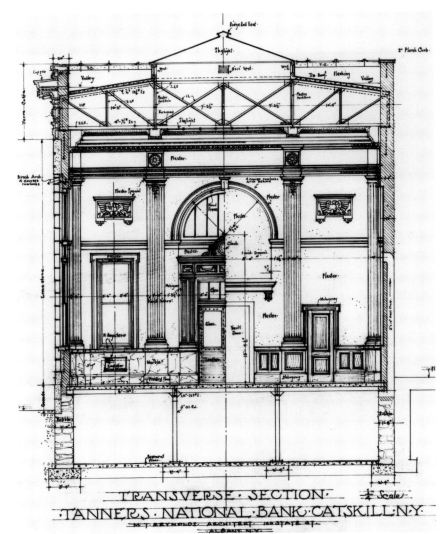

early Massachusetts coins, a form of bank decoration that Reynolds knew well from the Hooker facade of the New York State National Bank (Fig. 22). The lot on which the bank rose was an irregular trapezoid, and Reynolds used a busy pattern of coffers in the ceiling to hide the fact that the side walls are not parallel. The interior has an unusually cavernous feel, because the windows and the

Fig. 41. Tanners National Bank, cross section

Fig. 42. Franklin Savings Institution, Greenfield, Massachusetts, 1910-11, view from southeast

blind arches that mirror them are set high over very bare walls. The now-missing screen, however, projected into the center of the space and was made of marble and bronze.[73]

The first design for the Taunton Savings Bank in Massachusetts, published in 1912,[74] had a

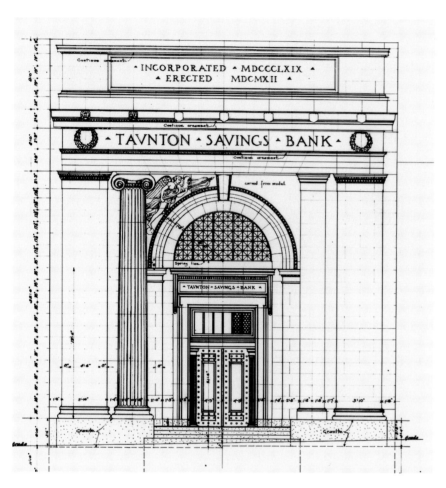

Fig. 43. Taunton Savings Bank, Taunton, Massachusetts, front elevation, first design, 1912

facade similar to that of the Catskill Savings Bank, but with an attic over the entablature instead of a pediment. The square of the facade (Fig. 43), measured from side to side and from the sidewalk to the cornice under the attic, prefigured the square plan and elevations of the cubic banking room (Fig. 44). Inside, the walls would have been articulated by pairs of pilasters, creating narrow bays that framed wider, round-arched bays. The deeply coffered ceiling would have reflected this A-B-A division of the walls, and in its center there would have been a square skylight. Budgetary considerations led to the adoption of a lower, one-story scheme, which forced Reynolds to redesign the facade.[75] The second facade lacks the punch of the first. Too many elements, not carefully worked out, destroy the sense of focus the first facade had.

On the lower interior a proliferation of forms led to a diminution in the force of the design. The facade still stands, but the interior has been altered beyond recognition.

The Amsterdam Savings Bank ranked alongside the savings bank in Catskill as one of Reynolds's two or three best banks,[76] but it has suffered seriously from remodelings.[77] The bank announced its presence in Amsterdam with a Corinthian portico (Fig. 45) capped by an attic that gives the dates of the founding of the institution and the erection of the building.[78] The rectangular porch and the rectilinear door set up the surprise created by the curves of the interior. Free of buildings to either side, the banking room is lit by large, round-arched windows and by glazed coffers set into the segmental barrel vault (Fig. 46). The cross bands of the vault continue the rhythm of the walls into the ceiling. (The walls do not actually support the vault, which is suspended from a steel truss.) The whole system of alternating arches and paired pilasters under a coffered barrel vault ultimately goes back to Alberti's Sant' Andrea at Mantua, but seventeenth-century France and eighteenth-century England have intervened, as well as a particular early twentieth-century American building, Cram, Goodhue and Ferguson's Chapin Hall at Williams College of 1910.[79] The six-columned Corinthian portico of Chapin, raised on a podium of steps, leads through an entrance hall (omitted by Reynolds) into a wide auditorium lit by round-arched windows in the side walls and covered by a segmental vault with cross bands. While the Cram, Goodhue and Ferguson interior remains closely tied to its prototype, James Gibbs's Senate House at Cambridge of 1722, the Reynolds interior speaks a richer, more detailed classical language. Not the least memorable of the details of the Amsterdam interior was the dark marble-and-bronze screen, whose segmentally curved front echoed the shape of the vault above (Fig. 46). Reynolds won this commission, his last major new bank, not through connections but through the success of earlier bank designs. The first vice president, Luther L. Dean, visited a number of banks in New York and other states before Reynolds was picked as the architect.[80]

Did Reynolds, one might ask, make distinctions in his designs among various types of banks? Are his national or state banks different from his savings banks, from his trust companies, from his

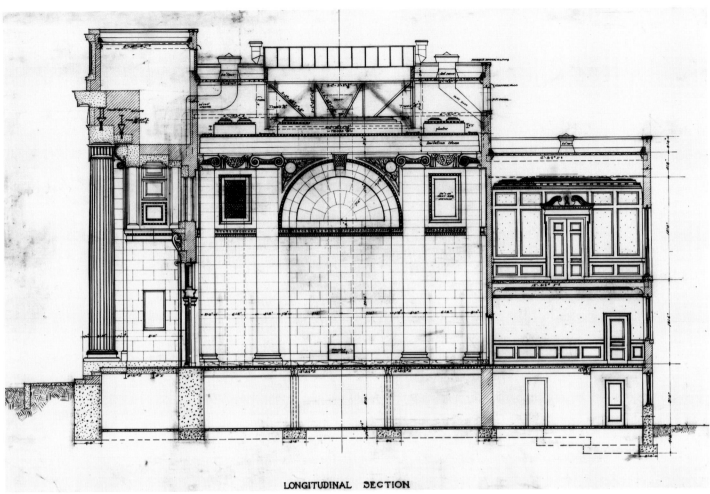

LONGITUDINAL SECTION

Fig. 44. *Taunton Savings Bank, longitudinal section, first design, 1912*

safe deposit institutions? The answer seems to be yes, but not consistently.

Of his banks, only one is for safe deposit. The Security Safe Deposit in Troy lacked the tellers'-screen in the main room, because there was no need for one. Instead, the space was choked by a vault, in a manner analogous to the way Michelangelo's staircase chokes the entrance hall of the Laurentian Library. The walls, below the rather complex lunettes and skylight, were remarkably bare, perhaps to emphasize the looming presence of the safe deposit vault. In the facade, which referred to a museum, the window grilles were given a particular emphasis, to suggest their role in protecting items deposited for safe keeping (Fig. 21).

Two are trust companies, Albany and Glens Falls. None of Reynolds's other bank designs look anything like the Albany Trust Company (Fig. 17). This fact may result in part from the position of the building in the cityscape, both in terms of its corner location and of the architectural influences exerted on Reynolds by surrounding build-

ings and by the previous building on the site. Part of the difference comes from the fact that the building offered six stories of rental offices. But the unusual appearance doubtless also had to do with the fact that the building served a trust company, rather than a commercial or a savings bank. Albany Trust was the first in the city, founded in an era in which trust companies, particularly in New York state, were booming, because they were subject to far less state and federal regulation than other kinds of banks and so could provide the convenience of one-stop banking.[81] James H. Manning explained the difference between trust companies and other types of banks with exemplary clarity: "The trust company has been not inaptly termed 'the department store of banking,' in that it can do for a man whatever he needs done in a financial way, dead or alive. It can accept deposits, make loans, receive savings accounts, and buy a bond or a share of stock for a client, but it cannot issue banknotes. It has broader powers than either national or state banks, for it is endowed by law with 'trust powers' denied to all the others."[82] It may very well be that John Parsons, the ambitious and energetic president of Albany Trust, and its equally energetic founder, Judge Randall Le Boeuf, wanted their building to suggest through its architectural difference the greater range of services their company could provide. Inside, that abundance of services was made instantly clear and accessible to customers by the circular tellers'-screen praised by the *Albany Evening Journal*. Reynolds never arranged a tellers'-screen in this way again.

On the other hand, the Glens Falls Trust Company (Fig. 34) does not seem nearly so different from other Reynolds banks. Its brick-and-stone exterior was surely chosen both to make it fit and to differentiate it from the brick buildings of the center of Glens Falls. The exterior has much in common with Reynolds's national bank in Whitehall (Fig. 32) and the savings bank he projected for Cohoes (Fig. 35). The interior, with its pilasters and coved vault with a skylight, is very much like the interiors of the New York State, Tanners and Manufacturers banks and of the Taunton Savings Bank. Unlike the tellers'-screen at the Albany Trust, the one at Glens falls was laid out on the hard-for-the-customer-to-see island plan.

Commercial banks were chartered by the federal or state governments. The National Banking Acts of 1863 and 1864 created the process by which national banks could be chartered directly by the federal government. Such banks were allowed to issue the bank notes that became the universal currency of the country. The prestige of having the word "national" in a bank's name was mitigated by strict governmental requirements for start-up capital, for maintaining reserves and for issuing loans. By Reynolds's day, those requirements had come to seem a liability, and newly created national banks were rare. In 1900, the government lowered the capital requirement for starting a national bank in a town with a population of less than six thousand from $50,000 to $25,000, but this seems to have had little effect on the commissions Reynolds received.[83] The relatively parlous condition of national banks in this era may perhaps be glimpsed in the only store-front banks Reynolds designed, the First National in Albany and the Union National in Schenectady (Fig. 29), which either could not or chose not to put much money into architectural advertising. Instead, they opted for rental property above the banking room behind relatively inexpen-

sive commercial facades. No trust company or savings bank for which Reynolds worked made a similar choice. The New York State National Bank, of course, did opt to spend quite a bit on a its new building, but the money was used in part to reinforce the prestige that the old facade by Philip Hooker gave the bank (Figs. 23 and 26).

Among Reynolds's national and state banks, there is considerable variety, at least in the exteriors. There is the Colonial "Survival" of the New York State National Bank's Hooker facade, the treasury-like facade with columns *in antis* of the Whitehall National Bank, the Beaux-Arts razzle-dazzle of the Tanners National Bank, and the rather solemn dryness of the state-chartered Manufacturers Bank at Mechanicville. This variety may suggest that Reynolds felt more freedom with this type of bank than he felt when he was designing savings banks. Or it may suggest that no overarching ideas guided the design of national and state banks.

With the exception of the store-front banks, the national and state banks have remarkably similar interiors: walls generally articulated by pilasters and generally supporting coved vaults penetrated by skylights. These interiors run the gamut from very lavish in the New York State National Bank to very plain at Whitehall, but their ceilings in all cases were less elaborate than the ceilings Reynolds designed for savings banks. On the whole, the officers and directors of national and state banks seem to have been somewhat less eager to spend money on architectural effects than the presidents and trustees of savings banks, at least in the case of buildings designed by Reynolds. But the richly appointed directors' room of the State Bank (Fig. 25) suggests that in some cases they were happy to spend money to make themselves seem and feel important.

Reynolds's savings banks form his most consistent group, and they also include some of Reynolds's best work. James Manning spoke eloquently, if effusively, of the role of the savings bank in society:

For it is one of the marvels of all the ages that this single institution has actually changed the once miserable dependents of Society into self-reliant, self-respecting citizens, the real bone and sinew of the land; that it has transformed the former paupers of all lands, who were content to seek ever the crumbs that fell from their masters' tables, into its real capitalists, the product of whose industry and self-denial has built and is building our homes, our schools, our factories, our ships, our roads, our bridges, our railroads, our canals.[84]

"And all of this," Manning continued, "has been done — at least by the Mutual Savings Banks of the land — without money and without price. *In other words, these institutions have cost their depositors nothing beyond the legitimate running expenses.*"[85] The depositors' savings were then invested in real estate mortgages and bonds, to finance all the economic growth of the land. The return to the depositors was threefold: the encouragement of habits of thrift, the interest paid on their deposits and, most important, the income produced through the jobs created by the banks' investments.[86]

The trustees and presidents of savings institutions took no pay; their efforts for the banks were considered charity work. The men who ran savings banks were "noble, high minded and unselfish… acting solely in the interest of the public, of those least able to get ahead…. They were helping them help themselves."[87]

Savings banks were seen by men like Manning, and doubtless by Reynolds, as transformative institutions from which the lower orders received moral uplift, economic security and social salvation (they became capitalists), all in return for their small but regular deposits. Arguably, this perception of the role of the savings bank stood behind the quasi-religious nature of the interiors of the National Savings Bank (Fig. 20), the Catskill Savings Bank (Fig. 37) and the Amsterdam Savings Bank (Fig. 46), the only interiors to which Reynolds gave barrel vaults or domes. In the cases of Hudson, Greenfield and Taunton, the flat ceilings had, or would have had, a more elaborate play of coffers and skylights than we find even in the relatively rich ceiling of the Tanners National Bank. At Hudson, and in the first design for Taunton, the flat ceiling, moreover, was essential to create the interior cube of the bank room (Fig. 44), a pure form that Reynolds used for no other type of bank.[88]

Manning is silent on justifying the expenditure on lavish buildings of profits that could otherwise be returned to the depositors. Presumably, to be considered a legitimate operating expense, pricey architecture had to give the depositors something that money alone could not buy. What architecture bought was a greater sense of confidence in the bank. That confidence, in turn, produced more depositors —more newly metamorphosed capital-

ists. As an anonymous writer in *Architectural Record* put it:

The conclusion is inevitable, that the designing of a bank is an important factor in its success, especially for an institution which depends upon the patronage of a very large number of depositors. The effect of the structure must be one of great importance and dignified simplicity. It must make on the depositors the impression of being a perfectly safe place in which to leave their money and valuables.[89]

Savings banks were in a difficult competitive

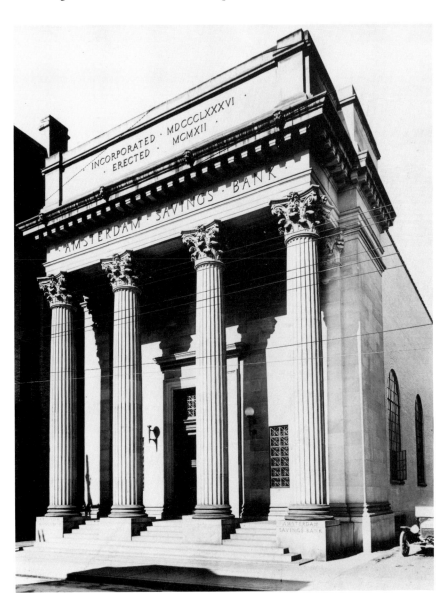

Fig. 45. Amsterdam Savings Bank, Amsterdam, New York, 1912-14, view from southeast

position because laws severely restricted their conduct of business. They could only take in deposits, pay interest and make safe investments. They could not provide checking accounts, trust services, or commercial loans. Trust companies and commercial banks could provide all these latter services, and they could also pay higher interest because their investments were not legally restricted to the "safe" ones of real estate loans and bonds.[90] Since the only real competitive advantage a savings bank held was the greater safety of its investments, architecture that bespoke safety was clearly to the bank's advantage. Growth of savings bank deposits meant increased business activity between savings banks and the commercial banks and trust companies of which their trustees were

mous writer invoked classical architecture at the outset. He noted that the ancient Greeks and Romans kept treasure in temples and that during the Renaissance the center of finance remained in an Italy whose architecture continued Roman traditions.[93] The writer insisted, however, that "modern bank buildings are the architectural expression of a problem which really has little or no definite precedent in antiquity."[94] His simulta-

Fig. 46. Amsterdam Savings Bank, interior

generally also directors and stockholders[91] and from which those directors and stockholders could expect larger dividends. Thus altruism might bring rewards beyond the moral.

Assessing Reynolds's use of a classical vocabulary for banks is a complex proposition, not easily achieved until we have a thorough study of bank architecture against which to set his work.[92] An article on banks that appeared in *Architectural Record* in 1909 provides some help, however, by discussing the problem of reconciling old architectural styles with modern functions. The anony-

neous citation and rejection of precedent left readers in an ambiguous situation, typical of the period. How was an architect to operate between the need, generally felt, to anchor buildings to appropriate precedents, and the need, universally acknowledged, to meet the demands of modern functions?[95]

Still, every bank the author discussed, with the exception of Louis Sullivan's Farmers Bank in Owatonna, Minnesota, of 1906-8,[96] used a classical vocabulary. If nothing else, that tells us of the widespread popularity of classical forms for banks at the time. (As we travel around the country, our own eyes tell us the same thing.) Clearly, Reynolds was giving his clients the kinds of banks that people expected bankers to build, and that bankers expected to build, if they were to be seen as responsible, trustworthy, prosperous members of the profession that undergirded the enormous success of the American economy.[97] It would be very surprising if Reynolds, in like manner to Sullivan, had chosen to use a style other than the antique.[98]

The *Architectural Record* writer's sense of the visual, physical and even spiritual effect of a bank was laid out in carefully chosen words:

The importance of the bank's prestige as established by its quarters is a matter which is nowhere better appreciated than in the United States, where the prevailing note in a well-designed bank building is a consummate expression of the importance of the institution and a certain mystery which adds immeasurably to the dignity of the management. The impression which it is intended to convey by these words is a perfectly familiar sensation to the average American, whether he frequents banks a great deal or very little.[99]

This hint of mystery in the common experience Americans had with banks is an important qualification, which rings true, one suspects, for most of us who have experienced a great classical bank interior. For a building to be mysterious, it has to be out of the ordinary, and Reynolds's banks, in their small city settings, are certainly that. Their mostly monochromatic exteriors, of carefully proportioned classical elements, depart from (and in their own way add to) the visual cacophony of an American Main Street. They are cool, orderly, self-contained, expensive, and they invoke the weight of the past. Inside the world of the street is banished and the light of nature is modulated. The space is tall and open and articulated by large-scale classical forms set in deliberate contrast to nearby shops and offices, whose chief embellishments might be a pressed-tin ceiling and an occasional molding.

Once admitted to the visual splendor of a Reynolds bank, the customer was barred from

most of the interior by the advancing tellers'-screen, behind which the officers and employees were partly hidden (Fig. 46). There is something of the Byzantine iconastasis in the tellers'-screen. Few ceremonies are more mysterious than the Byzantine liturgy, during which the clergy are mostly hidden from the congregation by the wall of the iconastasis. The tellers'-screen turns the customer into a communicant, who is sometimes admitted into the realm of the initiates behind the cages, to discuss business with the banker or to retrieve a safe deposit box in the vault. One suspects that Reynolds favored the island screen precisely because it made his interiors seem mysterious, his bankers more powerful. The "democratic" Louis Sullivan, we should note, eschewed the island plan in all his banks.[100] He preferred the more accommodating U-shaped screen, or the screen to one side, as Reynolds had placed it in Whitehall.

Although the analogy should not be pushed too far, further relationships exist between Reynolds's banks and religious architecture. In at least two banks, at Greenfield and at Amsterdam, he used elements ultimately derived from Renaissance churches. His bank vaults are invariably on axis, where the altar would be in a church, and surmounted by clocks almost as frequently as Christian altars are marked by crosses. The clock was a convenience to customers in a era when many people of modest means did not own watches. But it was also highly symbolic, not just of the old cliché that time is money, but also of time itself, which endures like the security of the vault, whose impregnability stood, of course, for that of the institution itself. Over all this presided a well-tailored and often well-upholstered gentleman in banker's grey, rather than bishop's purple.[101] Unlike churches, banks had to be brightly lit, so that you could see your money and the balance in your passbook.[102] No shadowy dealings in a money-changer's temple.

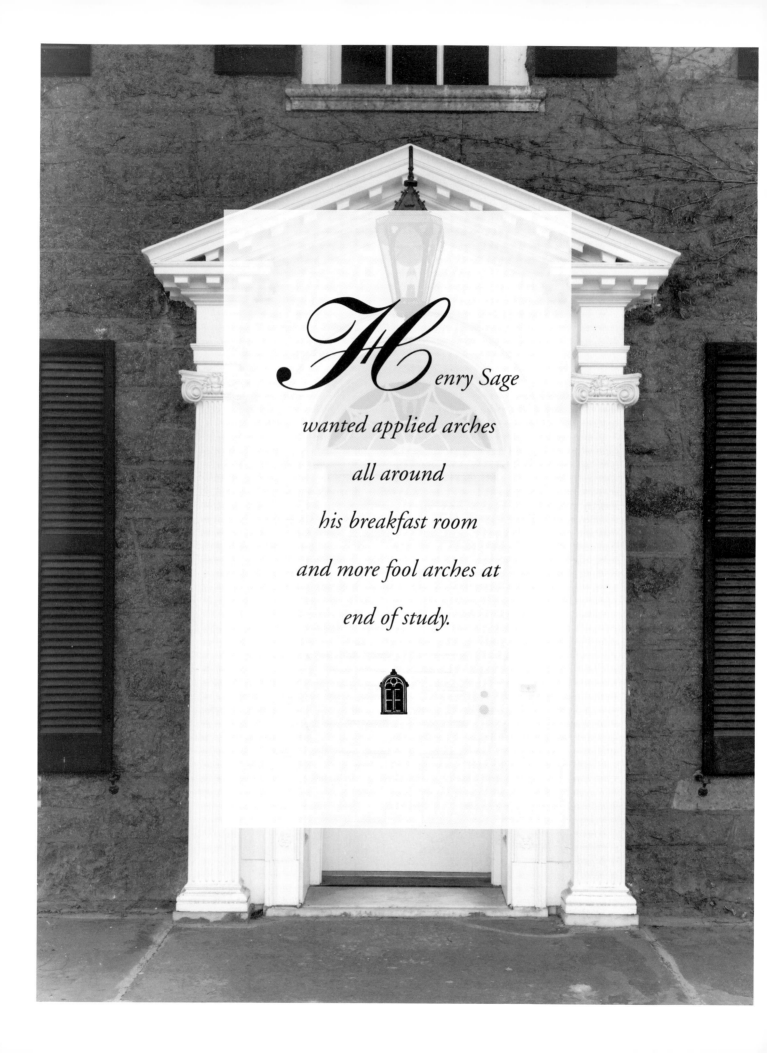

$\mathcal{H}$*enry Sage*

wanted applied arches

all around

his breakfast room

and more fool arches at

end of study.

CHAPTER 3

HOUSES

T OWN HOUSES
Architects often begin their careers by designing houses for relatives or friends. Marcus Reynolds was no exception. Almost the first important commission that came his way after he returned from his wanderings in Europe was a row of three houses on State Street, Albany, for his cousins, William Bayard and Howard Van Rensselaer (Fig. 47). The resplendent Italian Renaissance palazzo facade that Reynolds designed for them integrated the three houses into one commanding visual presence that dominates the northeast corner of Washington Park.

Reynolds used the basic elements of Italian palace facades: a flat, rectangular block punctuated at regular intervals by round-arched and rectangular openings and capped by a strong cornice. Onto this basic block the young Reynolds lavished such exuberant detailing as the alternating bands of fish-scale and vermiculated (as in worm-eaten) rustication. The vermiculated blocks, which seem all different at first glance, are actually all alike. They were made of terra cotta, a process that allowed Reynolds to achieve cheaply through mass produc-

tion the effect of hand-carved irregularity. The rich, North Italian quality of the ornament reflect both Reynolds's encounters with such buildings as the Palazzo del Consiglio in Verona and with American buildings that depended on the same sources, such as Stanford White's Herald Building in New York. But Reynolds's designs have an eclectic chutzpah, to use Charles Moore's delightful phrase, that goes beyond even Stanford White at his most decorative.

The ornament includes Van Rensselaer heraldic devices: woven baskets issuing flames, placed over the second-story windows and under the crowning cornice, and *croix à moulins* in the capitals of the half columns of the second-story windows. These decorations suggest that the three houses were originally intended to be occupied by three Van Rensselaers: William Bayard, Howard, and their mother, Laura. The houses, Reynolds's first published work, appeared under the title "Three Residences for Messrs. Van Rensselaer, Albany, N. Y."[2] Designing the three houses to appear to be one wide palace, covered with the heraldic devices of one family, gave them a presence in Albany

Facing page. Henry Manning Sage House, Menands, New York, 1919-21, east door

Fig. 47. Van Rensselaer Houses, 385-389 State Street, Albany, 1896-97, facade

unrivaled by almost any other house in the city. As head of the Van Rensselaer family, William Bayard was entitled to think of himself as Prince of Albany, a notion the facade did nothing to undermine. Louisa Greenough Lane Van Rensselaer, his Boston Brahmin wife, reportedly regarded Washington Park as her private front yard.

In the end, however, only William Bayard and Louisa Van Rensselaer came to live in one of the houses, that to the right. The other two, at 387 and 389 State Street, were sold soon after their completion to a felt manufacturer, F. C. Huyck, and to the president of the United National Bank of Troy, appropriately named Samuel S. Bullions.

Fig. 48. William Bayard Van Rensselaer House, 385 State Street, Albany, dining room

Fig. 49. Gerrit Yates Lansing House, 294 State Street, Albany, 1899, plan

William Bayard had reorganized the family land holdings, widely dispersed through inheritances, into a trust that he headed. He himself embarked on a career in law and banking, an act that marked a change from the patterns established by his forbearers. The patroons of the Van Rensselaer manor had been the feudal lords of an enormous tract of land, which they ruled from the manor house that William Bayard had destroyed in 1893. The Renaissance palazzo that Cousin Marcus designed for him proclaimed the new, urban, mercantile focus of his activities. In the early 1880s, McKim Mead & White's Villard Houses in New York had begun a fashion for well-to-do Americans to house themselves in the man-

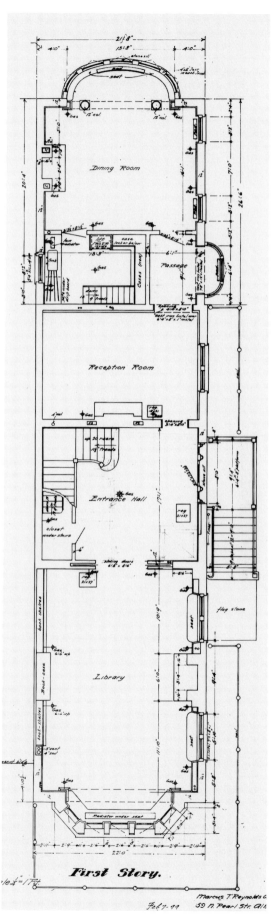

First Story.

44

ner of Italian aristocrats. The palaces of merchant princes of the Renaissance were deemed appropriate prototypes for the urban dwellings of modern American barons of trade.

The Van Rensselaer Houses are all three rooms deep: in the front a parlor, in the center a living hall and staircase, and in the rear a dining room with adjacent butler's pantry. All three houses had L-shaped plans that allowed for windows in the north walls of the living halls and in the side walls of the dining rooms. Privacy was maintained in the living halls and dining rooms by using stained glass.

The interior of the house at 385 State Street has been chopped up into several apartments, and the mantelpieces on the ground floor have been removed. In the dining room and parlor, however, are decorative details from the old manor house that Reynolds skillfully integrated into the new design. To frame the west window of the dining room he used the large staircase opening of the 1760s, with Ionic pilasters flanking a segmental arch surrounded by rich foliate ornament in the spandrels. The arch is reflected in the dining room mirror in an old photograph of the interior (Fig. 48). The door frames with broken pediments came from the manor house also.[3] Even as William Bayard Van Rensselaer set a new course for himself and his family, he did so surrounded by bits of Van Rensselaer history.[4]

In 1899 Reynolds chose non-Italian sources for his design for the Lansing House at 295 State Street. Gerrit Yates Lansing, the eighth generation of his Dutch family to live in the Hudson Valley,[5] was a classmate of Reynolds at Williams.[6] Lansing

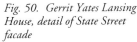

Fig. 50. *Gerrit Yates Lansing House, detail of State Street facade*

Fig. 51. *Canon George Carter House, 62 South Swan Street, Albany, 1901-2, facade*

established himself as a businessman in Albany and quickly achieved the success that required a handsome residence on State Street. He bought an old house at the southeast corner of Dove Street, which Reynolds enlarged and remodelled. Reynolds took advantage of the corner site to move the entrance to the side facade on Dove (Fig. 49), so that the front room would not have to give up space to an entrance hall, as it had in the old house.

Reynolds replaced the old front stoop with a bay window (Fig. 50), whose scroll pediment and the tapered pilasters suggest English and Dutch furniture designs of the early eighteenth century, so that the window seems a curious inversion of outdoor and indoor forms. The seal of the Dutch West India Company in the stained glass of the bay window surely celebrates Lansing's Dutch ancestry. In the Dove Street facade, a bowed window with a fanlight suggests eighteenth-century England, from whence came the forebearers of Lansing's wife, Susan Rathbone Townsend. Indeed, one is tempted to see in this pastiche of a house a celebration of the joining of Dutch and

Yankee cultures that characterized Albany since the early eighteenth century.

The house for Canon George Carter on Swan Street (Fig. 51), designed in 1901 and completed a year later, has an elaborate facade that recalls German and English houses of the sixteenth century, where one can find similar bays projected on corbels and articulated by richly decorated pilasters. The linenfolds in the panels under the second-floor windows (Fig. 52) are typical of English architecture of this period, but they are much more commonly found on interior wood panelling than on exteriors. Here, as at the Lansing House, Reynolds seems to have moved forms developed for interiors onto the exterior. The Englishness of the sources was appropriate, of course, for a canon of the Episcopal Church.

Some of the facade decoration provoked the good canon's disapproval. On September 28, 1901, he objected "to his grotesques." Nonetheless, the grotesques were placed under the steep eaves of the roof. The canon's displeasure may lend some credence to a bit of Reynolds's family lore, which has it that he loathed the impecunious canon's rich wife and gave her a replica of a famous French or Belgian (the story varies from teller to teller) bordello. Whether this story is true or not, Reynolds certainly possessed a sardonic

Fig. 52. Canon George Carter House, detail of second floor facade

Fig. 53. Ryder Apartments, 355 State Street, Albany, 1903-5, early design, elevation

46

humor that made him capable of pulling such a
trick on a client he disdained.

M. L. Ryder, a contractor and real estate entrepreneur with whom Reynolds frequently did business,[7] approached Reynolds about designing an
apartment building[8] in July, 1903, but Ryder did
not accept the final plans until January, 1904.[9]
The Ryder apartments brought to State Street in
Albany the kind of luxury apartment living already
established in Manhattan.[10] Each floor contains
two apartments, with public rooms along the State
Street facade, a kitchen and a maid's room in the
middle, and family bedrooms to the rear. The
ground-floor apartments also contained professional offices with separate entrances from the
common entrance hall.

Reynolds produced several facade designs
before a final scheme was settled upon. The earliest, a seven-story building (Fig. 53), Reynolds
treated as a vertically stretched palazzo, with a rusticated ground floor surmounted by five identical
floors reaching up to an attic under the cornice.
The only break with the palazzo tradition is the
insertion of two vertical strips of bay windows that
run from the second to the sixth stories. A six-
story scheme followed, with a few changes.

The final, four-story scheme (Fig. 54) saw more
fundamental changes in the facade. The rather
pure classicism of the ground floor was replaced by
rougher rustication, by droopy consoles around
the door, and by other consoles, large enough to
make Michelangelo blush, that support the almost
weightless wooden bay windows (Fig. 55). The
cornice became much heftier, with great consoles,
metamorphosing from triglyphs, surmounted by a
high balustrade that tries to replace the three stories the building had lost in height. The upper
consoles are paraphrases of a detail of the cornice
of the earlier house immediately to the west of the
apartment facade.

A town house of 1904 for Edmund Niles and
Jesse Van Antwerp Huyck (Fig. 56), for whom
Reynolds had earlier designed a country house,
followed swiftly on the heels of the Ryder apartments.[11] It should be no surprise, then, that the
two buildings have many details in common. In
the entablature of the Huyck House, however,
paired triglyphs carry the verticals of the brick wall
through the entablature into the piers of the
balustrade, whereas the triglyphs of the apartment
block have essentially no connection with what
goes on below them. The large scale of the Huyck

*Fig. 54. Ryder Apartments,
facade*

*Fig. 55. Ryder Apartments,
detail of facade*

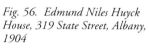

Fig. 56. Edmund Niles Huyck House, 319 State Street, Albany, 1904

Fig. 57. Sen. Curtis Douglas House, 4 Elk Street, Albany, facade remodelled 1899

Fig. 58. Harmon Pumpelly Read House (left), 7 Elk Street, Albany, facade remodelled 1915, and Judge William Wallace House (right), 6 Elk Street, facade remodelled 1908

triglyphs offers a telling contrast to those of the much earlier wooden house immediately to the west. When Reynolds worked in a Colonial Revival mode, he eschewed the diminutive and even self-effacing scale of its classicized style.

Reynolds also remodelled the facades of three town houses on Elk Street. The first, carried out in 1899 for the lumber magnate Curtis Douglas at number 4 (Fig. 57), involved only a few changes to a Greek Revival facade of 1824.[12] New frames, derived from sixteenth-century Italian Renaissance sources, were placed around the door and windows of the first floor, and a new attic story continued the Renaissance detailing in its squashed volutes. The reliefs in the attic suggest a happy marriage: Cupid peers out from the central panel, while the side panels display his torch and quiver. The second, at number 6, designed in 1908 for Judge William Wallace (Fig. 58, right), involved more extensive changes to an earlier facade.[13] A new brick wall supports an attic story, which, in its flat whiteness, seems to suggest early nineteenth-century London. The ground floor windows were given round arches that contain marble reliefs of women who hold musical instruments and lean against tripods that support wicker baskets issuing flames. This heraldic device recalled the fact that the house was originally built in the 1820s by

William Van Rensselaer. The third house, number 7 (Fig. 58, left), was done over for Reynolds's great friends, Harmon Pumpelly and Delphine Read, in 1915.[14] He shared Reynolds's interest in genealogy, while she, of French origin, gave splendid dinner parties that the sybaritic Reynolds was all too delighted to attend.[15] The bounty of her table is suggested by the cornucopias in the lintels above the second and third-floor windows. All three Elk Street facades are remarkable for their restraint, particularly in comparison to the facades of the Van Rensselaer and Carter houses. Reynolds seems not to have wanted to break too much with the simplicity of the facades of the other Greek Revival houses that remained on the street.

HOUSES IN SMALL CITIES

Reynolds's houses in small cities differ markedly from his town houses of Albany. They are more like country houses on relatively small lots rather than urban row houses. In this sense they are suburban, without being in suburbs. Because Reynolds had relatively few such commissions, he used few styles: half-timbered, Jacobean and Colonial. Sometimes Reynolds alone made the decision on the style; sometimes he offered the clients a choice. In the instance of a house of 1904 for a banker, Charles Van Deusen, in the small city of Hudson (Fig. 59), we know that Reynolds

prepared two designs: a picturesque and a classical; the Van Deusens chose the classical.[16]

By almost any standard, the house for Addison Beecher Colvin of 1901 in Glens Falls was one of Reynolds's least successful works. The unimaginative plan is enclosed in simply massed, asymmetrical walls with a touch of half-timbering in the front gable and some gratuitous herms tacked onto the front porch posts (Fig. 60). As one comes to understand the self-made and tirelessly self-promoting Colvin,[17] one begins to suspect that Reynolds deliberately gave him a bad house.

Born in 1858, Colvin was orphaned at an early age.[18] At eighteen he began publishing the *Glens Falls Times*, the first daily newspaper in the state north of Troy, and in 1883 he married Marie Louise Hees, the sister of J. Ledlie Hees, a banker from Fonda and Gloversville for whom Reynolds had done a cottage at Sacandaga Park in 1899.

A tireless joiner and an entrepreneur with major interests in publishing and banking, Colvin also had literary pretensions. Under the pseudonym Harvester Hiram he wrote two novels, of which this author has read only *"Lumberman Lew."*[19] That insufficiently short work begins with the equivalent of "It was a dark and stormy night.": "The shadows of the trees on the mountains back of the settlement known as Warrensville, at the foothills of the Adirondacks,

Fig. 59. Charles Van Deusen House, Hudson, New York, 1904, facade

Fig. 60. Addison Beecher Colvin House, Glens Falls, New York, 1901, front elevation, demolished

Fig. 61. Morgan Jones House, Hudson, New York, 1903-6, facade

were lengthened indefinitely as the sun sank deeper and deeper into the West." As the novel sinks deeper and deeper into quicksyntax, we encounter such literary dazzlers as "She had burned the fire of doubt at one end of the candle against the flame of hope at the other extreme, and finally the two met and extinguished one another, leaving her groping in the darkness of awful despair." In 1906, Colvin took his wife and daughters on a four-month tour of Europe, an account of which he sent his friends

as a Christmas letter upon his return.[20] The account ended with Colvin's statement that Paris was a nice city, but it needed a good American hotel. Colvin brings to mind the species H. L. Mencken identified as *Boobus Americanus*. It is hard to imagine that Reynolds could have taken him seriously. Colvin liked his house well enough, however, to return to Reynolds for other work.[21] It is hard to know if the poor design turned other clients away.

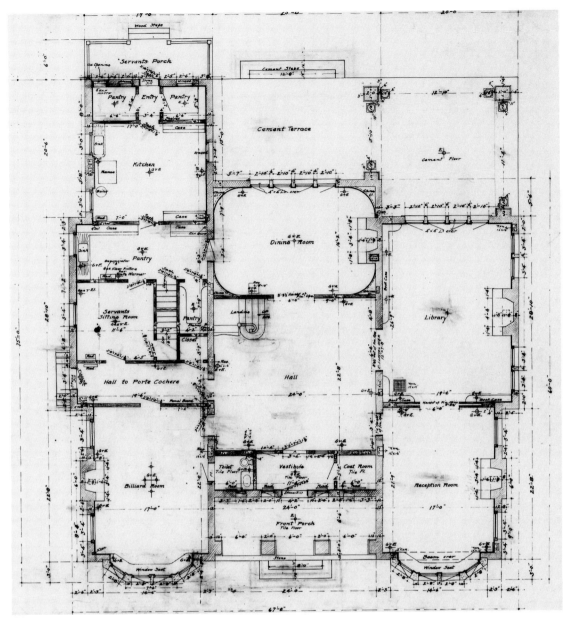

Fig. 62. Morgan Jones House, first floor plan

What Reynolds could do for a client he liked, and who had deep pockets, is clear from the Morgan Jones House in Hudson, designed in 1903 and completed in 1906. The brick-and-stone house, with its twin, scrolled gables that recall Dutch and Jacobean prototypes (Fig. 61), is a commanding presence among the large and imposing houses of Allen Street. The interior is one of Reynolds's richest and most successful. The plan (Fig. 62) is basically symmetrical, with variations at the rear to accommodate the service wing. The porch opens, through a door decorated with stained-glass panels of knights in glowing armor, to a vestibule which gives onto a two-story entrance hall. A great staircase rises up to a balcony that connects the upper rooms and frames a view of the beamed ceiling holding stained-glass panels. The hall leads on axis into the dining room, whose

paneled walls are surmounted by a plasterwork, rinceaux frieze of grape vines and birds that suggest a Bacchanalia (Fig. 63).[22] In the wood-paneled library scenes of stag, bird and boar hunting appear in the stained-glass transoms. The dining room and library once opened through glass doors onto a terrace and a covered porch. Both overlooked a narrow garden laid out by the landscape architects Townsend and Flemming of Utica.

The Jones House cost some $20,000,[23] a princely sum in comparison to what other Reynolds clients were prepared to spend at the same time.[24] Edmund Niles Huyck's town house on State Street (Fig. 56) cost $12,000, and Charles Van Duesen's Colonial house in Hudson (Fig. 59) $8,000.[25] Although still a college student when he commissioned the design, Jones was prepared to spend about twice as much as a very successful

Fig. 63. Morgan Jones House, dining room

Fig. 64. Thomas Kerley House, Ballston Spa, New York, 1905-7, exterior

manufacturer and a prosperous banker. Jones's father, who died in 1894, had invested in Sapolio,[26] a cleaning agent that was "the most widely known commercial product of the time, thanks to the company's Spotless Town jingles."[27]

Morgan Jones graduated in June, 1904, from Williams College at the age of twenty-four. His career at Williams, where he was a member of

Reynolds's fraternity, was hardly remarkable. He was manager of the golf team in his senior year and president of the New England Intercollegiate Golf Association. Six of his classmates voted him best dressed and seven, biggest bluff. On a senior questionnaire he gave "loafing" as his favorite diversion and "silence" as his ideal quality in a woman.[28] After graduation, he entered the insurance and mill supply businesses in Hudson, where he also became vice president and a director of the First National Bank.[29] In 1911 he married a woman from Hawaii, Clarissa Chapman Weaver. The sources are silent on her silence. In 1915 he reported to his classmates that he was "busy trying to make Hudson, N.Y., a modern town."[30] The next year he gave that up and moved to New York, where he worked as a business counsellor and lived until his death in 1965.[31]

Perhaps what Jones was trying to achieve in his house in Hudson was a college boy's dream of a great house. Certainly the decorations — the knights in the front door, the hunting scenes in the library, the Bacchic imagery of the dining room — all suggest a slightly sophomoric idea of the baronial good life. Such a vision was hardly restricted to men in their twenties. In 1902 a great Jacobean house designed by T. Henry Randall had been completed in Tuxedo Park for Henry William Poor, a Wall Street millionaire thirty-five years Jones's senior.[32] There are enough similarities between the two houses to lead one to ask if Jones's house may not be a reduced version of Poor's.[33]

Thomas Kerley of Ballston Spa was another small-city banker who hired Reynolds to design his house as well as his bank. Reynolds's work on the Ballston National Bank was modest, but the house he designed for its president was not. Like the Morgan Jones House, the Kerley House has a commanding presence in the town. Between 1905 and 1907 Reynolds transformed an older, Greek Revival dwelling into a Colonial Revival house of considerable charm (Fig. 64). It is not clear if the choice of style was the client's or the architect's. Reynolds went back to the earliest example of the Colonial Revival style, McKim, Mead & White's H. A. C. Taylor House in Newport, Rhode Island, of 1882-86.[34] The Kerley House has a hipped roof pierced by dormers, a semicircular front portico, and, perhaps most tellingly, a balustrade whose handrail drops abruptly from the main posts.

Inside, there was a good Georgian center hall plan, with the exception of the staircase, which rose from the living hall at the right rear. The staircase was moved when the house was converted into offices and apartments. Many of the elegant details Reynolds designed for the interior remain, however, including all the woodwork and the fireplace in the dining room, and the fireplaces in the main bedrooms upstairs.

COUNTRY HOUSES

Among Reynolds's earliest country-house designs may have been two at Selkirk, a favorite summer resort of Albanians, just south of the city on the west bank of the Hudson. There James B. Lyon, the owner of the largest printing firm in Albany, had acquired in 1886 a two-hundred-acre tract that had belonged to General John Taylor Cooper, brother of James Fenimore Cooper. On the site was a nineteenth-century Gothic cottage to which Reynolds, according to Lyon family tradition, added a library. Although the house has burned, old photographs (Fig. 65) preserve a sense of the Arts and Crafts library, with its wooden ceiling,

Fig. 65. J. B. Lyon Cottage, Selkirk, New York, library (attributed to Marcus T. Reynolds), c. 1896-98, demolished

Fig. 66. Dr. William MacDonald Chalet, Selkirk, New York (attributed to Marcus T. Reynolds), c. 1896-98, view fron southwest

FRONT ELEVATION.

brick-and-tile fireplace, leaded windows and decorations that included casts of the Parthenon frieze, the Venus de Milo and the Nike of Samothrace. In the center was an Italian marble table of such prodigious weight that a special foundation had to be constructed to support it.

In 1890, Lyon gave a piece of his Selkirk property to a good friend, Dr. Willis G. MacDonald, who built a Swiss chalet that Lyon family tradition also attributes to Reynolds.[35] Neither the Lyon nor the MacDonald house is mentioned in Reynolds's diaries. Because the diaries do not begin until 1899, after Reynolds had been practicing for about three years, it seems likely that both commissions date from the years 1896-98. A brain surgeon, MacDonald had developed a taste for chalets while studying medicine in Switzerland. Particularly fine is the south facade, with its pair of balconies overhanging the ground floor and its clever play of windows in the gable (Fig. 66). The interior contains several details sufficiently reminiscent of other Reynolds buildings to make the family tradition plausible. In the dining room a large arch frames a big bay window, just as arches frame the bay windows of the dining rooms of the three Van Rensselaer Houses on State Street in Albany of 1896-97 (Fig. 47).

Among his earliest country-house clients were Edmund Niles and Jesse Van Antwerp Huyck, for whom Reynolds designed a house in Rensselaerville (Fig. 67) sometime before 1899.[36] The Huyck fortune came from the family company, F. C. Huyck and Sons, the leading manufacture of papermakers' felts and jackets in the United States. The success of the company, founded in 1870, was related to the remarkable growth

of the United States paper and pulp industry during the late nineteenth century. The founder, F. C. Huyck, moved the factory from Rensselaerville, in the Helderberg mountains southwest of Albany, to Rensselaer, directly across the river from Albany. After he died in 1907, his son, Edmund, ran the company. In the 1890s, F. C. Huyck had bought the middle of the the Van Rensselaer Houses on State Street.

Edmund Huyck graduated from Williams in 1888.[37] He was the same age as and a close friend of William Barnes, Jr., who later became Reynolds's single most important client. Huyck had been a member of Delta Psi (Saint Anthony) fraternity, while its new Shingle Style fraternity house by McKim, Mead & White (Fig. 7) was constructed between 1884 and 1886.[38] Its porch, covered by a curving roof pierced by dormers and supported by wooden posts rising from a stone wall, may well be echoed in the porch of the summer house that Reynolds designed for the Huycks about a decade later.[39] In his articles on Roman villas, which appeared in 1897, around the time he was working on this house, Reynolds had decried the excesses of the Shingle Style. In the Huyck House one sees him stripping away much of its picturesque quality for a simplicity of statement in keeping with the modesty of the clients themselves.[40]

The Huyck House is sited on a broad, long, gently sloping lawn bordered by old stone walls, onto which all the principal rooms of the house face. The center of the house is a living hall, entered diagonally from the entrance porch at the side (Fig. 68). The most exciting space in the house is this hall, where the staircase climbs up to a seat beneath a two-story bowed window and then leaps over the hall to join an upstairs landing curved like the side of a piano. Beyond the staircase a fireplace welcomes the visitor. On the other side of the fireplace is the dining room, while to the right of the entrance a large library slips out of the main suite of rooms toward the lawn. The library was given particular prominence in the house because books occupied a large place in the lives of the Huycks. Huyck wrote poetry, and the family frequently spent the evening reading out loud or engaging in literary conversation with friends.

The terrace and garden porch give onto the lawn down a diagonally placed staircase that reflects the diagonal movement of the visitor through the house. The curved terrace, a response to the movement of the library, shows Reynolds adapting a form he knew from Renaissance gardens to the exigencies of an American country house. The terrace forms a transition between the geometry of the house and the openness of the landscape.

Uphill from the house, in 1901, Reynolds built a stable,[41] somewhat less modest than the house, with a glorious polygonal turret raised on heavy,

crude, stone piers. The irregular octagonal turret contained a billiard room. The stable burned in 1904, and Reynolds replaced it with the simpler building that now houses the dining hall of the Rensselaerville Institute.

Dr. Samuel Fessenden Clarke, Professor of Biology at Williams College and a botanist and arborculturist, called on Reynolds for two projects, an addition to his house in Williamstown[42] and a new summer house at Seal Harbor, Maine. Designed in 1897-98, "The Eyrie," named for its high site on a cliff over the sea, is a fine if belated exercise in the Shingle Style (Fig. 69). The mixture of stone and wood, the half-timbering,[43] the octagonal tower, the big dormer windows, the asymmetrical massing and the ample porch or piazza, partly roofed and partly covered with a trellis, are all familiar elements of that great moment in American domestic architecture. The wooden porch of the north facade, with a triple opening and a flaired roof, was both welcoming and sheltering.

The house had a particularly happy plan (Fig. 70). The center was occupied by a large living hall, by the late nineties a somewhat old-fashioned

Fig. 68. Edmund Niles Huyck House, first floor plan

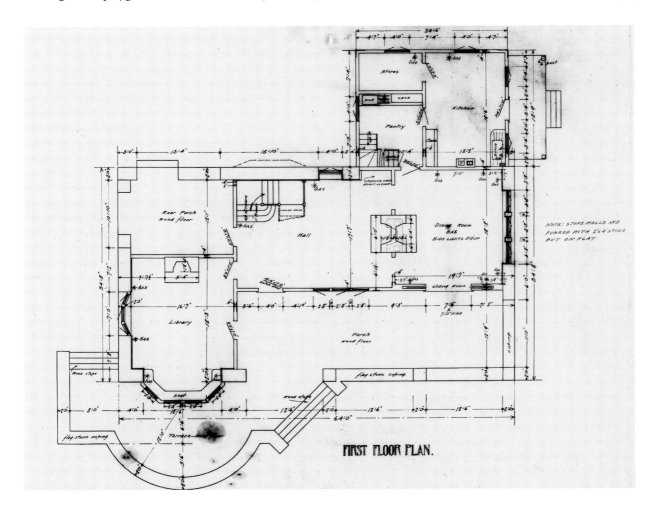

FIRST FLOOR PLAN.

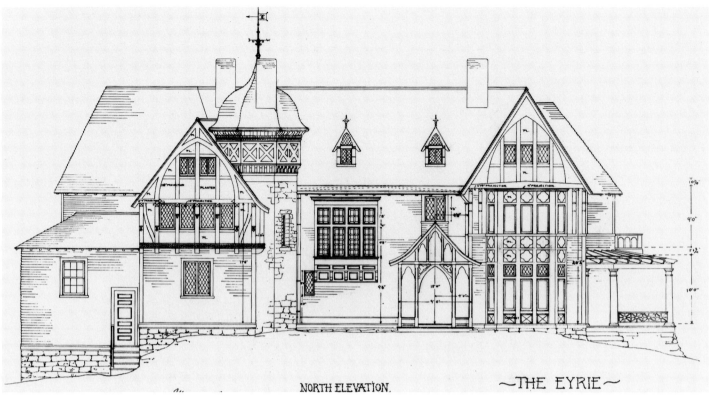

NORTH ELEVATION.   ~THE EYRIE~

Fig. 69. The Eyrie, Samuel Fessenden Clarke House, Seal Harbor, Maine, 1897-99, north elevation, demolished

Shingle Style form to which Reynolds gave the more up-to-date name of "Living Room Hall".[44] Toward the sea two bay windows and a door opened onto the columned piazza that made a transition between interior and nature. Angled to either side were the dining room, free of the piazza and open to the sea through a great bay window, and the library, which was only partly sheltered by the trellis that covered the adjacent porch. The house consciously embraced nature in a way not at all common in Shingle Style plans.[45]

Operating in a Darwinian world, Clarke managed to be both a devout naturalist and a devout Christian. He reconciled his two passions by insisting that the complexity of nature revealed the Divine; he "taught Biology for the glory of God."[46] A wildflower prize was offered in his honor to Williams students. Clarke's house opened up to the works of the Great Gardener, as he referred to his God, like a wildflower to the sun. In later life Clarke recalled his experience of nature from this house:

Seal Harbor was a wonderful spot for a summer home. We must all travel up there again some happy day, delight our eyes again with the happy grouping of mountains and valleys, the picturesque rocky shore line with its coves and partly wooded cliffs, old ocean and the lovely islands. We shall see again one of the memo-

rable sunsets, breathe again that air from over the pine woods, and be again reverently grateful for the inspiration of it all. Then — to let ourselves down to earth again — we will pick a lot of those delicious blueberries and have a Yankee expert make us a noble blueberry pie, inches and inches deep and ever so large around.[47]

The high location of Clarke's 150-acre property, perched over water, captured the fancy of none other than John D. Rockefeller, Jr., who purchased The Eyrie in 1910[48] and in 1915-16 had it vastly enlarged by Duncan Candler, a New York architect.[49] Reynolds's house, however, remained the core of the Rockefeller establishment, and Candler repeated the half-timbering and the flaring roofs of the dormers in his additions. The house was torn down by the Rockefeller family in 1963.[50]

A third country house of this early phase was built at Sacandaga Park in 1899[51] for J. Ledlie Hees, a banker from Fonda, New York. Hees was president of the Fonda, Johnstown and Gloversville Railroad, which took passengers from the main line of the New York Central at Fonda to Sacandaga Park, a resort the railroad had opened in the 1880s. The resort consisted of a thick development of cottages on small lots in a pine forest near the banks of the Sacandaga River. Hees kept a large tract of land for himself, on which he situat-

56

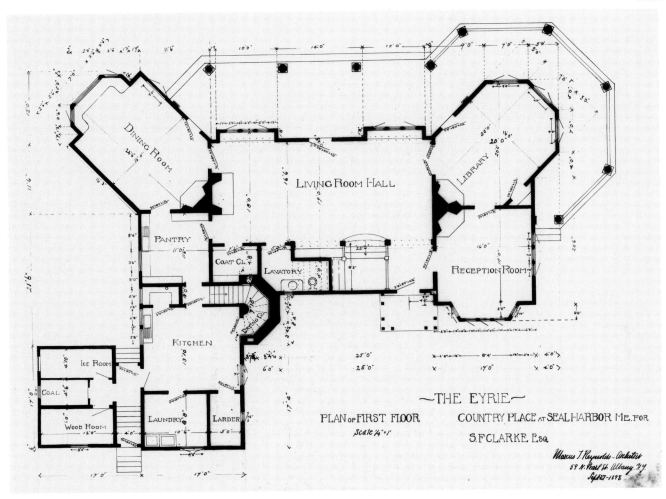

~THE EYRIE~

PLAN of FIRST FLOOR   COUNTRY PLACE at SEAL HARBOR ME. FOR

Scale ¼"=1'   S.F.CLARKE. Esq.

Marcus T. Reynolds - Architect
59 N. Pearl St. Albany N.Y.
Sept 27-1898

ed a pretentious cottage with which he may have hoped to attract a wealthier clientele to the development.

The cottage, dubbed Heeswyck, represents Reynolds's version of the Dutch Colonial (Fig. 71). He seems to have been inspired by such old Dutch houses as the Verplanck House in Fishkill, New York,[52] where the eaves of the lower part of a gambrel roof, pierced with dormers, were extended to form a porch. Reynolds's dormers were more aggressive, and the porch was "improved" by the use of Tuscan columns, but he left the elements of the prototype essentially intact. The plan (Fig. 72), with two rooms flanking a central hall, was also based on a typical early Dutch house plan, but Reynolds added an Anglicizing, Colonial Revival piazza with a semicircular projection. Like the contemporary Lansing town house, the Hees cottage was an Anglo-Dutch hybrid. A service wing adjoined the rear of the modest, three-room ground floor. Needless to say, such a wing would not have existed in much harder Colonial times.[53]

In 1909 Reynolds designed an unexecuted laundry and servants' quarters that would have been larger than the original cottage.[54] Upstairs there were to be eight bedrooms and one bath for the female servants, while downstairs there was a sitting room in which they could receive male callers. Separated from this room by a 24' x 14' laundry room were bedrooms for the butler and two chauffeurs, with their accompanying bath. Laundry in country houses was a major item. The Heeses and their guests could easily run through one hundred large linen napkins a week, each of which had to be washed and ironed. With bed linens, bath linens, undergarments, gentlemen's shirts, and the elaborate summer dresses that ladies changed several times a day,[55] it is no wonder that the little laundry room off the original kitchen became cramped.

By 1911-12 Hees's fortunes had taken a great leap forward that propelled the cottage into the realm of the "Country Residence," as the elevation of an enlarged design by Reynolds (Figs. 73 and

Fig. 70. The Eyrie, first floor plan (south at top)

57

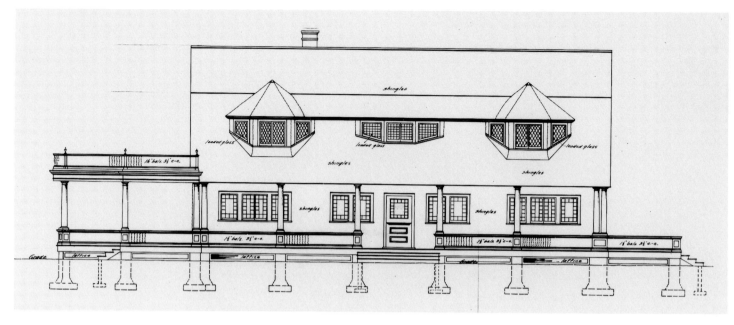

Fig. 71. Heeswyck, J. Ledlie Hees House, Sacandaga Park, New York, 1899, front elevation, demolished

Fig. 72. Heeswyck, first floor plan

74) is labeled.[56] By this date, Hees had divorced his first wife and remarried (his second wife's past was more mysterious than local society preferred),[57] and the new marriage probably played a role in the enlargement of the house. The front entrance stayed in the same place, centered under

the original dormers, but the front door became much more elaborate. The old dining room was enlarged into a new library, beyond which was a new dining room with a new semicircular piazza opening off it. The chamber to the right of the hall was doubled in size to become the "Dutch Living

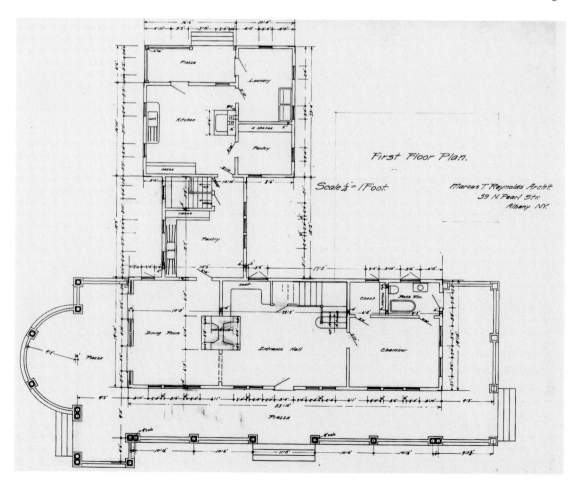

Room," the decoration of which included murals of windmills and tree-lined Dutch canals.

The house for the Superintendent of Albany Rural Cemetery in Menands, dated 1899 (Fig. 75), is different from these early country residences in that it is square in plan. The geometric purity of the form is underscored by an uncharacteristically (for Reynolds's country houses) Italianate treatment of the window surrounds and pediments, of the attic story under the roof and of the overhanging eaves. The handsomest detail on the exterior is the vertical integration of the pedi-

Fig. 73. Heeswyck, addition, 1911-12, front elevation, demolished

Fig. 74. Heeswyck, addition, 1911-12, first floor plan

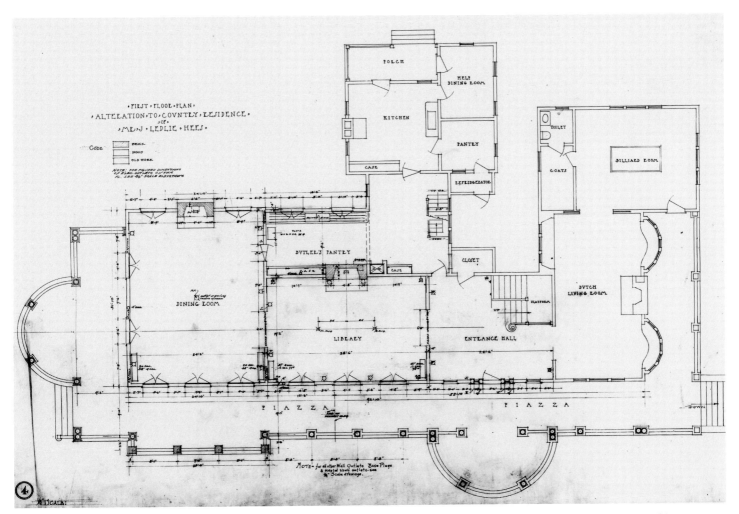

Fig. 75. House for
Superintendent, Albany Rural
Cemetery, Menands, New York,
1899, view from southwest

Fig. 76. House for
Superintendent, Albany Rural
Cemetery, detail of windows

Fig. 77. Samuel Hessberg House,
Selkirk, New York, 1909-10,
south elevation, demolished

mented windows of the ground floor with the second-floor windows, which are surmounted by
panels that seem to float in a very mannered way
(Fig. 76). The Italian Villa character of the house
is undercut, however, by shingling the walls below
the stuccoed attic to create an Americanized
hybrid. Reynolds doubtless chose an Italian Villa
style for the house because it rose in a very well
tended garden, the picturesque Albany Rural
Cemetery. The classical form stands in deliberate
contrast to the cemetery's carefully designed, irregular landscape. Reynolds introduced, apparently,
no formal garden to make a transition from the

building to "nature" — perhaps because here
nature had already been denatured.

The house once had two porches. The larger on
the east is now crumbling, and the smaller, facing
south toward the cemetery, is now destroyed. The
roof of the south porch sheltered a plaque with an
inscription giving the date of 1899 in Roman
numerals and the words, "Marcus T. Reynolds

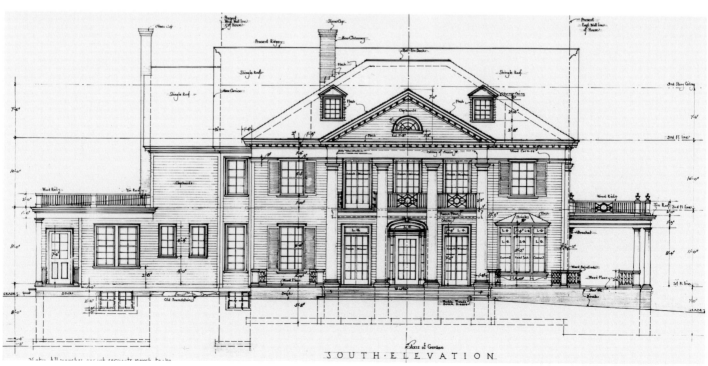

SOUTH·ELEVATION

Architect." This may be the earliest instance of a building "signed" by Reynolds, a practice he continued throughout his career, although with no obvious pattern. Perhaps here he hoped to attract mourners who would call on him to design funerary monuments.

For Samuel and Rose Hessberg Reynolds in 1909 designed a Colonial Revival house at Selkirk. (Four years earlier he had done an addition to their house on Willett Street in Albany.) At the same time the Hessbergs approached Reynolds for the Selkirk house, they asked Bryant Flemming of Ithaca to provide a layout for their garden. Flemming's garden plan arrived on November 5, and on November 29 Reynolds presented a design for the south elevation, a "colonial porch" with a giant order of four Tuscan columns set on the axis of the Flemming plan (Fig. 77). To the east Reynolds laid out a more modest and private one-story porch facing the river.

In the plan (Fig. 78), one of Reynolds's most open, he pulled the axis of the garden through the center of the house, while allowing the rooms and porches to develop around the axis in a relaxed asymmetry. Although the south side is relatively closed off, the ground-floor rooms on the east and north opened through a phalanx of French doors onto broad porches that mediated between the interior and exterior. The rooms and porches could be combined to accommodate large parties. In contrast, a cozy library with few windows, dominated by a fireplace, offered the Hessbergs a retreat on a chilly summer evening. The house had an admirable combination of public and private rooms, grand and intimate scales, open and closed spaces, held together by a classicizing image which imbued the owners with not just a sense of grandeur, but also, through the Colonial Revival style, a sense of truly belonging to the land that they owned.

Samuel Hessberg, the son of a shoe merchant who had immigrated from Germany in 1845, had amassed a considerable fortune as a banker and broker. In 1889 he had become the manager of the Albany office of Bache & Co., stockbrokers, and in 1893 he became a member of the firm. Five

Fig. 78. Samuel Hessberg House, first floor plan

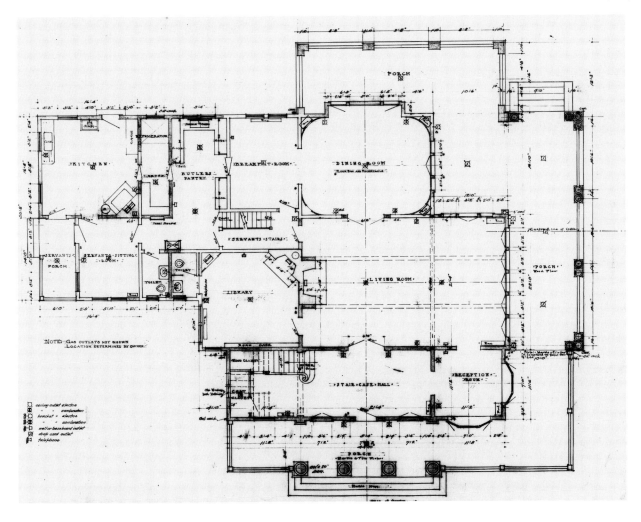

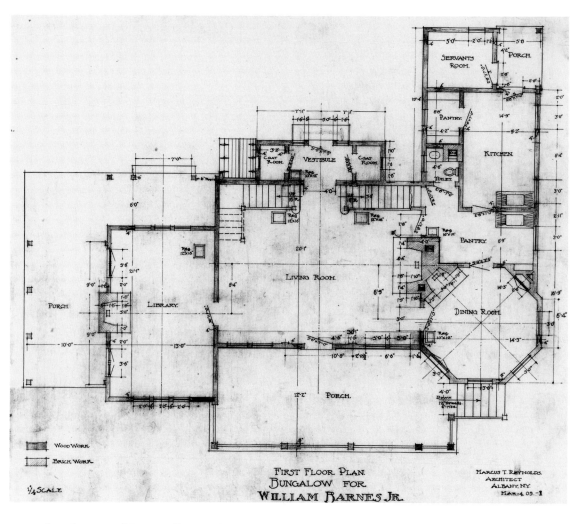

FIRST FLOOR PLAN.
BUNGALOW FOR
WILLIAM BARNES JR.

WOOD WORK

BRICK WORK

¼ SCALE

MARCUS T. REYNOLDS.
ARCHITECT
ALBANY, N.Y.
MAR. 4, 09.-1

Fig. 79. William Barnes, Jr., Bungalow, Albany, 1909, first floor plan, demolished

years later he married Rose Brilleman, the daughter of a leading jeweler of Albany.[58] In their Selkirk house the Hessbergs may have used the Colonial Revival style to assimilate themselves, as Jews, into the upper-class WASP culture of upstate New York, to which their money and taste, but not their ancestry, gave them entree. In the late eighteenth and early nineteenth centuries the old Dutch and Yankee families of the Hudson Valley had built columned mansions on the high ground beside the river.[59] Reynolds had already designed a Colonial Revival summer house with a two-story portico at Selkirk for General John H. Patterson and his wife, Grace Learned Patterson.[60] The Patterson portico of 1901 was followed by the similar porch of Sylvania, built in 1904 by Charles A. Platt for John Jay Chapman and his second wife, Elizabeth Chanler Chapman, on her family's nineteenth-century estate near Rhinebeck.[61] Published in 1908,[62] Sylvania, as well as the Patterson House, may have served as inspiration for Rose Hessberg; her great-nephew, Albert Hessberg, believes his aunt was probably the brains behind the house.[63] On her 250 acres beside the Hudson, this daughter of a German-Jewish jeweler

lived in a house that looked very much like one built for a descendent of an early Chief Justice of the United States.[64]

In the early twentieth century, when the bungalow became wildly popular in this country, the word was very elastic in its meaning. As generally understood today, bungalow conjures up images of small houses for the middle and lower-middle classes — houses with low roofs, ample porches and deep eaves, made of natural materials such as stone, wood and brick.[65] Bungalows projected the image of a relaxed lifestyle in the country, even though most of them were built on tiny city lots. But the rich and powerful also built bungalows; in 1909 Reynolds designed one for William Barnes, Jr., near the Albany Country Club.[66] Barnes had a town house on State Street for everyday living. The bungalow was a suburban retreat for his family and a few friends, where life could be lived with a freedom not permitted downtown.[67]

Reynolds's design had a relaxed, picturesque asymmetry reminiscent of his earlier house at Seal Harbor for Samuel Fessenden Clarke (Figs. 69 and 70). Indeed, the plan (Fig. 79) was close to that of the Clarke House, but tighter. A vestibule on the

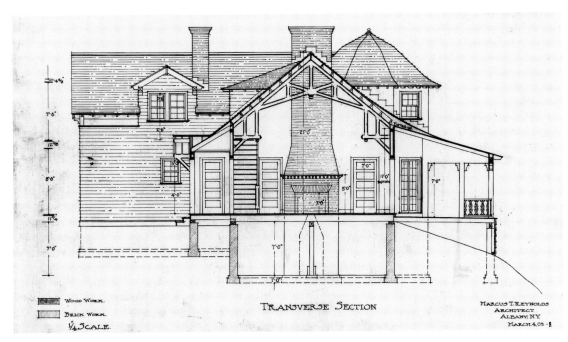

TRANSVERSE SECTION

MARCUS T. REYNOLDS
ARCHITECT
ALBANY, N.Y.
MARCH 4, 09 - ₤

WOOD WORK.

BRICK WORK.

¼ SCALE.

closed north side led into the living room, which opened the full height of the house into a roof supported by wooden trusses (Fig. 80) — there was something of the hunting lodge here. (In later years, until the house burned, this room served as the chapel for the SUNY-Albany campus.) Twin staircases flanked the entrance hall and led up to two separate bedroom areas. That above the library accommodated the Barnes' two sons, that over the dining room and service wing the bedrooms and sleeping porch of the parents.[68]

The exterior was treated with great restraint. There was a nice tension on the north facade between a generally symmetrical arrangement and

the compromises function dictated in that symmetry. The dining room and bedroom formed a picturesque tower that made the south side (Fig. 81) asymmetrical. The house was completely surrounded by woods, so that the south porch, unlike that of the Clarke House, had no view. The extension of the eaves of the south roof to cover the porch harked back to early Dutch houses that Reynolds had already celebrated in the Hees cottage (Fig. 71). Otherwise, the building is more remarkable for a lack of historical reminiscences than for a knowing use of historical prototypes. As the private pleasure house of a public man, the bungalow had no need to make a public statement

Fig. 80. William Barnes, Jr., Bungalow, section through living room

Fig. 81. William Barnes, Jr., Bungalow, south elevation

SOUTH ELEVATION.

MARCUS T. REYNOL
ARCHITECT
ALBANY, N.Y.

¼ SCALE.

63

through a knowing use of historical sources. Reynolds was a frequent guest at the bungalow. There he and Barnes played poker, and it was undoubtedly at the Barnes poker table that some of the planning for the great Albany river-front project that resulted in the Delaware & Hudson and Albany Evening Journal Buildings took place.

Henry Manning Sage, a lumber baron, and his second wife, Cornelia Cogswell Sage, were ardent collectors of Americana;[69] it is small wonder that Marcus Reynolds should have remodelled their large house in Menands in the Colonial Revival style (Fig. 82). Her father, Ledyard Cogswell, was president of the New York State National Bank when Reynolds designed both its new building behind the Philip Hooker facade in 1902 and the addition of 1916. Her brother, Ledyard Cogswell, Jr., was a collector of American art and antiques. Her brother-in-law, Edward Wales Root, wrote the first monograph on Philip Hooker[70] and formed a collection of American painting, a part of

which is now in the Munson-Williams-Proctor Institute in Utica. Sage's sister, Susan Sage Cooper, and her husband, James Fenimore Cooper II, were also collectors of Americana, particularly paintings and furniture related to the early history of Cooperstown, New York, his ancestral seat. Other members of the family were interested in other kinds of art. One of Sage's daughters from his first marriage was the surrealist painter Kay Sage, who married the French painter Yves Tanguy.

Henry Sage was a state senator with very close ties to William Barnes, Jr. In 1920 Barnes tried but failed to gain for Sage the Republican nomination for governor of New York. In 1910 Reynolds had done some minor work on the Sage house, a porte-cochère and a mantel. When the Sages decided to do something more elaborate to the house in which Sage had been born, they turned to Reynolds once again. In the end, Reynolds's remodelling of Sage's ancestral home cost the Sages $150,000.[71]

To say that the Sages were demanding and difficult clients hardly does them justice. The pages of Reynolds's diaries from 1919 to 1921 are filled with bickering between architect and clients and with incessant changes in plans. The east and west porches of the house were particular bones of contention. The Sages frequently insisted on details Reynolds did not like. On March 28, 1921, Reynolds noted: "Henry Sage in and wanted applied arches all around his breakfast room & more fool arches at end of study." All of this took place during the first months of Prohibition. On January 17, 1920, amidst entries on the Sage house, Reynolds wrote: "At 12:01 A.M. the sad death of Old Mother rum was announced and this damned hypocritical country went 'dry'." A little over a year later, still working on the Sage house, he noted: "Began on my last 5 gal jug of gin."[72] Given the relationship he had with the Sages, it is small wonder that his liquor supply was running low.

The plan of the house is not satisfactory in its circulation patterns, an area in which Reynolds sometimes lacked strength. Particularly frustrating to Reynolds was the fact that he could never achieve a center hall connected on axis to the principal doors of the east and west facades.[73] The biggest problem, in terms of the planning, was the addition of the great room, forty-four feet long, to the south side of the old house. To accommodate the slope of the land, the room had to be set several

Fig. 82. Henry Manning Sage House, Menands, New York, 1919-21, west facade

Fig. 83. House, Chatham Center, New York, c.1825(?)

steps below the rest of the house; this arrangement caused Reynolds to insert a staircase into the southwest corner of the music room. Reynolds tried to mask the awkwardness by placing an elegant frame from a house on Washington Square in New York on the doorway into the great room.[74] Using parts of old buildings was a commonplace in this house,[75] and this collage of old architectural parts formed a backdrop for the Sages' extensive collection of early American furniture.

If real pieces of old buildings were not available, Reynolds could copy them. The Sages spent time in Reynolds's office going through architectural books, and they also took inspiration from buildings they happened to see while travelling. Reynolds's diaries clarify the source of the west porch of the house (Fig. 83). On September 15, 1920, Reynolds went "to Old Chatham & measured up porch for Sage house." A house at Chatham Center (Fig. 84) had been featured in the October, 1919, issue of *The White Pine Series*, where Reynolds undoubtedly saw it, as did, perhaps, the Sages.[76] Reynolds used several details of its porch: the diamonds within ovals in the entablature, the fringe-like reguli under the raking cornice, and the leading in the sidelights. To adapt the Chatham porch to the broad west wall of the Sage House, Reynolds shortened its proportions and widened the central bay, which was given a lower, segmental barrel vault to which Reynolds added coffering. The Palladian window over the porch must also have been inspired by the house at Chatham Center, and other details from this building appear elsewhere in the Sage House.[77]

The stone veneer of the exterior sets the Sage House apart from the large early brick houses of the Albany area, such as the Van Rensselaer Manor

House or the Schuyler Mansion. Reynolds, who had written about these houses in his early years,[78] obviously knew this tradition well, as did the Sages, who made the decision to have ashlar cladding. The choice of grey stone, from quarries at Schoharie, New York,[79] may have been inspired by the summer house that Sage's sister, Susan, and her husband had built at Cooperstown in 1911.[80] That house deliberately recalled a Central New York tradition, dating from the early nineteenth century, of stone masonry combined with classically detailed white woodwork. Cooper, an important Albany lawyer, handled Sage's legal affairs; the relationship between the two couples was thus more than familial. Perhaps there was even an element of sibling rivalry. The east porch of the Sage House was more pretentious architecturally than any part of the Cooper House.

Certainly the best part of the Sage House is the east facade (Fig. 85), which faces a vast expanse of the Hudson Valley and gives scale to the house in the face of the landscape. It also forms the centerpiece of one of Reynolds's most felicitous designs, in which there is a very skilful manipulation of planes and a careful management of the disparate scales of the elements of the design to create parts, elegant in themselves, that form a coherent ensemble. The giant order of four Tuscan columns, like that of the Hessberg House at Selkirk, referred to American colonial architecture and to earlier Hudson Valley houses. Here, however, the columns were not so much employed to confer social status as to create a fictitious architectural world, one that seemed more fitting than the "real" house in which Sage had been born to shelter a collection of Americana.

Fig. 84. Henry Manning Sage House, west entrance

Fig. 85. Henry Manning Sage House, east facade

In the garden of the dead.

CHAPTER 4

MONUMENTS AT ALBANY RURAL CEMETERY

Albany Rural Cemetery is among the most remakarble nineteenth-century cemeteries in the country, and a few of its outstanding monuments are by Marcus T. Reynolds. In almost every case these monuments incoporate sculpture. Frequently, his buildings have a more interesting three-dimensional presence than drawings or photographs lead one to suspect. In his funerary monuments, which act as both architecture and sculpture, his abilities to deal in three dimensions are particularly apparent.

Jessie Walker Hamilton and her husband, Andrew Hamilton, lost their only son at age seven in 1898, and he was buried in Albany Rural Cemetery beneath a simple headstone.[1] In March, 1900, Jessie Hamilton commissioned a monument to her son from Reynolds, and the resulting cross was delivered to the cemetery in January, 1902 (Fig. 86). At the bottom right corner of the base of the cross is the barely readable name, Marcus T. Reynolds Archt. Another name below it has been so obliterated by time as to be illegible; surely it recorded John Francis Brines, the sculptor.[2] Higher up on the base is an inscription recording the life of young Andrew Hamilton.

Set on a two-stepped plinth, the cross rises in three parts: a squat base, a tall, tapered shaft, and a cross of four equal arms. The two upper parts, which derive ultimately from Celtic crosses, are richly carved with complex strapwork based on Anglo-Irish forms and with an array of figures and symbols. Albany Rural Cemetery contains a number of free-standing crosses based on Celtic prototypes that were erected between the 1880s and the 1920s. Almost all are characterized by the flat strapwork of their ornament and by a lack of figural decoration. They also share a characteristic fusing of a cross with four equal arms with a circular motif that either connects the arms or occupies the center of the cross. Reynolds and Brines created a highly original variant on this popular type. The profusion of figures on the cross seems more Catholic than Protestant, even though Albany Rural is a Protestant cemetery. Hamilton was a

Facing page. Hamilton Cross, Albany Rural Cemetery, Town of Colonie, New York, 1900-2, front, John Francis Brines, sculptor

Fig. 86. Hamilton Cross, back

Catholic, his wife a Protestant. Presumably the son was being raised in the father's church.

On the front, Christ in Judgment in the center of the cross is surrounded by the four Evangelists in the arms, while below on the shaft are Christological symbols: the fish, the Agnus Dei, and the pelican rending her breast to feed her young. The latter two bespeak Christian salvation through Christ's sacrifice. These medallions are surrounded by grapes, another symbol of Christ's

Fig. 87. Parsons Monument, Albany Rural Cemetery, 1905-6, front, Oscar Lenz, sculptor

sacrifice, which overlap the strapwork.[3] On the rear (Fig. 86), in the center, the entertwined letters Chi Rho, flanked by Alpha and Omega (all symbols of Christ), are surrounded by symbols of the crucifixion - a crown of thorns into which nails are woven. Below are three medallions. One shows wheat, which denotes the blessed - the good seed that Christ will separate from the chaff on the Day of Judgement. In the center medallion, the eagle, a symbol of Christ's ascension, grasps fleur de lis, which signify purity. A more abstract eagle in the bottom medallion, perched on a globe (perhaps a reference to Christ as ruler of the world), is surrounded by a mandorla of peacock feathers, which refer to immortality and to Christ's resurrection. The iconography stresses salvation obtained through Christ's sacrifice and resurrection.

The redemptive value of the iconography of the cross may have represented not only hope for eternal bliss for the son but also thanksgiving for a quasi-miraculous recovery that the father had experienced. According to Hamilton's obituary, several years before his actual death he had been pronounced dead from heart disease by two attending doctors. A third, however, saw signs of life, and the three physicians revived him.[4] A lawyer specializing in insurance, Hamilton, like many of Reynolds's clients, was well read, and he owned an excellent library. Most important, perhaps, for the appearance of the cross, his "collection of paintings was unusually fine. He was a connoisseur in art."[5]

Unfortunately, Hamilton's luck in recovering his health did not presage continued good fortune for himself or his family. He died in 1908, a year after his wife. His three daughters all perished in a train wreck on October 3, 1912, as they were returning to New York from a funeral in Hartford. Their deaths wiped out the whole family. The daughters were buried alongside their parents and their brother in front of the cross. The accident was the lead story on the front page of the *New York Times*, not only because of the horror of the wreck, but also because one of the Hamilton daughters was married to James Cox Brady, a son of Anthony Brady, "one of the great business figures of America," a director of scores of corporations, and a power in the traction, gas, electric and tobacco businesses.[6]

In December, 1904, John D. Parsons, President of the Albany Trust Company and a collector of paintings, died suddenly, just before his fifty-eighth birthday. Two years earlier, Parsons had commissioned Reynolds to design a new building for the Trust Company. In January, 1905, Agnes Chase Parsons, his widow, approached Reynolds to design a monument.[7] On August 17 Reynolds went to New York to talk about the monument with a representative of the New England Granite Company and with a "young sculptor (took sculptor to lunch)." The young sculptor was Oscar Lenz, with whom Reynolds would collaborate at least twice. On December 16, 1906, the second anniversary of Parsons' death, the monument arrived in Albany.

The pink granite monument (Fig. 87) consists of two major parts, a base and a cross. The base forms a platform and a backdrop for the angel of the Resurrection, who steps forth from the arched entrance to Christ's tomb to address us with the words, carved on the arch, "He is risen. He is not here."[8] Above rises a tall cross, another variant on the Celtic. The conjunction of Christ's cross and empty tomb stresses the Christian concept of life after death made possible through His sacrifice. In

Fig. 88. Parsons Monument, detail of bronze freize, Oscar Lenz, sculptor

Fig. 89. Palmer Monument, Albany Rural Cemetery, 1906, front and side

the center of the cross, a flaming urn surrounded by an oak wreath symbolizes that eternal life. The Christian faithful are represented on the monument by a frieze of bronze figures that begins in

Fig. 90. Walter Launt Palmer, Georgiana Myers Palmer Monument, Albany Rural Cemetery, front and side, 1895

the center of the back with two groups of singing men and boys straight out of Luca Della Robbia (Fig. 88). The throng follows the kneeling Marys to the tomb to hear the good news of Christ's resurection and thus of their salvation.

The Parsons curved headstones are meant to be read as horizontal arches, the surfaces of which have been tilted to make legible the names carved on them. The headstones are symbolic portals through which the souls of the Parsons may pass, just as the Risen Christ left His tomb through the round arch from which the angel emerges. The upturned hands of the angel summon the couple

to eternal life. Simultaneously, this gesture that visually connects the monument to the headstones also suggests that the angel speaks to the viewer.

The frieze is inscribed, "Copyrighted — Oscar L. Lenz Sc. -1906-." Lenz had a meteoric but brief career that ended with his death in 1912 at age thirty-eight. In 1886, a prodigy of twelve, he entered the Rhode Island School of Design. At seventeen he moved to the Art Students League in New York, where he attracted the attention of Augustus St. Gaudens, who thought so well of Lenz that he "gave him part of the modeling of the statue of Diana on Madison Square Garden tower to execute."[9] After making figures for the Court of Honor of the World's Columbian Exposition, he went to Paris for study and then returned to carry out monumental commissions in Charleston, South Carolina, and Buffalo, New York, and on Pennsylvania Station in New York. The now-forgotten Lenz was a sculptor with a good name in his day.

Reynolds's third major funerary monument was for Albany's most important nineteenth-century sculptor, Erastus Dow Palmer, who died in 1904, and for Palmer's son, Walter Launt Palmer, a painter of note in his own right. The whole commission, which came from Walter Palmer, seems to have started and finished in 1906, the date beside the signature, Marcus T. Reynolds Architect, on the lower right corner of the monument (Fig. 89).

A rectangle of white Vermont marble set on a granite plinth and capped by a granite lid embellished with volutes, the Palmer monument seems to take its form from a small bronze monument that Walter Launt Palmer had designed (Fig. 90) in 1895 for his first wife,[10] Georgiana Myers Palmer, who had died in 1892 in childbirth. Georgiana was the daughter of John Myers, who owned Albany's leading department store, and the sister of Jessie Myers Hilton, who would commission a monument from Reynolds after the death of her husband in 1909. From this handsome bronze object, Reynolds seems to have taken not only the general Italian Renaissance character, but also the rectangular shape and the wreaths of laurel tied with ribbons,[11] the cornice and the volutes. To these details Reynolds added some of his own, particularly the weeping (and punning) palms below the name of Erastus Dow Palmer and the burning torches at the corners. Into the tomb Reynolds

incorporated versions of two of Palmer's most
popular works, the marble reliefs of Morning and
Evening,[12] whose Desiderio-like delicacy Reynolds
attempted to give an appropriate setting in the
Renaissance character of the monument. Wreaths
of the laurel of eternal life frame the roundels.
Over the head of Morning is a flame said to be
that of a burning torch, even though Palmer did
not represent the torch itself.[13] Reynolds took
Palmer's torch seriously enough to keep it burning
on all the corners of the monument. Generally,
torches on tombs are inverted. Here they stand
erect, perhaps to suggest that the flames of the
Palmers's art are not extinguished.[14]

On October 7, 1909, George Porter Hilton
died unexpectedly at the age of fifty of a cerebral
hemmorrhage. The tomb which his widow, Jessie
Myers Hilton, commissioned from Reynolds (Fig.
91) is very restrained architecturally – a largely
undecorated grey granite box enclosing four
coffins and supporting a large bronze relief by
Oscar Lenz.[15] In the relief, a winged, draped figure of Sleep hands her somniferous poppies to a
seated man, who is nude except for a drape across
his lap. Based on the Ludovisi Mars, the man has
put aside his spears, shield and helmet for his lyre,
which he lays down at his side as his eyes are
drawn to the flowers. His shield hangs from a post
with a sundial on its face and a pine cone on top.
The absence of a gnomon on the sundial suggests
that time has stopped. Below the relief is the
inscription "I Have Fought a Good Fight. I Have
Finished My Course. I Have Kept The Faith."
The rhetoric of this relief may have gotten a bit
out of hand. Hilton held the rank of colonel in the
New York State National Guard,[16] hardly a war
hero's status. His musical abilities had carried him
to the point of being tenor soloist at St. Peter's

*Fig. 92. Dalton Cinerarium,
Albany Rural Cemetery,
1928-30, front*

Episcopal church. The allegory is also a bit euphemistic: the gentle figure of Sleep instead of a more fearsome Death.

Hilton was the son of a very important engineer, Charles Hilton, whose Hilton Bridge Company had built two major structures in Albany, the Hawk Street and Northern Boulevard viaducts. In 1902 George Hilton had taken over the estate of his father-in-law, John G. Myers, the largest department store owner. His marriage to Jessie Myers in 1899 seems to have been only one strand in the web of connections that tied him to the circle of Marcus Reynolds's clients. He had been a pallbearer at John Parsons's funeral,[17] and he was a director of the First National Bank, for which Reynolds had designed a new building in 1907. His wife's sister, Georgiana, had been married to Walter Launt Palmer, another Reynolds client. Even though the Hilton tomb, completed in May, 1911, is not very interesting architecturally, it nonetheless tells us a lot about the closely knit society in which Reynolds operated and of the way that society chose to view death.

The Dalton Cinerarium (Fig. 92) occupies a corner plot far across the cemetery from most of Reynolds's other designs. William Dalton, from Schenectady, stood outside Reynolds's usual circle of clients, and so it is perhaps fitting that this monument, more architectural than anything else Reynolds did in the cemetery, should also stand apart. Dalton had already been a Reynolds client for some time[18] when he had lunch with the architect on July 25, 1928, to discuss "a columbarium for ashes of family." At that lunch Dalton gave Reynolds some "sketches of Greek Doric circular temple – fluted columns of black granite [,] polished circular drum of some other white granite – rose pink marble interior."[19] On September 12 Reynolds recorded: "Mr. Dalton ... decided to have cinerarium of marble & engaged columns like Choragic Monument." Reynolds meant, of course, the Choragic Monument of Lysicrates in Athens, which, like the cinerium, is monochromatic.

From the outset, the building was centrally planned, even though it went from round to ten-sided to twelve-sided to round again. Once begun in August, 1929, the structure went up fairly quickly. The last stone of the dome was put in place on November 14, and the interior appointments were installed by the end of January, 1930.

The cinerarium had risen as the stock market crashed. It was not a cheap building; an early estimate from the Vermont Marble Company put the cost at $38,000.[20]

The cinerarium is one of Reynolds's finest classical designs. During the year in which the tomb was designed, there was little work in the Reynolds office, and so the staff could spend days at a time designing and redesigning details. The glazed bronze door set in the marble wall allows a view of the interior. There, the light that falls through the oculus of the blue Guastavino tile dome illuminates an open book of marble, on which were "written'" the names of the Daltons whose ashes were placed beneath the floor. Space on the pages of the book ran out before William Dalton died in 1968, at the age of ninety-nine. His name is on a modest bronze plaque attached to the wall to the left of the book.

A chief engineer for the American Locomotive Company in Schenectady, Dalton was a man who designed enormously powerful machines. But when it came to monuments, he wanted nothing to do with modern engineering; he wanted the traditional dignity associated with classical forms. A hero of industrialism, Dalton wanted himself remembered like a hero of antiquity.[21] In this desire, he was not unlike others of that remarkable group of brilliant engineers who lived in and around Schenectady in the first decades of this century. Employed by General Electric and American Locomotive, these men invented technological marvels such as radar and television. For their houses, however, they chose not the visual forms of technology but rather traditional architectural styles.[22]

A development and an intensification of itself.

CHAPTER 5

DELAWARE AND HUDSON AND ALBANY EVENING JOURNAL BUILDINGS

Few railroads companies have built headquarters for themselves that could be taken for a state capitol, but that is exactly what some visitors to Albany assume the Delaware & Hudson and Albany Evening Journal complex[1] to be — so imposing is its size, so dominant its tower, so rich its ornamentation, and so prominent its location at the foot of Street Street (Fig. 93). Also, unlike most railroad company headquarters, the building is Gothic in style. That it sits where it sits and looks the way it looks is largely due to two men who frequently sat at the same poker table: Marcus T. Reynolds and his friend, William Barnes, Jr., the Republican political boss of Albany.[2] They had as a collaborator Colonel Leonor F. Loree, president of the D & H in one of its greatest periods of expansion and a remarkable figure in the history of railroads.[3]

Now the administrative center of the State University of New York, the Delaware & Hudson and Albany Evening Journal Buildings form a complex structure that consisted of at least six main parts. At the north end, hidden behind the nineteenth-century Federal Building, was a long, sparsely decorated warehouse of reinforced concrete (Fig.94) that no longer stands. South of the warehouse site rises a square block with corner turrets and a steep roof (Fig. 95). A diagonal arm, five stories high, stretches southeast to connect the square block to the central tower of thirteen stories. These four parts of the building were constructed in 1914-15. When the building opened, it was already too small to house all the D & H employees, and so another five-story arm was immediately designed to rise south of the central tower (Fig. 96). At the south end of that arm a second tower rose to house the Albany Evening Journal (Fig. 97), whose owner, William Barnes, had decided in 1915 to build a new headquarters, connected to that of the D & H. The entire building, completed in 1918, was 660 feet long.

A remarkable characteristic of this building is its great length. To paraphrase Louis Sullivan, it is the long *and* tall building artistically considered –

Facing page. Delaware & Hudson and Albany Evening Journal Buildings, Broadway at foot of State Street, Albany, 1912-18, view from south

Fig. 93. Delaware & Hudson and Albany Evening Journal Buildings, view from northwest

a building in which the horizontal expanse is carefully framed at each end, rhythmically punctuated by the leaps of the dormers into the roofs and skillfully sliced not quite in half by the skyward thrust of the tower. The unequal arms of Reynolds's structure embrace a public plaza, laid out by Reynolds on an irregular plan (Fig. 96). The two breaks in the line of the building that make it fit the plaza are clearly articulated by slender, round towers that act as hinges. Immediately to the right of the central tower, a church-like facade announces the entrance to a passageway that once led through the building to the river. The building is essentially two-sided. The west face forms a backdrop to the plaza and acts as a setpiece to the end of Albany's main thoroughfare, State Street. The east side, now at the edge of Interstate 787, once stood on the banks of the Hudson and marked the entrance to Albany for those arriving by boat (Fig. 109).

Like the structural frame of the warehouse, that of the north arm is reinforced concrete, while steel was used to frame the tower, the south wing and

Fig. 94. Delaware & Hudson Building, warehouse wing, demolished

Fig. 95. Delaware & Hudson Building, Albany, square block and north wing

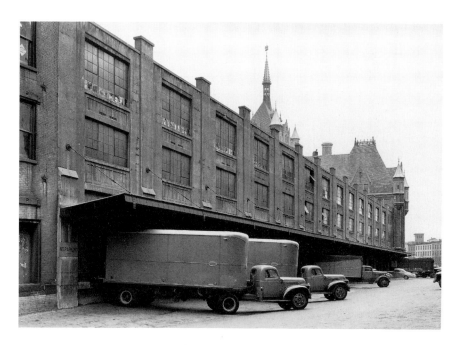

the Journal Building. Over this is laid a complex revetment of granite, cast stone and terra cotta designed in a Late Gothic mode.[4] The interiors, with one major exception, were unremarkable — simple office floors partitioned into the spaces the owners found useful. The space at the top of the central tower, where today we might expect to find an observation deck or a restaurant to take advantage of the view, was used merely for storage. On

the outside, however, rich and sometimes arresting decorations were lavished. On the north tower and arm, beavers flank the dormer windows (Fig. 98). At the top of the tower were seals of New York State and the city of Albany (Fig. 99), while the stringcourse above the eleventh floor boasts a group of squatting grotesques who glower down on us. An eight-foot-high copper replica of Henry Hudson's ship, the *Half Moon*, designed by Reynolds, sails over the steep flèche of the tower as a weathervane.

The decorations of the south part of the building are even fancier. The gables bear coats of arms of early Dutch settlers of the Hudson Valley (Fig. 100), while the frontispiece of the passageway that once led from the plaza to the river bears coats of arms of Francis I of France, of the States General of Holland, and of the Duke of Albany, for whom the city was renamed when it came under English rule in the late seventeenth century (Fig. 101). All these had to do with the early history of the area. On the ground-floor arch of the frontispiece is the coat of arms of Henry Hudson and the date 1609. In that year Hudson sailed the *Half Moon* up the river that now bears his name, perhaps as far north as the very spot on which the D & H Building rises. On the Evening Journal Building there are large cast-stone reliefs reproducing the marks of famous figures in the history of printing, such as Aldus Manutius and William Caxton (Fig. 102).

For this building, Reynolds's office executed hundreds of drawings. The few that have survived attest to the loving care with which his office

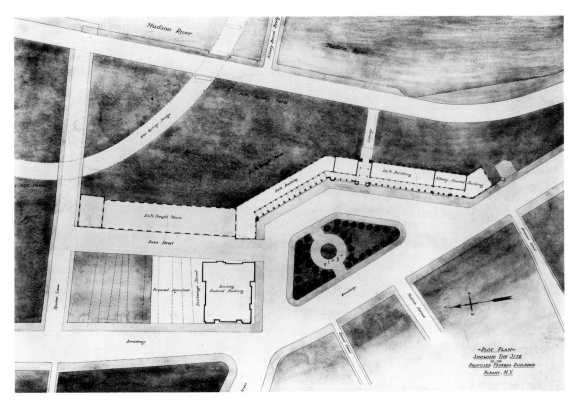

handled details. Two drawings for the subway frontispiece, one for the ground-level archway and the other for the gable, are particularly rich in a variety of the Gothic forms. It would have been too expensive, as well as mind numbing, to cover the whole building in such ornament. Reynolds preferred to marshall his ornamental forces in the places where they might do the most good. He chose neither the placment of his ornaments nor the Gothic style of the building casually.

In the early twentieth century, when the D & H Building became the centerpiece of a new Albany, the city was a busy river port for freight and passenger service, as well as the major railroad center that connected New York and Boston to the Great Lakes cities of Buffalo, Cleveland and Chicago, and, through them, to the vast territories of the western United States. Of the six railroads that served Albany, the most important were the New York Central and the Delaware & Hudson. The New York Central tracks came up the east side of the Hudson and crossed the river just north of State Street to enter Union Station, a Beaux-Arts design of 1898 by the Boston firm of Shepley, Rutan and Coolidge. The Delaware & Hudson tracks, running along the west bank of the river, created south of Union Station a tangle of streets and quays that made boarding the boats that joined Albany to New York a dangerous occupation.

Union Station had been planned to replace a

Fig. 98. Delaware & Hudson
Building, exterior, detail of
square block

dilapidated old shed of a station in the last year of
power of the Democratic administration that preceded Barnes's takeover in 1899.[5] Opened in
December, 1900, it gave Albany a grand new gate-
way between train and city. But travelers arriving
by water or rail from New York still had a grim
first view of the city. The river bank was marred
by rag-tag industrial buildings, decaying piers and
raw sewage rotting in the basin of water at the foot
of State Street (the basin had been created by a
pier built out in the river in the 1820s, after the
opening of the Erie Canal). One of Barnes's chief
objectives, from the moment he took power, was
the improvement of the whole Albany river front.[6]
The D & H Building is the final result of those
plans.

It took Barnes almost twenty years to realize his
river-front improvements. Initially, his ideas were
fairly modest: an interceptor sewer line that would
gather the city's effluent and dump it into the
middle of the Hudson below State Street, plus
some modest improvements at the water's edge
and to nearby streets.[7] The purpose of this work
would be to impress travelers and improve
property values in the river-front area.

In 1903 the basin was dredged and the wreck-
age in it removed.[8] By 1906, however, Barnes's
newspaper was able to announce a far grander project, the "transformation of the old pier at the foot
of State Street into a recreation pier and a park of
beauty."[9] A new bridge would lift pedestrians over
the D & H tracks and the basin and deposit them
on the pier, which would have docks for excur-
sionists and facilities for rowing, canoeing and
yachting. There would also be a little park —

complete with trees, shrubbery, grass and gravel
walks – with a bandstand for summer concerts.
The state legislature authorized $1 million for this
endeavor. New sea walls were to be built by the
owners of the land alongside the basin, the largest
of those being the New York Central and the D &
H. Much squabbling ensued throughout 1907,
largely because a number of citizens felt that the
city was giving away property it owned (the land
beneath the water of the basin) to the railroads.[10]
By 1909, however, the plans had been approved
and construction begun on the new pier and the
bridge to join it to the mainland.

On June 11, 1910, the readers of the *Albany
Evening Journal* were treated to a bird's-eye view of
their city (Fig. 103) that contained a new and even
grander proposal for the embellishment of the
waterfront.[11] At top center of the drawing is the
great mass of the New York State Capitol. Just
below it and to the right rises the tower of H. H.
Richardson's city hall. From the Capitol, State
Street falls steeply eastward, lined by four more
towers, those of St. Peter's Episcopal Church by
Richard Upjohn, of the Albany City Savings Bank
and the Albany Trust Company designed by
Marcus Reynolds, and of the French Renaissance
Federal Building, built between 1878 and 1883
after designs of William Potter that had been modified by James B. Hill.[12] This drawing, produced
in Reynolds's office, was made to show a
Reynolds-Barnes proposal, a triangular park to
replace the decaying buildings that stood between
the foot of State and the river. The proposed new
bridge would connect this park to the new pier,
which was already under construction.[13] In a

sense, Reynolds was Barnes's house architect. In 1909 he had designed for Barnes a spacious bungalow adjacent to the Albany Country Club (Figs. 79-81), and in the very months of 1910 in which the river-front scheme was being worked on, Reynolds was drawing up a boathouse for Barnes's summer place on Nantucket.[14]

In 1924 Reynolds recalled his role in this phase of the project (complete with an erroneous date): "In 1912 he [Reynolds] conceived the idea of demolishing all that portion of Albany which lay south of State Street and between Broadway and the Hudson River. This was the oldest portion of the city, and by reason of the narrow tortuous streets and its low-lying site, which subjected it to annual submersion during the spring freshets, had fallen into decrepitude."[15]

To float the fifty-year bond issue that would allow Albany to acquire the land for the park, the city needed authorization from the state legislature. The required act Barnes's fellow Republicans swiftly provided, but the bill was vetoed by another Republican, Gov. Charles Evans Hughes,[16] only a short time before he resigned his office to take a seat on the United States Supreme Court. One suspects that Hughes gleefully stopped Barnes's project in retaliation for the grief Barnes and the *Evening Journal* had given him as governor.[17] There was also opposition from local citizens, who argued that the park was a waste of valuable commercial space, and, worse, it was ludicrous to put a public park alongside a noisy, filthy railroad track that might imperil the lives of children at play. According to a speech given to the City Plan Association on February 28, 1912, by the vice president and general manager of the Delaware & Hudson Company, C. S. Sims, the opposition had been aimed at his company as well. The *Albany Evening Journal* reported that Sims stated:

Now a year or so ago there was talk of improving the river front and someone dubbed the scheme "Cinder Park." It was next said that the Delaware and Hudson company wanted it. Now, just imagine a railroad running its train through a park. Why, one broken down store house is worth more to the Delaware and Hudson company than all the parks you can construct. We did not want it, my friends, but the plan was killed just because someone said we did.[18]

Despite the veto of Governor Hughes, Barnes continued to push the project. In April, May and June, 1911, the river-front scheme showed up again in Reynolds's diaries. On May 22 a committee met and approved the designs that had been worked up in Reynolds's office, and on the afternoon of June 1 Reynolds explained the plan to the chamber of commerce, which had formed a committee to study the whole river-front issue. In

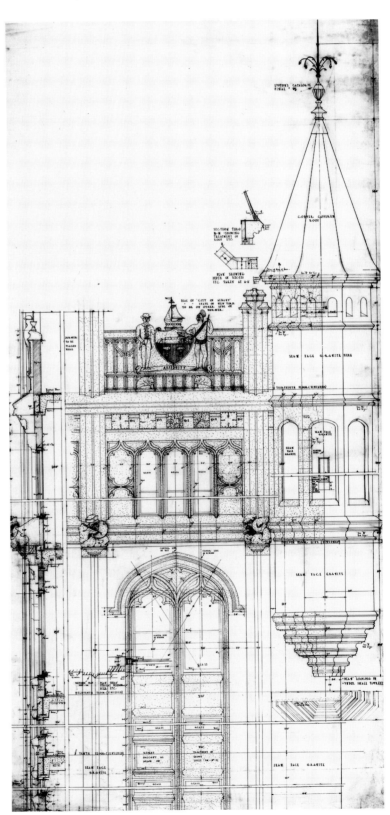

Fig. 99. Delaware & Hudson Building, elevation of southwest corner of upper part of central tower

November the committee, chaired by a two-time Reynolds client, Edmund Niles Huyck, presented its report to the chamber and then to the mayor.[19]

Huyck was a widely respected businessman, as well as a friend of Barnes. He and his fellow committee members insisted that "any plan which beautifies but does not recognize the necessity [for commercial utility] must be a failure."[20] Thus, they argued, the river-front project had to take into account three factors: sanitation, economic purpose and beautification.[21] This conclusion was a hardly subtle condemnation of the Reynolds scheme, which included "Cinder Park" but no commercial property.

The Huyck committee report forced the city to look around for an outside advisor. Thus, in the winter of 1912 Arnold Brunner, an architect and city planner from New York, entered the picture, at the same time that the legislature took up consideration of another bill to authorize the city to improve the river front. The *Albany Evening Journal* noted on February 3:

Preparing to engage an expert city planner pursuant to an ordinance recently passed by the common council, Wallace Greenalch, commissioner of public works, is now communicating with other committees that have adopted city plans. This morning he received reports from Rochester, Cleveland and Columbus. In each of these cities the experts have recommended certain specific improvements as well as to make suggestions for street improvements and the care of parks. The plans for

Rochester and Cleveland were prepared with the aid of Arnold W. Brunner, one of the jury of award that selected the design for Albany's soldiers and sailors' memorial.[22]

Brunner was called to Albany to take a look at the whole city, for which he subsequently proposed a master plan of parks and parkways, of which Reynolds's open space on the waterfront formed only one part. There is no evidence that Reynolds would have been prepared to draw up so comprehensive a plan for the city.

Brunner's analysis of Albany, which he published in 1914 in the *American Architect* and in expanded form in a small volume entitled *Studies for Albany,*[23] was sensitive to its site and history. The plan of the original Dutch settlement was irregular, like that of its sister town, New Amsterdam. The unusually wide State Street was the major east-west thoroughfare. When the city expanded at the end of the eighteenth century, it did so in a typical American grid, but that grid had always to take into account the terrain, cut by deep ravines that either limited the expansion of the grid or forced it into a roller-coaster ride prophetic of the layout of San Francisco. Of this layout Brunner wrote: "today Albany is essentially picturesque. Situated on hills on the west bank of the Hudson, its natural growth has been irregular and it possesses an individuality among our cities that is most pronounced. I have endeavored to take these characteristics into account.... It would seem a calamity to attempt to formalize the City of Albany or to try to change its plan to make it resemble those stately cities where the architecture is formal and where the streets all cross each other at right angles and where steep hills do not exist."[24]

The purport of this statement is made particularly clear by setting it against the background of some of Brunner's previous work as an urban planner. In the first decade of the century Brunner, together with the now better known Daniel Burnham and John Merven Carrère, had been responsible for the ambitious plan for Cleveland, Ohio, of 1903 – an important moment in the history of the City Beautiful movement in America. Burnham had been the architect in charge of the planning of the World's Columbian Exposition of 1893 and the author of the great plan to encircle Chicago with parkways. Both schemes were crucial to the development of City Beautiful notions, as was the recently completed New York Public Library by Carrère & Hastings. The centerpiece of the Cleveland plan was a T-shaped square connecting the commercial heart of the city to the lakefront. At the north, or lake end of this enormous Beaux-Arts space, based on the Place de la Concorde in Paris, was to rise a never-built railroad station.[25] Brunner realized that this kind of flat, classicizing scheme was wrong for Albany, with its hilly landscape and irregular Dutch plan. He wrote, "I feel strongly that whatever changes are made in the future, the spirit that originally dominated the city should be respected, and that the future Albany should be a development and an

Fig. 101. Delaware & Hudson Building, frontispiece of subway

Fig. 102. Albany Evening Journal Building, detail, printers' marks of William Caxton and Jehan Petit

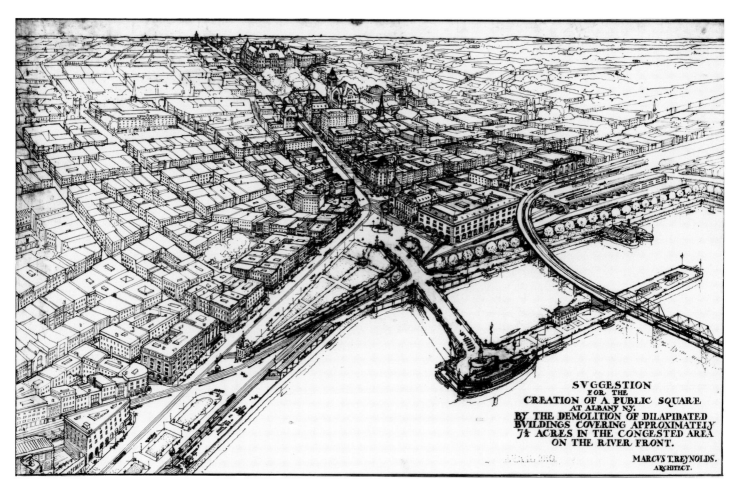

SVGGESTION
FOR THE
CREATION OF A PUBLIC SQUARE
AT ALBANY N.Y.
BY THE DEMOLITION OF DILAPIDATED
BVILDINGS COVERING APPROXIMATELY
7¼ ACRES IN THE CONGESTED AREA
ON THE RIVER FRONT.

MARCVS T. REYNOLDS.
ARCHITECT.

Fig. 103. "Suggestion for the Creation of a Public Square at Albany, New York," 1910, drawing by Charles Cobb

intensification of itself."[26] Hurray, in other words, for the *genius loci*. Brunner's respect for this genius of Albany led to his accepting something highly unusual, if not even unique, in the annals of City Beautiful schemes — Reynolds's "Cinder Park," a large public space laid out on an irregular instead of a classically symmetrical, geometrical plan.

In Brunner's scheme, however, Reynolds's park of 1910 was no longer to be open toward the river. Instead, its eastern side would be defined by a long building with a central tower rising on the axis of State Street (Fig. 104). Brunner's justification for this long building was visual rather than functional. He noted that many Albanians wanted a view down State to the Hudson. But his studies, he argued, had led him to the realization that this would not be a view of the river, but of railroad tracks, trains, the New York Central bridge over the Hudson and the "unfortunate Round House on the other side of the river." "Accordingly," he continued, "it seemed much better to obliterate

this so-called 'view' and create a Plaza surrounded by buildings that would effectually screen these activities from sight."[27] Brunner, Burnham and Carrère had already proposed a similar scheme for Cleveland. There, long colonnades would have extended east and west from the railroad station to hide the tracks from the grand square they had designed. In both cases Brunner chose to conceal the modern reality of a railroad behind a screen of historicizing architecture.[28]

The proposed building for the Albany site that appeared in a Brunner drawing dated June 4, 1912, takes its cue, in terms of roof line and pyramidal roof shape, from the adjacent Federal Building. Brunner was also respectful of buildings with towers in the city, including city hall and the Capitol. For Brunner, Albany's towers added to the picturesqueness he found in the city as a whole. He pointed out that the Capitol is not centered on the axis of State Street, but rather dominates the top of the street with its southeastern corner tower. The central tower in his drawing would terminate State Street to the east just as the Capitol tower terminates it to the west. The effectiveness of the tower in the urban environment was made clear in two illustrations published by Brunner in 1914 (Figs.105 and 106), one a photograph of the east end of State Street "as it is now" and another in which a drawing of the D & H tower as designed by Reynolds was added between the converging lines of the sides of the street.[29]

According to a statement Brunner made at a hearing in Albany a week later, this building was to house "offices for the railroads and trolley companies and the steamboat lines." That variety of prospective tenants probably accounts for the way Brunner's design is broken into various parts. As early as June 1, however, the D & H was slated to build on the plaza, and Reynolds, Barnes's poker partner, not Brunner, was its anointed architect. Reynolds noted in his diary on June 1, 1912, "Met Brunner and his man Andrews. Andrews City Engineer and Greenalch in for first time about D & H office building at end of new public square." Brunner, then, established the footprint of the building to which Reynolds would give form.

Details of the negotiations with Lenor Loree that led to his decision to build the D & H Building are not known, but apparently Edmund Niles Huyck played a major role. A fellow member of his chamber of commerce committee recalled that "Mr. Huyck…was finally successful in effecting agreement that proved mutually satisfactory to all parties concerned."[30] Huyck had served his friend, Barnes, and his architect, Reynolds, well.

By 1912 the expanding D & H was in need of considerable new office space, and Loree's ambitions for the railroad quite likely required that office space be housed in an important architectural statement. Loree had already had an impressive career. In 1889, as an employee of the Pennsylvania Railroad, he was put in charge of wrenching order from the chaos of the Johnstown flood. That he is said to have accomplished in two weeks. By 1901 he was president of the Baltimore & Ohio, and in 1907 he moved over to the same job at the Rock Island. In 1907, E. H. Harriman, who had bought the D & H in the panic of that year, made him its president.[31] Loree, described as "shaggy and elephantine, with quick, amused eyes and the lumbering, soft-footed walk of a bear,"[32] turned the D & H into a marvel of modern efficiency. Its main business was hauling coal from Pennsylvania mines to the Hudson Valley, particularly New York City. To make hauling more efficient, Loree by 1910 had doubled the number of freight cars owned by the company and had bought or ordered 79 new engines of a very large size,[33] which would reduce costs by enabling one crew to do the work of several crews using older, smaller engines.[34] The heavier new engines needed "stronger bridges, longer roundhouses, better roadbeds, longer turntables, easier grades, … more water and better service at terminals and shops."[35] In 1912, the railroad opened at Colonie, just

Fig. 104. Arnold Brunner, project for plaza and office building, Albany, 1912

STVDY for PLAZA
ALBANY
ARNOLD W. BRVNNER
ARCHITECT
JUNE 4 · 1912

Fig. 105. State Street "as it is," photograph 1914 (to the left of the Albany Trust Company is the First National Bank facade)

Fig. 106. State Street with proposed Delaware & Hudson tower, drawing, 1914

north of Albany, a vast new yard containing ten acres of floor space and costing $2.5 million.[36]

Since its founding in 1823 as a canal company, the D & H had kept its headquarters in New York. In 1873-76 it built its own building, designed by the eminent Richard Morris Hunt, at 17-21 Cortland Street, also called the Coal and Iron Exchange.[37] In 1906 it sold this structure and moved into rental space. In Albany, the railroad offices were housed in a building at 58 North Pearl Street, which the D & H bought in 1892.[38] The expansion of the company's business and the paperwork required by increasing federal regulation of the railroads made the need for more office space desperate. The sale of the Hunt building left the railroad without what we would call today a corporate image.[39]

Reynolds began design work on the new D & H building in July, soon after the Albany aldermen had authorized the plan for the new plaza at the end of State Street. Designing the building that would face this square was neither quick nor easy. In September Reynolds took plans for a four-story building 800 feet long to New York to show to officials of the railroad. One of the officers asked for a three-story building, but Brunner, who had the right to pass on Reynolds's designs, approved the four-story scheme, which had a tower. On September 21, however, Reynolds produced a design for a three-story building with an arcade and a "small central feature," and on

October 19 he presented a cheaper design for a three-story building, flat of roof and considerably shorter in length.

On January 24, 1913, there is a curious entry in Reynolds's diary, considering all he had written about the D & H building the year before: "The beginning of the D & H office building on the Plaza. Sims telephoned at 2:00 and wanted sketches for $225,000 office building ready by following Saturday." On February 2 Reynolds submitted a new design with "two symmetrical 64' wings with pavilions. Andrews objected." With that plan shot down, Reynolds gamely started over. On February 3 he wrote: "Began plan for D & H building with three splayed sides, the first starting at angle from the P.O. This was Sims' idea." On February 7 Reynolds recorded: "Brunner turned down my plan drawn by Sims' instruction of three long stretches all at an angle with pavilion on axis of State. Brunner subsequently suggested that we build only to axis where place a five or six story tower. The other parts four stories."

Finally, on February 10, something like the present design made its first appearance in Reynolds's diary: "River Front for D. H. commencing Gothic design with 8 story office building on axis of State Street." On the nineteenth Sims accepted this design, and on February 28 "Brunner approved Gothic design for building for foot of State St." There were more problems with Brunner, but by late winter, 1913, the general layout and the Gothic style of the building were settled. In that same winter finishing touches were being put on Cass Gilbert's Woolworth Building in New York, to ready it for a spring opening.[40] Reynolds traveled to New York frequently, and he could scarcely have been unaware of a building that was creating an enormous outpouring of public enthusiasm. It is altogether likely that the excitement generated by Gilbert's Gothic building led to the relatively quick acceptance of Reynolds's Gothic design for the D & H.

Reynolds specifically called the style of the D & H Building Flemish Gothic.[41] Indeed, he made considerable use of the greatest of all Flemish Gothic secular buildings, the Cloth Hall at Ypres, begun around 1200, as a prototype.[42] The great length of the Cloth Hall worked well for a building that had to screen hundreds of feet of railroad tracks,[43] while its central tower provided the vertical that both he and Brunner wanted to place on the axis of State Street. As a secular build-

ing, the Cloth Hall was a fitting precedent for a building that would house the offices of a great business enterprise. Mature capitalists of modern Albany could identify with the fledgling capitalists of medieval Flanders, should it ever occur to them to do so.

Fig. 107. Delaware & Hudson and Albany Evening Journal Buildings, view from south

Fig. 108. Albany Evening Journal Building, printer's mark of François Regnault, drawing, 1916

For Reynolds, the choice of Flemish Gothic also seemed peculiarly appropriate to commemorate the Netherlandish origins of the founders of his city. He noted in his publication of the building in the *American Architect*: "As the site was very irregular in outline, it was obvious that some type of picturesque rather than formal architecture should be selected, and the Flemish Gothic seemed most appropriate as recalling the nationality of the original settlers."[44] In the Middle Ages, of course, Flanders and Holland were one.

In two earlier Albany public buildings Reynolds, ever conscious of his city's history, had already recalled the nationality of the original settlers. In 1900 he designed the Pruyn Free Library (Fig. 119) to look like houses built in Albany in the seventeenth and early eighteenth centuries by Dutch settlers. In 1910, during the months when the "Cinder Park" project was being discussed, Reynolds designed a fire station on Delaware Avenue (Fig. 121) which is derived from the Meat Market in Haarlem.[45]

The fire station is decorated with beavers that refer to the original Dutch settlement at Albany, called Beverwyck. The same animal appears in an equally prominent role in the earlier part of the D & H Building. Flanking the dormers that penetrate the roof are pairs of beavers (Fig. 98) that both celebrate the early history of the city and give the building an unexpected touch of whimsy.[46] The beaver's embodiment of industriousness accords splendidly with the Albany motto, "Assiduity"; on the city's shield a beaver gazes proudly at a just-felled tree. Further symbols of Albany's history were displayed at the top of the thirteen-story tower: the seal of the city and the replica of the *Half Moon*. The *Half Moon* had recently been on Albanian minds. In 1909 a replica, accompanied by a copy of Robert Fulton's *Clermont*, had sailed up to Albany, to be met by a celebratory crowd estimated at 70 thousand people.[47] For the subway that led to the river Reynolds composed an inscription that encouraged the visitor to imagine, on the site of the D & H Building, both the primeval landscape on the day of Henry Hudson's arrival and the first buildings of the Dutch settlement:

Here where the ship Half Moon
Ended its cruise of adventure.
Between fields of Indian corn
A Kill made its way to he river.
Called by the Dutch — The Füyck —
A stream abounding in beaver.

Here was the first trading post
Beversfüyck the name of the hamlet.[48]

In 1916, when Reynolds designed the part of the D & H building south of the tower, he expanded its historical allusions. On the dormer gables are the names and coats of arms of important early Dutch settlers (Fig. 100), together with the dates of their arrival.[49] These arms join those on the frontispiece that bespeak the roles of the French, Dutch and English in the history of the area. In the gables the Dutch connection is doubly stressed, through the style of the architecture itself, and through the history lesson, or at least the genealogy lesson, that the coats of arms teach. The personal importance of this history lesson for Reynolds can hardly be overstated. Included is Hendrick Cuyler, from whom Reynolds was descended on his mother's side. Cuyler was a modest tailor. The main reason for listing his name alongside those of Van Rensselaer, Schuyler and Livingston was that he was Reynolds's direct link to the Dutch in the Hudson Valley.[50]

The addition of the Albany Evening Journal Building at the south end (Figs. 97 and 107) was conceived only in 1915, when William Barnes made the decision to move his newspaper offices and printing plant to the new plaza that he had brought into being. According to Reynolds's diaries, in December, 1912, Barnes talked with his architect about expanding the old Evening Journal plant on James Street. Barnes revived that scheme in January, 1915, but on March 24, 1915, Reynolds noted: "Barnes in for first time about independent building for Journal on NW corner of Hamilton. I suggested piece on Broadway at end of city property on Plaza. Got map of layout from D & H." Reynolds took advantage of Barnes's dissatisfaction with his James Street site to propose an addition to the D & H Building that would allow the ensemble to form a wall along the entire eastern edge of the new plaza. Barnes took Reynolds's advice, and the result was a building with a complex massing that shows Reynolds at his best. The new Evening Journal structure contained not only newspaper offices and a printing plant, but also an elegantly appointed, if awkwardly planned, apartment for Barnes at the top of the tower. From there he enjoyed a view south and east over the waterfront he had rejuvenated and west over the city he ruled. For the Evening Journal Building, Reynolds conceived a remarkably apt decorative scheme, relief sculptures based on early printers' marks (Fig. 102). Through these marks Reynolds connected Barnes with the most notable early masters of the trade from which his client derived his wealth.[51] A building for a Republican politician naturally had to include the elephant of the French printer François Regnault (Fig. 108).[52]

Although Barnes is largely forgotten today, in the first two decades of the century he was a powerful force in Republican politics, not just on the local and state levels, but also on the national scene. On his mother's side, he was the grandson

regained control of the Evening Journal, which had passed out of family hands, and had taken over leadership of the moribund Republican party in Albany. So skillfully did he play the game of politics and so cleverly did he use his newspaper to push his ends that by 1899 he was able to have a Republican elected mayor of Albany for the first time, thus solidifying his hold on the city, which he ruled until 1921, when a very shrewd group of Democrats overthrew him and installed the still-reigning regime.

of Thurlow Weed, one of the founders of the Republican party in New York State, as well as the founder of the Albany Evening Journal. Through his father, he traced his ancestry back to one of the original settlers of Hartford in the 1630s. His august Yankee lineage, together with his magna cum laude degree from Harvard, suggested to some a more genteel career that the rough-and-tumble one he took up in politics. One writer called him "the most successful combination of university graduate and strong-arm politician in public life."[53] Enormously energetic and ambitious, Barnes had, by the age of twenty-five,

Barnes rose to power by combining ruthlessness with accommodation. He drained the previous Democratic machine by keeping many of their best people in office, thus winning them over to his side. He played to the dissatisfaction that various immigrant groups, particularly Germans, felt with the old machine, and he brought a large number of wealthy Democratic businessmen over to his side by creating a climate favorable to their interests. Barnes ran a wide-open city, in which almost any vice was available. At the same time he embarked on a campaign of public works, including the elaborate Brunner plan for the beautifica-

Fig. 109. Delaware & Hudson Building, under construction in 1914, view from north

Fig. 110. Delaware & Hudson Building, bay system of north wing

tion of the whole city, of which the scheme at the foot of State Street was only the most ambitious part. He increased police and fire protection (for example, Reynolds's firehouse), established public baths, built schools and increased public spending on libraries. Under Barnes, there was something for almost everyone, except recalcitrant Democratic politicians. Or fundamentalist preachers. He once told an irate man of the cloth that a group of ministers bore no more weight with him than a like number of saloon keepers.

As Barnes increased his power in Albany, he reached out for influence in the state Republican party. He managed Theodore Roosevelt's successful campaign for governor in 1898, and after Roosevelt moved onto the national scene, Barnes acted as T.R.'s political weathervane in the state. In 1907 Roosevelt appointed him Inspector of the Port of Albany, the only political office Barnes ever held. In 1911 Barnes became chairman of the New York State Republican Committee.

As Barnes's power and influence waxed, so did the public display of his innate conservatism. In 1908, at the state convention in Saratoga, he opposed the renomination of Charles Evans Hughes for governor. He had fallen out with Hughes over the issue of direct primaries. That break, in turn, led to a more fateful break with Theodore Roosevelt in 1910, when Roosevelt also came out for direct primaries.

In the summer of 1912, when design of the D & H Building was beginning, Barnes reached the apogee of his power and influence. At the Republican National Convention of 1912, he renominated the President, William Howard Taft, and he directed the floor fight that gained Taft the nomination. This, of course, was one of the great Pyrrhic victories in American politics, for Taft's victory led to Roosevelt to bolt the party and run under the Bull Moose banner. That, in turn, secured the election for the Democratic nominee, Woodrow Wilson. But Taft's future loss to Wilson was on no Albanian's mind when Barnes returned home victorious from the convention in Chicago. He was met at Union Station by a throng of citizens who formed a parade to escort him to his house on State Street. According to the delirious account in the *Evening Journal*, the parade stretched from Broadway up State as far as the capitol. Barnes had defeated the man he had come to call "Citizen Roosevelt."

His break with Roosevelt in 1910 had widened disastrously in 1911 over an issue that Roosevelt championed: judicial recall by popular vote. Barnes was a man frightened by the rising specter of socialism — a genuine fear in an era which saw many American cities elect socialist mayors and found ten socialists in the New York legislature in 1918[54] — and by the evils of mob rule. Barnes saw the judiciary, with its reliance on precedent, as the surest safeguard against the tyranny of a volatile majority, easily swayed by demagogues such as Roosevelt or (even worse) William Jennings Bryan. Barnes made a distinction between representative and democratic government; he believed in the former and recoiled from

The iconography of the south end of the D & H Building and of the Evening Journal Building fitted Barnes's political philosophy admirably. The coats of arms were of the "favored upon this earth," the most distinguished, industrious and successful of the Dutch settlers. The arms speak of individual achievement, the very thing that Barnes felt gave him the right to lead. By treating passers-by to a parade of *uomini illustri*, the building exhorted modern Albanians to trust men like Barnes to govern. The printers' marks on the Journal Building play a similar role. They put Barnes in the company of the most distinguished historic members of his profession, again men of individual achievement.[56] In the inscription at the main entrance to his newspaper Barnes elevated his own ancestry to this company: "Albany Evening Journal. Founded by Thurlow Weed. 1830."[57]

The conscious switch from generic beavers to specific historic figures was conceived only during the second phase of the building, when Barnes was directly involved in the design. At that moment Barnes found himself, and his conservative wing of

Fig. 111. Delaware & Hudson Building, cast-stone panels for south wing, drawing, 1916

the latter. As Barnes's biographer put it, his "entire political career demonstrated his belief that the base instincts of the majority of men should be controlled by those who had proven by inherited or acquired wealth that they were the favored upon this earth."[55] For Barnes, the great mass of humanity was to be manipulated to maintain the control of those who had the right to lead.

the party, increasingly embattled. During the heat of the 1912 presidential race, T.R. had publicly branded him "Boss Barnes of Albany, a corrupt boss." Barnes sued for libel. The case, tried in 1915 in Syracuse, attracted national attention and produced a remarkably enigmatic verdict, in which the jury found against Barnes, but required Roosevelt to pay the court costs.[58] The battle with

89

Roosevelt made Barnes a liability to the party, which was searching to regroup through reconciliation. At the same time, Barnes's increasingly strident claims for his conservative point of view were seen as more and more out of step with the nation at large. Moreover, his "brutal directness that is offensive and arouses resentment"[59] had made him a large number of enemies, eager to see him fall. Barnes's growing stress on ideology, reflected in the decorations of the D & H and Journal Buildings, cost him the flexibility that had brought him to power. As one contemporary writer presciently put it, "As far as mere force will take a man he will go; but when he reaches the point where influence is required he will fail to 'make good.' He will not last long."[60] Ironically, the completion of the Journal Building, the physical expression of Barnes's political power and the culmination of his drive to beautify Albany, coincided with the beginning of his fall.[61] The tower of the Journal Building, with Barnes's apartment at the top, looks like nothing so much as a castle keep. By 1918, when he moved in, he was already beginning to spend less and less time in the city over which he reigned. The keep was the residence of an increasingly absentee lord, who in three years would no longer be lord at all. When the Democrats took over in 1921, Barnes moved to Mount Kisco, where he lived until his death in 1930.[62] Reynolds attended the graveside services at Albany Rural Cemetery.[63]

With the Delaware & Hudson and Albany Evening Journal Buildings, then, Reynolds consciously gave Albany a structure appropriate in style to its geography, its Dutch foundation and its architectural character. His picturesque, medieval design, unusual in the annals of City Beautiful planning,[64] is simultaneously a lesson in Albany's history, in the history of William Barnes's métier, and in the history of Reynolds's own roots. Formally, it "intensifies" (to use Arnold Brunner's word) the picturesque character of the city, just as iconographically it intensifies the city's sense of its own history. It is also a clear statement of the political values held by a powerful man.

All of this emphasis on history, of course, served present financial as well as political needs. The Gothic structure housed the offices of a railroad in a period of vigorous expansion and the printing presses of a modern political boss. Putting modern functions in a Gothic package was hardly unique to this building at this time. Indeed, the D & H Building stands chronologically between the two most famous Gothic office buildings of the period: the Woolworth Building and the Chicago Tribune Tower, designed in 1921 by Howells and Hood. Of the three, however, the D & H Building had the most complex rationale for the use of the Gothic style. For the Woolworth Building, the Gothic seemed the most flexible and vertically oriented historical style for a "cathedral of commerce" that would be the tallest building in the world. The Gothic exterior of the Tribune Tower was essentially an afterthought, something chosen by the architects after working out the building's plan and structure.[65] One wonders, of course, if Howells and Hood may have been influenced in their choice of Gothic for the Tribune Tower, owned by the politically very conservative Col. Robert McCormick, by Reynolds's use of Gothic for the Evening Journal Building.[66]

Such thoughtfulness about style seems to be something Reynolds learned as a student at Columbia. While he was there, one of his teachers, A. D. F. Hamlin, published an article entitled "The Battle of the Styles."[67] Even if Reynolds never read the article, he must have heard the ideas in the classroom. According to Hamlin, there was no one "right" historical style for an architect to choose (purists of various stripes disagreed, of course). Hamlin argued for "the appropriateness of the style... to the special purpose of the building."[68] We might state Hamlin's position (to paraphrase Louis Sullivan once again) as style follows function.

In the D & H Building Reynolds clearly carried out that precept. A photograph taken in 1914 during construction (Fig. 109) shows the steel skeleton of the tower and the reinforced concrete piers and floor slabs of the north arm. Over this skeleton Reynolds laid a complex veneer of concrete, granite, cast stone and terra cotta that screened the building's modern structure in the same way the building itself screened the railroad.[69] Reynolds's Gothic overlay, however, did not mask the wide bays of the structural frame (Fig. 110). Here he also seems to have followed the pragmatic Hamlin, who argued that an architect should adapt all historical styles to modern exigencies of structure and function.[70] Every historicizing modification that Reynolds made to the rectangular grid of the structural system expressed an architectural notion that Reynolds found important: the articulation of the ground floor loggia, the arched termination of each bay at the fourth floor, the lively projection of the dormers into the steep roof to break up a very long facade, the historical detailing of tracery and, of course, the crucial appliqué of beavers or *uomini famosi*. What Reynolds achieved here was far from the "monstrous and factitious" juncture of modern structure and historical ornament that Edith Wharton excoriated on contemporary robber-baron houses in New York in the same year that Reynolds worked out the design of the D & H Building.[71]

Reynolds demanded that this masonry skin have an "old" and irregular appearance. "I wish to follow," he wrote to the Atlantic Terra Cotta Company, "as closely as possible the finish which would have been given by a stone mason of three hundred years ago. I do not want to have the suggestion of terra cotta, and I do not wish to have any smooth mechanical or modern finish."[72] The blocks of seam face granite had to be laid to achieve an effect of random coursing, and the cast stone surfaces had to be hand-tooled. Reynolds sent only sketchy drawings to the company that made the molds for the cast stone ornaments. He explained: "In making these models I am most anxious that the modeler should exercise his skill and take advantage of the pliability of the material …it has been my experience…that the better and more careful the drawings, the worse is the final result. One cannot show very carefully the proper feeling in a drawing. This can only be brought out by the touch of the modeler, and I wish to take advantage of his skill in this work."[73]

Even when he left the concrete frame bare, as he did in the warehouse wing to the north (Fig. 94), Reynolds manipulated the surface in a way that was visually arresting and that "explained" the functions of the various parts of the structural system. The protruding piers emphasized the vertical support system. The bottoms of the piers were thicker, because that part had a greater load to bear, while the stubby vertical projections above the roofline harmonized the warehouse with the more decidedly vertical aspirations of the rest of the structure. Behind the piers, a second plane was created by the wall that enclosed the interior and held the large, steel sash windows in place. A third plane marked the edges of the horizontals of the floor slabs, whose faces were carved back in two further planes that gave the slabs a visual interest that created a balance between the wider verticals and narrower horizontals.

For the beavers and most of the tracery of the rest of the D & H Building, Reynolds skillfully made use of cast stone, created through a repetitive industrial process that could be manipulated to produce a sense of variety. For both the north and south arms the Reynolds office designed cast-stone panels (Fig. 111) that were placed under the windows of the second floor where they would be most visible. Seven different panel designs were arranged in a carefully calculated, irregular pattern that created the illusion that each panel was unique.

While Reynolds mined the veins of historical architecture in a way consonant with Hamlin's theories, he simultaneously made use of a particular American tradition of commercial architecture exemplified by Richard Morris Hunt's design for the Delaware & Hudson Building on Cortland Street, New York, of the 1870s. Reynolds's concept of the office building owes a lot to the Hunt design. Hunt's D & H Building had the same strong piers, thin tripartite frames for the windows, low arches terminating vertical bays, dormers in the roof and strongly marked pavilions at the edges. Reynolds seems to have chosen to follow this specific American type of office building design to anchor the railroad in its own architectural past.

Even if one has quarrels with the Hamlin-Reynolds approach to using historical styles, it made more sense than one advanced by an Englishman, Edward A. Freeman, in the same volume of the *Architectural Record* in which Hamlin's essay appeared in 1891-92.[74] Freeman urged architects to return to the last truly indigenous architectural styles of their native countries and to start over again from there. The English, French and Germans, he argued, should go back to the Late Gothic, while Italians should return to the "Pisan Romanesque." But what should Americans, who had no history, do? (Freeman seems to have been ignorant or disdainful of the Colonial Revival.) They too, he pronounced, should take up the Pisan Romanesque, because they live at the same latitudes as Italians. In comparison to Freeman's theory, Reynolds's choice of the Flemish Gothic for Albany appears as sweet reason itself. Had Reynolds followed Freeman rather than Hamlin, a round, arcaded tower might lean over the plaza at the foot of State Street. The latitudes of Pisa and Albany are perilously close.

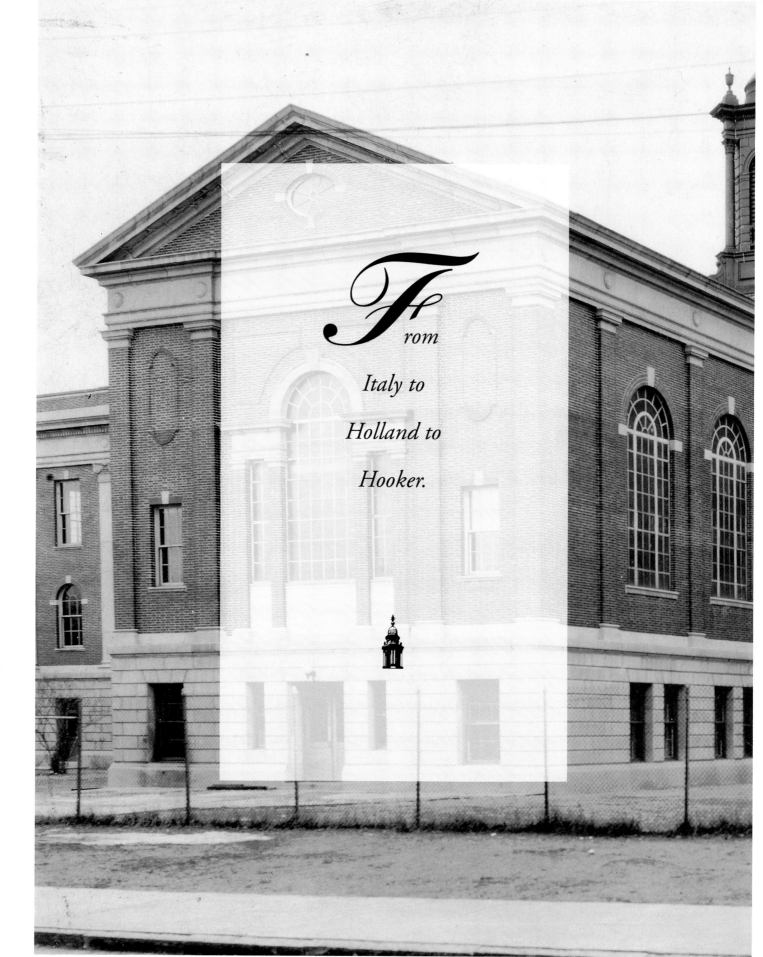

*F*rom

Italy to

Holland to

Hooker.

CHAPTER 6

OTHER COMMERCIAL AND PUBLIC BUILDINGS

Reynolds's commercial and public buildings offer a rich means of reconsidering the range of his interests, and even a chance to broach the question of stylistic development in his work. For Reynolds, however, stylistic development is not so much a question of moving from a personal early style through a middle period into a late phase as it is a question of adopting different historical styles as those styles seemed to fit current situations most aptly.

In his additions to the New York State National Bank (Figs. 23 and 26), Reynolds showed a remarkable ability to make something new that looked like what was already there.[1] Perhaps Reynolds's most astounding feat of designing a new part of a building to look like the old occurred in the Hampton Hotel (Fig. 112).

His involvement with the Hampton project began in 1904[2] and lasted at least until 1910. The project started out as a modification of the National Commercial Bank Building, a Romanesque structure of 1887 designed by Robert W. Gibson that had become available when the bank moved into its new York & Sawyer quarters a few doors to the west on State Street. Reynolds gave Gibson's six-story facade two additional floors. This part of the project opened on October 29, 1906.[3]

It is easy to look at the present facade and believe that, even though it is rather tall for its time, it is all of a piece. Reynolds removed the transoms of Gibson's sixth floor windows and their surmounting gables and left the lower parts of the windows and their flanking walls in place. Over the old windows he erected a new wall that continued the verticals and horizontals of the red sandstone window frames, and he added areas of checkerboard ashlar within a grid created by the red stones.[4] Over his new eighth floor windows he placed Gibson's old transoms and gables, as well as the waffle-patterned parapet that Gibson placed behind the gables. By continuing the basic framework established in Gibson's sixth floor, and by adding details that harmonized with what was already in place, Reynolds created the remarkable fiction that his new wall was old.

In Reynolds's early years, his fondness for Italian Renaissance architecture led him to design, in 1899, palazzi for the New York State Normal School and the Albany Railway Company. Both were the public equivalents of the Van Rensselaer Houses of 1896-97. The Normal School needed a large dormitory because it was in a period of considerable expansion, as it sought to become the main institution in the state for the training of high school teachers. It should be no surprise that the commission came to Reynolds, for his cousins William Bayard Van Rensselaer and Marcus T. Hun were directors. Unfortunately, the building seems never to have been built.

So Italianate was the dormitory project (Fig. 113) that the three upper stories would hardly have seemed out of place in Rome itself. From the rusticated basement of this blocky building, a

Facing page. Public School 4, Albany, Madison Avenue and Ontario Street, gymnasium from northwest, 1922-24, demolished

Fig. 112. Robert W. Gibson and Marcus T. Reynolds, The Hampton, 40 State Street, Albany, facade, 1887 and 1904-6

Fig. 113. *New York State Normal School Dormitory, Albany, project, 1899, front elevation*

Fig. 114. *New York State Normal School Dormitory, project, rear elevation*

grey-brick ground floor, pierced by large, round-arched windows, rose to a strongly projecting limestone and terra-cotta stringcourse. The main portal, another round-arched opening, was flanked by four engaged, fluted, banded columns. Above this floor rose three tightly designed stories of banded brick and terra-cotta masonry. The windows, grouped in pairs over the voids of the ground floor openings, produced a lively alternating rhythm. The top story, separated from those below by a rich stringcourse of bundled leaves, was decorated with heads, swags, wreaths and ribbons. Rectangular marble panels alternated with evenly

spaced windows to form a rhythm completely different from that established in the floors below. The upper story brings to mind Raphael's drawing for the facade of the Palazzo Branconio dell'Aquila in Rome. Reynolds must have known that design. Neither Raphael nor art in general had anything to do with the design of the rear facade of the dormitory (Fig. 114), where utilitarian construction took the place of architecture.[5] Reynolds chose the language of the Renaissance for this building because it was, for him, the most appropriate language for a large-scale urban housing unit to speak. Roman palazzi, which accommodated hordes of relatives and servants as well as their owners, were big not just to impress, but also to shelter a lot of people.

For the Albany Railroad Company at Broadway and Columbia Street, Reynolds's first proposal was a four-story block whose verticality was strongly emphasized by the quoins at the edges and the connecting frames of the windows in the second and third stories (Fig. 116). A similar window design occurred on the contemporary house for the superintendent of Albany Rural Cemetery (Fig. 76). The even rhythm of the window bays was played in syncopated fashion against the triplets of the attic-story consoles. When the building was shortened by one floor, the horizontal separation of the first and second floors became much stronger, and the central bay received a quite opu-

REAR ELEVATION.

94

lent treatment (Fig. 115). The detail is mannered. The cartouches that hang on the walls of the first floor, which visually but not physically support the paired columns of the *piano nobile*, recall Michelangelo's consoles under the paired columns of the entrance hall of the Laurentian Library. Under the pediment of the central window Reynolds inscribed the date of the building, 1899, and above, on the bottom of the aedicule, the words "Marcus T. Reynolds Archt." Like that on the cemetery superintendent's house, this inscription, on Reynolds's first major public structure in his native city, made sure that no one would be ignorant of the architect's name. The pride and ambition that led him to "sign" the building so prominently seem to have known few bounds at this point in his life.

The building opened on June 14, 1900, after the Albany Railway had joined with the Troy Street Railway in December, 1899, to form the United Traction Company.[6] A violent strike broke out against United Traction in May, 1901, climaxed by the attack of an angry mob on a streetcar at the corner of Broadway and Columbia where the office building stands. There, in front of the mannered richness of this facade that bears Reynolds's name, two men were shot and killed by troops called out to quell the riot. The eruption of a lethal labor riot before a mercantile palace designed by an aristocratic, learned and arrogant young architect offered a clear picture of the struggle between labor and capital that characterized turn-of-the-century America to anyone perspicacious enough to see it. One can even imagine the president of the company, Robert C. Pruyn, standing on the balcony over the main door, trying to calm the restive workers in the street below. But such a scene never took place.

For Pruyn, Reynolds produced a second Renaissance palace some fifteen years later (Fig. 117). Reynolds spent the summer of 1914 enjoying Italy, the European country of which he was most fond, and watching the early phases of the war develop beyond the Alps. When he returned, Pruyn gave him the commission for a new office building on State Street for the Municipal Gas Company. Pruyn had long been involved in important architectural events in Albany. He was one of the commissioners of the new city hall, designed by H. H. Richardson, and in 1887 he had commissioned Robert W. Gibson to design the National Commercial Bank that Reynolds

later converted into the Hampton. As president of that bank, Pruyn had an interest in the Hampton, and he had also been responsible for giving the commission for his new bank building to York & Sawyer.[7] He lived in a splendid house on Englewood Place, designed by Gibson, of which the carriage house still remains. Deeply interested in art, Pruyn collected Japanese ivories, for which he had developed a taste when he served as an aide

Fig. 115. Albany Railroad Company, 600 Broadway, Albany, 1899-1900, view from southeast

Fig. 116. Albany Railroad Company, elevation, early design, 1899

to his father, Lincoln's ambassador to Japan. Pruyn had also supported the study of the history of Albany by subsidizing the publication of Cuyler Reynolds's *Albany Chronicles.*[8]

Completed in 1916, the Municipal Gas Company was Reynolds's most Palladian — perhaps his only Palladian — design.[9] This sober, travertine facade, however, once had a rather playful, even gassy crown (Fig. 118). On the capping balustrade Reynolds placed flaming urns of carved stone flanked by two large iron tripods that looked capable of carrying real flames, whether they were or not.[10] Unfortunately, the urns and tripods are gone. What is remarkable about this facade, in contrast to those of the dormitory and the Albany Railway, is its sobriety. In the Catskill Savings Bank facade of 1907 (Fig. 36) and also in the pro-

ject for the Union National Bank, Schenectady, of 1908 (Fig. 27), Reynolds displayed a tendency toward simplification, an abandonment of his mannerist tricks of the late nineties. The Municipal Gas Company facade, which shares some ideas with the Union National project, may be seen as the culmination of that sobering up of Reynolds's architecture. During his trip to Italy in 1914 he seems to have been inspired by a different type of Renaissance architecture from the kind that had interested him during his first trip of twenty years earlier.

If Reynolds housed industries and their captains in Renaissance palaces, he installed civic functions in buildings that recalled the Dutch origins of Albany.[11] These Dutch buildings formed an ethnic architectural backdrop against which we can place the Flemish Gothic of the D & H Building (Fig. 93). Like that structure, they belong to the years when the Republicans under William Barnes, Jr., dominated Albany politics.

In 1900 Reynolds designed the Pruyn Free Library,[12] donated by Mrs. John Van Schaick Lansing Pruyn, the queen, or at least a grand duchess of Albany society, in memory of her husband (Fig. 119). Descended from early Dutch settlers of the city, Pruyn had been the lawyer who did the formidable legal work for Erastus Corning to combine many small railroads into the New York Central.[13] After the Vanderbilt takeover of the New York Central, Pruyn devoted himself to civic causes, particularly education; for more than twenty years he was president of the Board of

Fig. 117. Municipal Gas Company, 126 State Street, Albany, 1915-16, facade

Fig. 118. View of south side of State Street, Albany, with Municipal Gas Company, photograph c. 1920

Regents of the state university system of New York. He also laid the cornerstone of the new state Capitol.

Opened in 1901, the library stood on the site on North Pearl Street of the small Federal house in which Pruyn had been born in 1811. Reynolds replaced it with a building that looked like one of the houses built in Albany in the late seventeenth and early eighteenth centuries by Dutch settlers, thus giving Pruyn a genealogically correct, if fictitious, natal architecture. In his article on the colonial buildings of the Albany area, Reynolds had lamented the disappearance of the early Dutch houses that had given Albany a "striking individuality."[14] With the Pruyn Library, he tried to restore something of that quality.

When the growth of the city's population in the 1920s made an addition to the library necessary, Reynolds's office designed a building attached at right angles to the rear of the old that maintained scrupulously the Dutch character of the original (Fig. 120), even though Reynolds's other public buildings of the twenties were all in a classical mode. The $64,000 addition, of 1926-27, had to be faithful to the earlier, just as that "original" part had been faithful to structures that were truly original. Reynolds consistently added on to either his or earlier buildings in a style that was sympathetic to that of the older structure.

The interior of the first part of the library had been a large, well-lit, tall space covered with an open, timber roof. The addition provided readers with a congenially domestic setting. In *O Albany!*, William Kennedy recalls fondly his first encounters with books in the cozy interior of the Pruyn Library,[15] which provided, in the winter, the warmth of a fireplace for young readers from poor, and poorly heated, homes. The window decorations in the addition were reminiscent of those Reynolds had designed for the D & H Building.

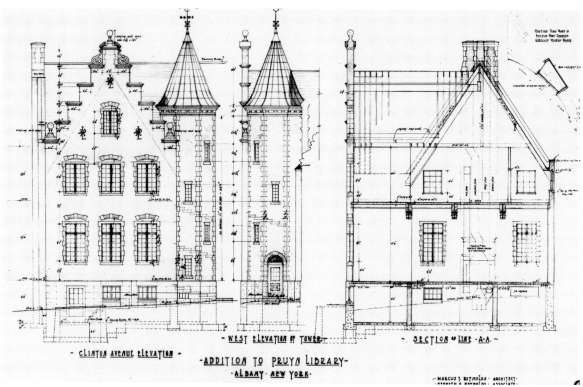

CLINTON AVENUE ELEVATION

WEST ELEVATION OF TOWER

SECTION ON LINE A-A

ADDITION TO PRUYN LIBRARY
ALBANY NEW YORK

MARCUS T. REYNOLDS · ARCHITECT·
KENNETH C. REYNOLDS · ASSOCIATE·

Fig. 120. Pruyn Free Library, addition, 1926, elevations and section

Fig. 121. Truck house no. 4, 360 Delaware Avenue, Albany, 1910, facade

Pruyn's daughter, Huybertie Pruyn Hamlin, recalled that the window insets included the seals of the West India Company, Holland, the New Netherlands, the British after 1664, and the Walloons, as well as representations of the *Half Moon*, the Six Nations, and "the famous beaver of Beverwyck."[16] There were also a tulip, a sturgeon and printers' marks.[17] The building was to be a history lesson for those who used it. Unfortunately, the city itself has not always given good lessons

in preserving its history. The Pruyn Library was sacrificed in 1968 for an interchange of Interstate 787. At that point, Albany lost one of the two Dutch buildings that Reynolds had given it. The other, unexpectedly, was a firehouse.

In 1910, during the months when the "Cinder Park" project for the river front was being discussed, Reynolds designed a Dutch fire station on Delaware Avenue (Fig. 121), in a part of town enjoying a rapid growth in wooden houses.[18] Formally, the building is derived from the Meat Market in Haarlem, and the Dutch connection extends to some of its most wonderful details, such as the four terra-cotta heads of seventeenth-century burghers that act as corbels for the arches of the truck doorways (Fig. 122). The building is coloristically arresting: purple brick, laid in Flemish bond, accented with olive green terra-cotta ornaments and gray moldings. The twin gables of the Delaware Avenue facade mark the twin openings for the fire engines, while a lower aedicule signals the door for people squeezed in between. Now, huge modern fire trucks back in and out of entrances designed for horse-drawn equipment.

Above, on pinnacles, guardian beavers, holding shields, are ever alert to the danger of fire. On the east gable of the facade, in a roundel, a beaver in relief runs so rapidly that its heavy tail flies behind it. These beavers refer to the original Dutch settle-

Fig. 122. Truck house no. 4, facade, detail of corbel

Fig. 123. Truck house no. 4, west elevation

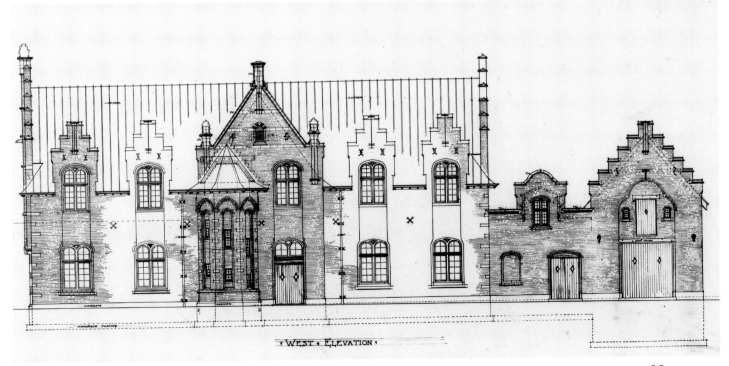

· WEST · ELEVATION ·

99

ment at Albany, called Beverwyck, or Beavertown, in honor of the hundreds of thousands of those creatures that the settlers of the Hudson Valley slaughtered to satisfy the taste of Europeans for that sensuous fur. (Rembrandt's *Syndics of the Cloth Guild*, for instance, wear beaver hats that may well have been made from the tummy fur of beaver pelts that passed through Beverwyck on their way to Amsterdam.) The beaver as a symbol of Albany appears in an equally prominent role in the north part of the D & H Building.

The long flanks of the firehouse (Fig. 123) are punctuated by rows of stepped dormers, and the

west facade is complicated by a projecting mass that holds a subsidiary entrance and the staircase tower to the sleeping quarters on the second floor. At the rear is a picturesque, lower structure for the horses, which had stalls below and a hayloft and oat bin above. The skillfully laid out firemen's quarters, over the room for the trucks, included an ample recreation room, lit from three sides.

The fire station is one of the more idiosyncratic building types to have developed in the United States. In them, "Architects tried out ideas ... that would have been considered too outlandish for any other type of building; no one ever complained about a fire station being undignified."[19] In Reynolds's case, however, there is more than wackiness at work, for the Dutch references were as serious here as they would be in the D. & H. Building.[20] This building, built by the city, celebrated both the city's original settlers and the furry animals that formed the economic basis of its foundation. There is no little irony in posting beavers, trapped almost to extinction by the Dutch settlers, to look out for the lives and property of later Albanians.

Reynolds's Dutch buildings in Albany continued a local architectural tradition whose examples had essentially been demolished by Reynolds's time. His Delaware & Hudson Railroad Station in Cooperstown, however, took up a local tradition still much in evidence. Built in 1915-16, the small station was designed in the "colonial" mode at the request of the client, C. S. Sims of the Delaware & Hudson Company.[21] In this case, "colonial" to Reynolds meant the early nineteenth-century stone architecture of Cooperstown, such as the house erected in 1804 by William Cooper as a wedding present for his daughter, Ann Cooper Pomeroy. Built by a Scottish stone mason, the house has herringbone patterns in the masonry that Reynolds repeated, at larger scale, in the station. Against the stone walls, Reynolds placed white wooden columns, a juxtaposition that recalls the house of 1804, as well as numerous similar local examples. The interiors of the station (Fig. 124) were treated more as domestic spaces than public ones. There were imitation Chippendale benches in the waiting room, which boasted a stone fireplace and copies of portraits of the leading early citizens of Cooperstown.

For industrial buildings Reynolds opted for a reduced Italian Renaissance brick style that gave his structures dignity but allowed them to be built

Fig. 124. Delaware & Hudson Station, Cooperstown, New York, 1915-16, waiting room

Fig. 125. Albany Industrial Building, 1031 Broadway, Albany, 1913-15, view from southwest

on the low budgets such commissions required. The blocky exterior of the Albany Industrial Building on Broadway (Fig. 125), for which Reynolds won the competition in 1913,[22] conceals the U-shaped plan, which creates a large light court at the rear. The reinforced concrete structure of piers and floor slabs is expressed on the outside by the widely spaced verticals and the wider, recessed horizontals that hold the large windows of industrial steel sash in place. Most of the building is treated with a directness that would make a functionalist proud. But it is the deviations from the purely functional, like the deviations in the contemporary warehouse wing of the D & H Building[23] (Fig. 94), that make the building interesting. The design went through several phases, the contract was let in February of 1914, and Reynolds settled finally with the contractor in June, 1915.[24] The ground floor is treated as a basement, separated from the upper floors by a stringcourse. On the long Broadway facade, at bays four and ten, the wall projects slightly to emphasize the stair towers that rise above the flat top of of the bulk of the building to terminate in water tanks. The small windows light small rooms off the staircases, while the diaper pattern of yellow brick in the broad expanse of dark red wall suggests the diagonal of the stairs within. The water tanks are blind, relieved by *Serliane* (or are they arches on strip frames bordered in red?) punctuated only by keystones. The upper parts of the towers certainly reflect Reynolds's study of Roman buildings of the sixteenth and seventeenth centuries, such as the flanks of Vignola's Gesù, in which classical architectural systems are reduced to a manipulation of shallow brick planes.

This kind of historicizing but simple industrial architecture does not seem to have received much scholarly attention. It was the subject, however, of an intelligent article in the *Architectural Record* in 1909.[25] The author, Robert D. Kohn, presents his own factory for H. Black & Company of Cleveland as a model that "might show it possible to build a common-sense, economical factory, practical in every particular and reasonable in cost, of simple, low-priced materials, and yet a building fairly *good looking*." Kohn achieved good looks by cleverly manipulating cheap materials to suggest historical forms, by paying attention to proportions and colors, and by turning the water tower into a sculptural accent for the whole. Reynolds seems to have taken Kohn's ideas to heart, although in the end he produced a handsomer design.

The Kohn article had appeared in the February issue of *Architectural Record* just before Reynolds

Fig. 126. *Public School 4, Madison Avenue and Ontario Street, Albany, south facade, 1922-24, demolished*

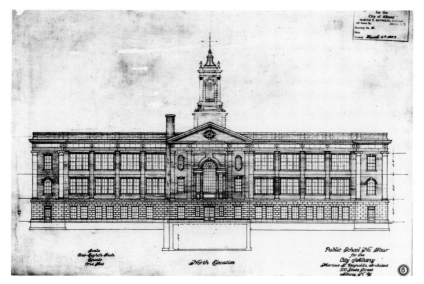

Fig. 127. *Public School 4, rear elevation*

Fig. 128. *Public School 4, first floor plan*

ings still stand, but the employment office has not been well treated. The employment office is a flat-roofed, two-story, brick building with minimal articulation. To the right of its facade a curving wall encloses the parking garage and leads to the garden area, which is deliberately irregular in plan. Beyond the garden are the trolley shed, its roof shaped like the letter C to embrace curving tracks, and the waiting room, a square brick block with a pyramidal roof. The whole complex of structures forced all workers and visitors to enter the plant through the gate next to the waiting room. [28]

For the entrance complex in Schenectady Reynolds also used his reduced Renaissance style. The waiting room, with its round arches and strip frames, suggests casinos in Roman Renaissance villas, about which Reynolds had written in the 1890s. The relative elegance of the architecture – even though it was built in cheap industrial brick – and its small scale mediated between the modestly scaled architecture of a small city and the huge industrial buildings of one of the most important factories in the nation. To take a leaf from Leo Marx, Reynolds made a little garden through which one passed into the world of machines. [29] The waiting room and shed served to shelter employees from the weather while they waited for the trolleys of the Schenectady Railway. [30]

was approached for the first time by George E. Emmons, general manager of the General Electric Company in Schenectady, to redesign the entrance to the GE plant. [26] Eventually the complex came to include the entrance gate, or waiting room, a trolley stop outside the gate, a fairly large grassy area enclosed by a wrought-iron fence, a parking garage for the automobiles of GE executives, and an employment office, the part of the complex closest to the center of Schenectady. [27] All of these build-

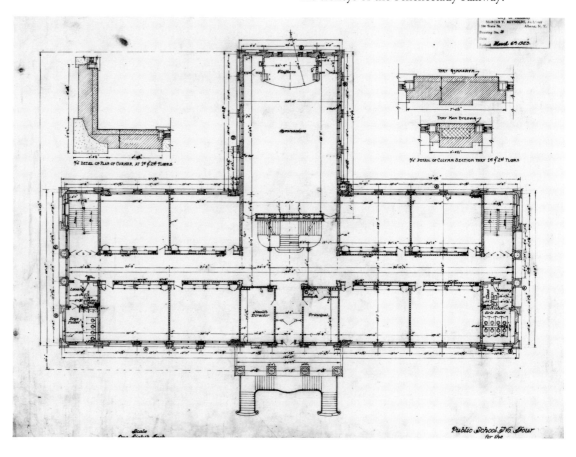

In the 1920s Reynolds's office was occupied with three school buildings in classical styles[31] that, together with the Clark gardens at Cooperstown, mark the end of his career as a creative architect. The first was a commission from the recently installed Democratic machine of Albany, whose mayor, William S. Hackett, had just asked Reynolds to design an addition to the Albany City Savings Institution.[32] Reynolds's diary entry for May 10, 1922, makes clear how things were done: "Edwin Corning at breakfast asked me if I wanted to do School 4 to replace one which was burnt.[33] Went with him to see Mayor Hackett who said O.K." Edwin Corning was the old-monied Protestant who had joined forces with the Irish Catholic Daniel O'Connell to oust William Barnes the previous year.[34]

For Public School 4, which stood until the 1960s at the corner of Madison Avenue and Ontario Street,[35] Reynolds gave Hackett a design that broke conclusively with standard school architecture in the city of Albany. Earlier Albany school buildings had largely been of a utilitarian character, with an occasional gloss of historical ornament

Fig. 129. William S. Hackett Junior High School, 45 Delaware Avenue, Albany, 1925-26, view from southeast

Fig. 130. Albany Academy, Academy Road, Albany, 1928-30, north facade

Fig. 131. Albany Academy,
detail of cupola

to suggest that the building was more interesting
than it actually was. Reynolds's design was graced
with an attention to proportion and detail that
lifted it above the ordinary, but its architectural
elegance was achieved only after a battle with
forces more interested in economy than architecture. In the end, Corning and Hackett, who wanted a good building for the city, saw to it that
Reynolds had his way.[36]

The school had a remarkably unified, yet varied
exterior. On the front (Fig. 126) Reynolds fused
the porch and the side walls by giving the interco-
lumniations of the classical portico the same width
as the modern industrial bays of the wings. The
columns of the porch and the pilasters of the end
pavilions were made more important by giving
them stone facing and Ionic capitals. The lesser,
brick pilasters of the industrial bay system have
Tuscan capitals. At the rear, to the north, (Fig.
127) each corner of the gym/auditorium wing was
marked by three pilasters, one on the north wall,
one on the corner and one on the east or west wall.
Those on the east and west walls (Fig. 128) indi-
cated the depth of the stage area inside, while the

Palladian window made clear that the stage was a
two-story space. The building was raised on a rusticated stone basement, with a double-ramped
staircase in front leading to a round-arched door in
the center of the main facade. The arch of the
door was echoed by the arch of the Palladian window at the opposite end of the north/south axis.
On the east and west facades, pairs of Ionic
columns set *in antis* recalled the four columns of
the main porch. Over it all rose a cupola that was a
reduced version of Philip Hooker's cupola for the
Albany Academy (Fig. 132), which was, to
Reynolds, the only appropriate form to crown a
school building in Albany. Inside, pupils moved
up and down as elegant a staircase as one is likely
to have found in a public school, anywhere.
Although the staircase is gone, some splendid
drawings from Reynolds's office are preserved to
remind us of its glories.

School 4 was part of the ambitious improvement schemes of Mayor Hackett, under whose
regime four new elementary schools and two
junior high schools were planned.[37] He also
improved the city water supply, built new and
improved old roads, and put in a new zoning ordinance. Described as a "human dynamo," Hackett's
popularity among Albanians increased almost geo-
metrically from election to election, so that the
third time he ran, in 1925, he received 15,000
more votes than his Republican opponent. On his
untimely death in 1926, he was said to be the
Democrats' natural choice to succeed to Al Smith
as governor,[38] an honor that fell instead to
Franklin D. Roosevelt. In a memorial statement
requested by the City Planning Commission,[39]
Reynolds wrote that under Hackett's "initiative
and guidance the city began to take on a new life
and to improve and expand in a manner compara-
ble only with the first decade of the last century,
when Albany ceased to be a village and began to
assume the aspect of a city."[40]

In his tower for the Albany City Savings
Institution (Fig. 31), Reynolds had looked back to
the architecture of Philip Hooker, and through
Hooker to Robert Adam, to commemorate
Hackett's Scottish and Scotch-Irish ancestry. The
architecture of School 4 seems to signal a general
ascendancy of English-speaking cultures in
Albany. English, after all, was the language taught
inside. The school also looked back to the classical
architecture of an earlier America,[41] probably to
the Jeffersonian roots of the Democratic Party, of

which Hackett was the Albany standard bearer. Certainly, the school marked a sharp break with the architecture of the Low Countries that Reynolds had used for public buildings during the Republican years of the Barnes machine — the Pruyn Library, the firehouse, and the D & H Building. The ambitious group of Democrats Reynolds now served would hardly have wanted those styles, redolent of Republicanism, repeated for them. The Democrats had to distinguish themselves architecturally from the Barnes regime by stressing a different architectural heritage.

The school served the largely middle-class neighborhood of Pine Hills, populated by an upwardly mobile mixture of ethnic groups. In *O Albany!* William Kennedy noted that the neighborhood contained Jews, Protestants and Irish Catholics. He quoted reminiscences of the neighborhood by Albert Hessberg, great-nephew of Samuel Hessberg, whose Colonial Revival country house Reynolds had designed in 1909: "I liked the kids I played with, liked their families. Most kids went to Public School Four, or to VI [Vincentian Institute, part of St. Vincent's Catholic parish], across the street. We all played together. It was a good, stable, law-abiding atmosphere in which to grow up."[42] Reynolds's school provided an architectural means for melting these diverse groups into the English-speaking American pot in which their parents or grandparents had chosen to live.[43]

The function of assimilating all the children of Albany, not just the relatively well-off of Pine Hills, into Anglo-American culture was performed by Reynolds's other public school building, William Hackett Junior High School (Fig. 129). Under construction in 1926 when Mayor Hackett died,[44] the new junior high school was immediately named for the man who had made it possible. It opened to about six hundred ninth-grade students in September, 1927, while still incomplete.[45] The junior high school movement had developed slowly in New York State. Of the larger cities, Rochester opened the first one in 1915; Albany finally fell into line twelve years later. The point of the system was to isolate seventh, eighth and ninth graders in a situation where the curriculum could be tailored to their special adolescent needs, not just in school but also in the world at large.[46] When the program for a junior high was presented to Mayor Hackett, a product of the Albany public school system, he "saw in it a new principle of education, giving such opportunity for training as he had never had, as this city had never offered."[47]

Reynolds chose as the historic source for this school the great English country houses of the eighteenth century that owed their origins to the villas of Andrea Palladio. Set on a curious diagonal on very large grounds on Delaware Avenue, the school offers its pupils a sense of architectural grandeur that was surely intended to enoble them, to dazzle them visually, and to introduce them to the world beyond their city — to suggest, in other words, the possibilities that an education might open up. The transverse entrance hall is lit by stained-glass globes decorated with maps of the world. Beyond is a broad, low passage, lined with casts of the Parthenon frieze — handsome youths and maidens on their best behavior, honoring their patron goddess at a formative moment of western civilization. The frieze figures lead into a great, two-storied central hall, from which two grand staircases rise to the second floor, where the climax of the building awaits the pupil — the large audi-

Fig. 132. Philip Hooker, Old Albany Academy, Academy Park, Albany, 1815-17, detail of cupola, reconstructed by Marcus T. Reynolds, 1930

torium that occupies the whole of the upper part of the projecting central pavilion. Amply lit by Palladian windows on two sides, the auditorium focuses on a stage flanked by domed exedrae embellished by elegant, Adamesque decorations. One feels that one has attained the intellectual and visual refinement of the culture of late eighteenth-century London, a pretty heady experience in an American public school.[48]

The decision to move the private Albany Academy to a new location in a residential area and to build a much larger building to house a far greater number of students, resulted in another of Reynolds's great school commissions, but one that turned out to be visually less successful than School 4 or Hackett Junior High (Fig. 130). Reynolds used the same basic division of parts, a

projecting, pedimented central mass capped by a cupola and flanked by long wings ending in shallow pavilions. The cupola (Fig. 131) is copied from that of the old Albany Academy (Fig. 132) with stunning fidelity, at least above the clocks. Reynolds literally reproduced the Academy's own architectural history on the roof of its new building. Other details of the Hooker building were invoked as well. The swags in the central panels of the lintels of Hooker's ground-floor windows reappear in the ground-floor windows of the central pavilion of Reynolds's building, as do the round-arched windows of the upper floor. Atop the cupola Reynolds placed the codfish and pumpkin weathervane saved in 1922 from the destroyed steeple of Hooker's Second Presbyterian Church.[49] Reynolds carried his devotion to

Hooker to the point of placing a copy of Edward W. Root's *Philip Hooker, A Contribution to the Study of the Renaissance in America*, hot off the press in 1929, in the cornerstone.[50] In 1935 Hooker's Academy building was refurbished under Reynolds's supervision."[51]

Built during the Depression at the hefty cost of $963,000,[52] the new Albany Academy has a thinness about its architecture that results from the corners that had to be cut to keep within what turned out to be a tight budget. The building also suggests, however, that Reynolds's powers as a designer were on the wain by the late twenties. Perhaps the Depression did him a favor, in that its limited opportunities for building saved him from commissions he might not have handled with the verve and skill he once commanded.[53]

Reynolds's interest in the art history of the city of Albany extended beyond architecture to painting. On March 22, 1923, just after the contracts for the Albany City Savings addition and School 4 had been let, Reynolds noted in his diary: "I bought the picture of Peter Schuyler said to be by Sir Geof [Godfrey Kneller] for $2.500 plus interest from Sept. 1920 of Westcott Burlingame,"[54] and a week later he offered the portrait of its first mayor to the city.[55] In a letter to Mayor Hackett, Reynolds noted that "While the painting has no great artistic merit, there is no reason to doubt the tradition of the Schuyler family, that it was the work of Sir Godfrey Kneller, an artist who enjoyed a higher reputation than his talents warranted."[56] Reynolds's attribution was dead wrong, and his assessment of the picture completely missed its rude vigor. In September, after Reynolds had returned from two months in Europe, Kenneth Reynolds started to design the frame in which the Schuyler portrait would hang in City Hall.[57] On May 22, 1924, the same day the statue of Mercury was raised atop the City Savings Bank, the frame (Fig. 133) was installed in the mayor's office.[58]

A dedication followed on June 3, the third day of the Albany Tercentenary celebration. The mayor made a little speech, in which he noted his initial reluctance to accept the "dark and shabby picture," as well as Reynolds's condition that it be firmly attached to the wall of his office, in a frame designed by the donor, so "as to reduce to a minimum the chance of its removal." Instead, Hackett now found the frame and mantel designed for the portrait "a happy result," and the picture, cleaned and repaired, to be "revealed enhanced by the mellowness which centuries have given it."[59] The mantel and frame, in an eighteenth-century mode, accord not with the Richardsonian architecture of city hall, but rather with the date of the portrait. When forced to choose between two historical moments, Reynolds opted for the one which spoke more clearly to him about Albany's history.[60]

Reynolds spoke only a few words. The Tercentenary had seen enough speeches, he said. But he must have felt very happy to have preserved for Albany a piece of its history. The hero of the moment, he was surrounded by a crowd (he called them "invited hot dogs") that in its diversity summed up many of his own interests.[61] There was a representative of the Netherlands. There was a clutch of historians, archaeologists and archivists, as well as some politicians. Several Schuylers and Van Rensselaers stood alongside two daughters of Mr. and Mrs. John Van Schaick Lansing Pruyn. Mayor Hackett, his principal client in these years, presided. There were clients from the past, all important figures financially and socially: Simon Rosendale, Benjamin Arnold, Henry and Cornelia Sage. Finally, there was his family: his cousin Howard Van Rensselaer; Louisa Van Rensselaer, the widow of William Bayard; his brother Cuyler; his nephew and partner, Kenneth Reynolds; and Lydia Hun, his cousin and Kenneth's fiancee. Those "hot dogs" represented most of what was important to Marcus Tullius Reynolds, as an architect and as a human being. All of them had an understanding of the importance of family and of history.

NOTES

INTRODUCTION

1. Edith Wharton, *The Age of Innocence* (1920, reprint New York: Charles Scribner's Sons, 1968), 345.
2. Reynolds was not the only member of his class to do so. For example, Chester Aldrich, from an old Rhode Island family connected to the Rockefellers, received a degree from Columbia the same year as Reynolds. Upper-class women at this time took up landscape architecture, particularly Beatrix Jones Farrand, a niece of Edith Wharton, and Ellen Biddle Shipman. For short biographies of contemporary architects, see Mark Alan Hewitt, *The Architect and the American Country House* (New Haven: Yale Univ. Press, 1990), 267-86.
3. Caroline Peltz Schultze, in an interview with the author, 1991.
4. Ibid.
5. The diaries are preserved in the McKinney Library of the Albany Institute of History and Art.
6. Diary of Marcus T. Reynolds (hereafter Diary), Oct. 3, 1934.
7. He was impatient with clients he found hopeless: "MTR felt better until Elinor Ransom of Crest Ridge East Chatham appeared for the first time & wanted plans for a bath tub among locust trees!"; Diary, April 29, 1935.
8. Letter from Atlantic Terra Cotta Co. to MTR, Oct. 6, 1916; McKinney Library, Albany Institute of History and Art.
9. FDR shared Reynolds' interest in the early Dutch architecture of the Hudson Valley; see his introduction in Helen Wilkinson Reynolds, *Dutch Houses in the Hudson Valley Before 1776* (1929; reprint, New York: Dover Publications, 1965).
10. MTR, "The Colonial Buildings of Rensselaerwyck," *Architectural Record* (hereafter *AR*) 4 (1894-95): 415-38.
11. Cuyler Reynolds, *Albany Chronicles, A History of the City Arranged Chronologically* (hereafter *Albany Chronicles*) (Albany: J.B. Lyon Co., 1906).
12. Cuyler Reynolds, *Hudson-Mohawk Genealogical and Family Memoirs* (hereafter *Hudson-Mohawk Memoirs*), 4 vols. (New York: Lewis Historical Publishing Co., 1911) and *Genealogical and Family History of Southern New York and the Hudson River Valley*, 3 vols. (New York: Lewis Historical Publishing Co., 1914).
13. I am grateful to Harry Yates, who lived in Reynolds's house in the last years of Reynold's life, for providing this photograph. A close-up photograph by Yates of the desk shows the view of Rome more clearly.
14. Mariana Van Rensselaer, "Recent Architecture in America. Public Buildings. I.", *The Century Magazine* 28 (May 1884): 49-50. This was the first of a nine-part series on recent American architecture she published between 1884 and 1886. Reynolds likely read these pieces.
15. This account of McKim, Mead & White's career is largely drawn from Richard Longstreth, "Academic Eclecticism in American Architecture," *Winterthur Portfolio* (1982): 55-82.
16. Ibid., 66.
17. So termed by Vincent Scully, *The Shingle Style* (New Haven: Yale Univ. Press, 1955).
18. Mariana Van Rensselaer, "American Country Dwellings. 3.", *The Century Magazine* 32 (July 1886): 428.
19. A.D.F. Hamlin, "Architectural Design," *Building* 7 (December 31, 1887): 222; quoted in Longstreth, 59.
20. Longstreth, 59.
21. A.D.F. Hamlin, "The Difficulties of Modern Architecture," *AR* 1 (1891-92): 141.
22. Hamlin, "Architectural Design," *Building*, 7 (September 17, 1887): 9; quoted in Longstreth, 59.
23. Hamlin, "Difficulties," 139-40.
24. Van Rensselaer, "Country Dwellings. 3.", 428.
25. James F. O'Gorman, *Three American Architects, Richardson, Sullivan, and Wright, 1865-1915* (Chicago: Univ. of Chicago Press, 1991) argues eloquently for the conservative and historicizing nature of Wright's early work, but Wright conserved different ideas and went back to different times and places in history.
26. Frank Lloyd Wright, "In the Cause of Architecture," *AR* 23 (March, 1908): 155.
27. Ibid., 158. For a study of Wright's clients, see Leonard Eaton, *Two Chicago Architects and Their Clients: Frank Lloyd Wright and Howard Van Doren Shaw* (Cambridge, Mass.: MIT Press, 1969).
28. Wright, "In the Cause of Architecture," 163.
29. Mariana Van Rensselaer, *Handbook of English Cathedrals* (New York: The Century Co., 1893), 36.
30. Wright, "In the Cause of Architecture," 165.
31. Mariana Van Rensselaer, "Country Dwellings. 3.", 426.

CHAPTER 1

1. *Hudson-Mohawk Memoirs*, 1726-27.
2. The life of Marcus Tullius Reynolds (1788-1864) is outlined in Ibid.,1843, and *The History and Descendants of John and Sarah Reynolds [1630?-1923]*, Marion H. Reynolds, ed. (Brooklyn: The Reynolds Family Association, 1924), 214. In both cases, the biographical information seems to have been put together by MTR.
3. The photograph of the slab shows it lying on its side in the workshop of John Evans & Co., 77 Huntingdon Ave., Boston, before being shipped to Albany; the name of the firm is stamped on the back. I am grateful to Norman Rice for providing the photograph.
4. MTR, for instance, was a major contributor to the volume on Reynolds family history cited in n. 2.
5. William Morgan, *The Almighty Wall: The Architecture of Henry Vaughan* (Cambridge: MIT Press, 1983), 89-100.
6. They are identified, left to right, as "[back row] Hobart Thompson - Edith Dove - John J. Pierepont, James Clapp Emma Olcott [front row] Will Warren - Mae Prentice. Fred N. Townsend, Marry Warren, Ogle T. Warren Sally Townsend. M.T. Reynolds"; none seems to have become a client. The photo is dated "Luzerne 1889."
7. Leland Roth, *The Architecture of McKim, Mead & White, 1870-1920, A Building List* (New York: Garland Publishing Co., 1978) (hereafter Roth [1978]), 168.
8. Talcott M. Banks, *First Report of the Class of 'Ninety* (Williamstown, Mass.: 1892), 24-25.
9. William R. Ware, *The American Vignola* (Scranton, Pa.: American Textbook Co., 1902), 2.
10. MTR, "The Housing of the Poor in American Cities," *Publication of the American Economic Association* 8 (2 and 3, 1893): 135-262.
11. Richard T. Ely, "Report of the Organization of the American Economic Association," *Publication of the American Economic Association*, 1 (1, March, 1886):5-6.
12. *Handbook of the American Economic Association, together with Report of the Sixth Annual Meeting* (January, 1894) lists the essays and the winners.
13. For a discussion of attitudes toward tenements and slums in Reynolds's day, see David Ward, *Poverty, Ethnicity, and the American City, 1840-1925* (Cambridge and New York: Cambridge University Press, 1989), 61-86; n. 107, p. 230, cites Reynolds's essay as a source for the fact that high tenement rents forced poor families to take in boarders or double up in single units.
14. In particular, Reynolds noted the accomplishments of the Peabody Trust and Sir Sydney Waterlow's Improved Industrial Dwellings Company, both founded in the 1860s. Their crucial role in the history of housing for the poor in England is pointed out by John Nelson Tarn, *Five Per Cent Philanthropy, An account of housing in urban areas between 1840 and 1914* (Cambridge: Cambridge University Press, 1973), 44-56.
15. The idea of cooperative kitchens was fairly widely discussed around 1890, according to Dolores Hayden, *The Grand Domestic Revolution*, (Cambridge: MIT Press, 1981). See also Elisabeth Bisland, "Co-Operative Housekeping in Tenements" *Cosmopolitan* 8 (November, 1889) cited in Hayden, 155. The first communal kitchen, 'The New England Kitchen' was established by Mary Hinman Abel and Ellen Swallow Richards in 1890 to complement tenement houses. The most likely sources for Reynolds were the Boston architect J. Pickering Putnam's ideas and plans for apartment houses that had communal kitchen and dining areas. See J. Pickering Putnam, *Architecture Under Nationalism* (Boston: Nationalist Educational Association, 1890), 13, and "The Apartment House," *American Architect and Building News* 27 (Jan. 4, 1890): 5.
16. *Albany Times Union*, March 18, 1937.
17. See the map of that area of New York in Leland M. Roth, *McKim, Mead & White, Architects* (New York: Harper & Row, 1983) (hereafter Roth [1983]), fig. 90. A host of McKim, Mead & White buildings, in a Renaissance mode, were completed or being completed just before or during Reynolds' years in New York. See Roth (1978), #186, 263, 282, 306, 399, 447, 448, 485, 500, 572, 727, 734, 869, 887, for examples.
18. While Reynolds frequently noted deaths in his diaries, he took no note of the death of Van Rensselaer on January 20, 1934.
19. *Hudson-Mohawk Memoirs*, 1734.
20. Did they ever meet? Another possible link to Wharton was her love of many years, Walter Van Rensselaer Berry, whose mother, Catherine Van Rensselaer Berry, was the aunt of W. B. and Howard Van Rensselaer; ibid., 22-23. For Wharton's life, see R.W.B. Lewis, *Edith Wharton, a biography* (New York: Harper & Row, 1975).
21. Hewitt, *The Architect and the American Country House*.
22. William B. Rhoads, *The Colonial Revival*, 2 vols., (New York and London: Garland Publishing Co., 1977), 21.
23. Rhoads, 21, notes that as early as 1869 Upjohn himself lamented the fact that the area was becoming a factory district. MTR, "Colonial Buildings," 433-4, gives a poignant account of the final situation of the house. In the previous issue

Montgomery Schuyler, "A History of Old Colonial Architecture," *AR* 4 (1894-95): 360-1, had also discussed the manor house.

24. He reported this commission in a letter of Sept. 30, 1894, to his Williams classmates; he also said he had won a competition to design the Albany Country Club, a half-timbered building to which he later made several additions. The country club was torn down to make way for the state office campus.

25. MTR to W.S.B. Hopkins, June 20, 1934: The Van Rensselaer Manor House had been unoccupied since the death of Mrs. Stephen Van Rensselaer in 1875, and wishing to improve what remained of the lands, my cousin, Bayard Van Rensselaer, had a spur from the New York Central constructed to a point which would serve this undeveloped territory.

A branch of this railroad passed directly through the west wing of the Manor House. Feeling that it was far better to destroy the entire building that [*sic*] to leave it in this disreputable condition, I persuaded him that it would be more creditable for the family to demolish the building in toto and he agreed readily to my proposal that the family should give me the stone trim and the timbers.
I am grateful to Norman Rice for providing me with a copy of this letter.

26. Rhoads, 132. Also Montgomery Schuyler, "State Buildings at the World's Fair," *American Architect* (hereafter *AA*) (Jan. 2, 1892): 10. The "real" Van Rensselaer Manor House would have stood between two ersatz colonial buildings: Peabody and Stearns's reconstruction of the John Hancock House for Massachusetts and Pennsylvania's reconstruction of Independence Hall, Philadelphia.

27. MTR to W. S. B. Hopkins: I...measured the building and made the plans, which I brought over to Williamstown and showed to the trustees at the time of the Centennial celebration of the College.

These contemplated rebuilding the entire building including the wings, one of which would contain and [*sic*] lodge room and the other the dining room, but even that left a good deal of area for social use on the main floor. The four large rooms I labeled "Study," "Library," "Lounge" and "Card Room." Wilhelmus Mynderse objected to considering any plan which provided for more than one public room as he held the fallacious idea that the students did more lounging than work.

As he had saved the life of the Chapter by maintaining the insurance at his own expense over a long period of time and as we relied upon him largely to finance the new operation, his decision prevailed, and I was told to prepare the plans for the re-erection of only the central feature. This I did and spent the entire winter in measuring up the stone trim as it was being removed from the building. Of course, much of the stone from the wings was incorporated in what we now call the east and west facades of the structure.

28. Marshall B. Davidson and Elizabeth Stillinger, *The American Wing at the Metropolitan Museum of Art* (New York: Alfred A. Knopf, 1985), 52-55.

29. Reynolds duplicated many of the features of the Sigma Phi House when he designed a house for the same fraternity at the University of Vermont in 1900.

30. MTR, "Colonial Buildings," 415-38.

31. Diary, July 2,1929: "MTR's anniversaries of July 2 Pres. Garfield shot — 1881. First went into a saloon - US Hotel Saratoga with W. B. Van R. Ate first olive. Was Graduated from Williams. Sailed...in 1894 for two years study abroad."

32. See n. 24 above. He also visited Athens (*Hudson-Mohawk Memoirs*, 1846).

33. MTR, "The Villas of Rome," *AR* 6 (1896-97): 256-88 and "The Villas of Rome, Part II," *AR* 7 (1897-98): 1-32.

34. Charles A. Platt, "Italian Gardens," *Harper's New Monthly Magazine* 87 (July, 1893): 165-80, and 87 (August, 1893): 393-406.

35. Charles A. Platt, *Italian Gardens* (New York: Harper & Brothers, 1894).

36. Ibid., 6-8.

37. Ibid., 153-4.

38. MTR, "Villas of Rome," 256-57. This was a theme taken up by Edith Wharton, *Italian Villas and Their Gardens* (New York: The Century Co., 1904), 7, who wrote of the "subtle transition from the fixed and formal lines of art to the shifting and irregular lines of nature" in Italian villas. Wharton, with her remarkable gift of seeing both essentials and complexity, combined ideas espoused by Platt and Reynolds into a far richer statement of the problems addressed in the Renaissance villa. Her bibliography mentions neither Platt nor Reynolds, but it is certainly possible that she had read one or both of them.

39. Diary, Sept. 20, 1923: "Stephen Clark called & wanted me to go to Cooperstown to plan his garden."

40. Information about Clark comes from Gilbert Vincent, who is preparing a study of Clark as a collector. I am very grateful to Mr. Vincent for his generosity in sharing with me his extensive knowledge of the Clarks and their house.

41. Because all the drawings for the gardens seem to have disappeared, as have large parts of the garden and adjoining house, it is difficult to reconstruct the history of Reynolds' design in detail. What follows is based on MTR's diaries, old photographs, Gilbert Vincent's detailed knowledge of the history of the house and grounds, and a site visit. Happily, the present owner has begun extensive repairs of what remains.

42. The steel frame is visible in a photograph taken during construction (New York Historical Assn., Cooperstown, PH 16,834). The first plans for the bridge had envisioned a concrete core. See Diary, Oct. 21, 1927. The three elliptical arches of the bridge recall those of the Ponte Santa Trinità in Florence.

43. The decision to build the pool and tennis courts was made only a year after Reynolds began work on the garden design; Diary, Sept. 9, 1924.

44. Diary, Aug. 16, 1927: "Miss Leeper in and I gave her the plan of the Casino & two photos of Villa Papa Giulio. She to make sketches and revise estimate."

45. The elaborate plantings in this largely architectural garden were designed by the landscape architect Bryant Flemming from nearby Ithaca, with whom Reynolds had collaborated on at least two earlier commissions.

CHAPTER 2

1. "His specialty has been the design of banks, of which he has been the architect of sixteen." *Hudson-Mohawk Memoirs*, 1846.

2. William J. Shultz and M. R. Caine, *Financial Development of the United States* (New York: Prentice-Hall, 1937), tables 35, 37.

3. Ibid., 457.

4. Alfred Hopkins, *The Fundamentals of Good Bank Building* (New York: The Bankers Publishing Co., 1929), 17.

5. Van Rensselaer was a figure of some importance in New York state banking circles; he served four terms as president of the New York State Savings Banks Association. In 1883 he became a trustee of the Albany Savings Bank, in 1897 vice president, and in 1901 president, "an office which his grandfather, General Stephen Van Rensselaer, had held when the Bank was chartered, March 25, 1820." See Frederick B. Stevens, *History of the Savings Bank Association of the State of New York, 1894-1914* (Garden City and New York: Doubleday, Page & Co., 1915), 692.

6. James H. Manning, *Century of American Savings Banks, Retrospective-Prospective Volume* (New York: B. F. Buck & Co., 1917), 147-8, provides a fine description of the interior of the Cobb bank.

7. Museum of Fine Arts, Houston, *Money Matters, A Critical Look at Bank Architecture* (New York: McGraw-Hill, 1990), 68-9. See also Richard Guy Wilson, *McKim, Mead & White Architects* (New York: Rizzoli, 1983), 41, and Roth (1983), 237.

8. From its foundation in 1850, the bank had been affiliated with the Albany City National Bank and had used their offices at 47 State. When that bank merged with the National Commercial Bank, the Albany City Savings had to find a new home. See William Law Learned Peltz, *The Banks and Savings Banks of Albany, New York* (Albany: American Historical Co., 1955), 47. According to James H. Manning, *Century of American Savings Banks, New York Volume* (New York: B. F. Buck & Co., 1917), 94-96, in 1905 the amount due depositors by the bank was $4,559,965.

9. *Albany Chronicles*, 768.

10. Robert A. M. Stern, Gregory Gilmartin and John Montague Massengale, *New York 1900* (New York: Rizzoli, 1983), 146.

11. Montgomery Schuyler, "The 'Sky-scraper' up to Date," *AR* 8 (1899): 231-57. In the same article Schuyler had nice things to say about Louis Sullivan's Bayard Building in New York. An illustration of the Washington Life Building had been published in *AR* 7 (1897-98): 477.

12. Diary, July 11, 1902: "began to move at noon."

13. Diary, May 7, 1902. The president of the bank was his former client for the Albany Railway and future client for the Municipal Gas Co., Robert C. Pruyn.

14. Diary, June 30, 1902: "Union Trust decided to...do nothing more until following year & then go the whole hog." They never did.

15. A thirteen-story design for the building was published in *AR* 12, 450, in a rendering by Hughson Hawley.

16. "Russell Sturgis's Architecture," *AR* 25 (1909): 404-10. Montgomery Schuyler, "Russell Sturgis," *AR* 25 (1909): 146, 220: "Mr. Richardson ... spoke of this building even with enthusiasm."

17. The placing of the structural members on the plan was not easy. Chambers, the engineer Reynolds hired to help with the structure, "telephoned that he could not prevent Albany Trust from blowing over." The next day Chambers and Reynolds "decided to move elevators and adopt interior wind bracing." Diary, May 27 and 28, 1902.

18. *Albany Evening Journal* (hereafter *AEJ*), September 2, 1904, 2.

19. Diary, May 9, 1902: "Nat'l Savings presented to Gen Rosendale."

20. Several examples are included in the survey provided by *AR*, "Recent Bank Buildings of the United States," 25 (1909): 3-66. Of these, McKim, Mead & White's Bank of Montreal and Girard Trust, Philadelphia; George B. Post & Sons' Cleveland Trust Co.; and Parker, Thomas & Rice's Metropolitan Savings Bank, Baltimore, all have domes on the exterior, while Cass Gilbert's Suffolk Savings Bank, Boston, has a dome visible only on the interior.

21. The domed Fulton County National Bank at Gloversville is probably not based on the designs Reynolds made for that bank in March, April and May, 1910.

22. Frederick S. Hills, *New York State Men, Biographic Studies and Character Portraits* (Albany: Argus Co., 1910), 122.

23. *The Fort Orange Club 1880-1980* (Albany: The Fort Orange Club, 1980), 12.

24. Diary, Oct. 8, 9 and 10, and Nov. 4, 1902.

25. James H. Manning, *Retrospective-Prospective Volume* (hereafter *Retrospective-Prospective Vol.*) and *New York Volume* (hereafter *N.Y. Vol.*). The former contains a general history of savings banks and an assessment of their place in the American economy, the latter "a brief, authentic history of each of the one hundred and forty-one Savings Banks in the State of New York."

26. The first was the Philadelphia Savings Fund Society.

27. *N. Y. Vol.*, 126. The new quarters reflected the rapid growth of the bank, whose deposits had increased from about $7.5 million in 1895 to $11.3 million in 1905.
28. *AA* 91 (1632, April 6, 1907).
29. Diana S. Waite, *Ornamental Ironwork, Two Centuries of Craftsmanship in Albany and Troy, New York* (Albany: Mount Ida Press, 1990), 71 and fig. 77.
30. *Troy City Directory*, 1902, 677, notes the change. In 1922 Security Trust Co., in turn, became the Manufacturers National Bank (ibid., 1922, 1014), and by 1923 five bays that copied those of the old cast iron bank had been added to its Fourth St. facade (drawing of expanded facade in ibid., 1923, 1014). Security Safe Deposit, however, retained its original identity.
31. Diary, Aug. 4, 1902: "I went to Troy & saw Mr. Van Santford (*sic*) for first time".
32. *Troy Times Record*, November 15, 1938, 8.
33. Seymour Van Santvoord, *The House of Caesar and the Imperial Disease* (Troy, New York: Pafraets Book Co., 1902). This handsome volume was designed by D. B. Updike, the leading American book designer of the time. The book is dedicated to Van Santvoord's father, a lawyer who had led him into the paths of learning. This tradition continued in Van Santvoord's son, George, the well-known headmaster of the Hotchkiss School.
34. Ibid., vii.
35. Seymour Van Santvoord, *Octavia, A Tale of Ancient Rome* (New York: E. P. Dutton, 1923), introduction. Even though he was a Protestant, he also wrote a life of St. Francis: *St. Francis, The Christian Exemplar* (New York: E. P. Dutton, 1928).
36. Seymour Van Santvoord, *The Roman Forum, An Address before the Albany Institute Historical and Art Society, Thursday Evening, January 25, 1906*. The Union College Library has a copy of this privately published pamphlet, the text of which was republished in Seymour Van Santvoord, *Random Addresses* (New York: E. P. Dutton, 1930), 100-34. The same volume includes: "Address Delivered in Troy, N. Y., February, 1908, The Excavations of Herculaneum," 150-63; "Introducing MGR. John Walsh, at an Entertainment in Music Hall, Troy, N. Y., in 1909 to Raise Funds for the Restoration of the Ancient Church of San Clemente in Rome," 164-7; and "Romulus and Remus! A New Story of Old Rome. Address at Troy, N. Y., 1914," 188-95, a report on recent excavations on the Palatine Hill.
37. For Hooker, see *A Neat Plain Modern Style, Philip Hooker and his Contemporaries, 1790-1814*, Mary Raddant Tomlan, ed. (Amherst: Univ. of Massachusetts Press, 1992).
38. *Albany Chronicles*, 773.
39. The leather, ordered in New York in June, 1903, was installed in Jan., 1904. Diary, Jan. 2, 1904. The bank had moved into its new quarters precisely two months earlier, on Nov. 2, 1903.
40. Diary, May 7, 1929: "Bought the Jean Goujon chimney piece from the State Bank." May 9, 1929: "Visited warehouse and saw marble mantel from State Bank Wrote Mr. Kent offering it as gift to Met. Museum."
41. Diary, April 10, 1902: "Met Cogswell, Van R [William Bayard Van Rensselaer, Reynolds's cousin, who was vice president]...about the new building for State Bank for first time." April 22, 1902: "Cogswell in all afternoon about State Bank." April 24, 1902: "Cogswell all afternoon about State Bank."
42. See *Murals in the State Bank at Albany Painted by David Cunningham Lithgow* (Albany: privately printed, 1943), 26-7.
43. MTR's proposal is apparently no longer preserved. In 1902, Reynolds had friends in high places in the bank; his relatives William Bayard Van Rensselaer and Marcus T. Hun were directors, and the former had become its vice president in 1900, when Cogswell became president. By 1925 Reynolds's relatives had long passed from the scene, and Cogswell had turned the presidency over to his son, Ledyard, Jr.
44. According to Peltz, 32, the First National merged with Albany Trust Co. in 1926 to become First Trust Company of Albany. Presumably the architectural merger followed thereafter. The facade of the First National Bank is seen on angle in Fig. 105, and a rendering of the facade appeared in the *Albany Evening Journal*, June 11, 1907.
45. There is a photograph of this structure in the Schenectady County Historical Society collection.
46. The bank opened on June 13, 1892, with assets of $163,591.92; 25 years later, to the day, they were $3,056,576.50. *The Schenectady Union Star*, June 13, 1917, 4.
47. One suspects that Reynolds's design was influenced by the facade of York & Sawyer's New York Historical Society Building, published in: "The New Building of the New York Historical Society," *AR* 21 (1907): 76-8.
48. Reynolds first had to talk the bank out of holding a competition and into giving the job to him directly. Diary, March 30, 31, April 3, 10, 1922.
49. Diary, April 6, 1922.
50. *In Loving Memory of William Stormont Hackett, Sixty-Seventh Mayor of Albany*, comp. by David M. Kinnear (Albany: Argus Co., 1926), 14-15, states: "He superintended the erection of the new bank and office building now known as 100 State Street, and the credit for that beautiful and commodious edifice is entirely due to him." For the impact of Hackett's career as mayor on Reynolds's work, see Ch. 6.
51. The present tower was arrived at with some difficulty: numerous entries, Diary, June and July, 1922.
52. In Albany the significance of the national origins of historical architectural styles was clear to many. Hooker's New York State Bank facade, for instance, was understood to have given "nineteenth century Albany its English look against the old Dutch

appearance" (*Murals in the State Bank*, 21).
53. The detested new National Savings Bank opened for business on Oct. 20, 1930, according to Peltz, 53. The diary for 1929 is filled with Reynolds's anguish at the proposed erection of what he viewed as a monster.
54. Hopkins, 26.
55. Ibid.
56. Reynolds published the Glens Falls Trust in *AA* 97 (1784, March 2, 1910).
57. According the the Glens Falls City Directory of 1907-1908, the bank had already moved into the new quarters at 154 Glen Street. By 1914 the bank's resources approached $1.3 million.
58. The building to the right of the Glens Falls Trust, the Saunders Dry Goods Store, was designed by Reynolds in 1908. Its brightly colored terra-cotta ornament represents a (unique?) Reynolds venture — and a somewhat tentative one at that — into the Art Nouveau, at least in the curved bands and laurel leaves of the side panels. Part of the store's facade is visible at the right in Fig. 34.
59. Diary, June 1, 1904: "invited to compete for savings bank Cohoes."
60. Diary, April 14, 1904, states that the Troy building opened for business that day.
61. Diary, June 25, 1904: "Cohoes perspective came from Hawley." June 29, 1904: "local man given Cohoes competition."
62. According to *N. Y. Vol.*, 121-23, the bank's deposits had almost tripled between 1895 and 1905, from $1,059,394 to $2,987,167.
63. Reynolds published the Catskill Savings Bank in *AA* 96 (Nov. 24, 1909), but he does not seem to have published the Tanners Bank.
64. In subsequent expansions, the bank has knocked out the side wall to the south and the rear wall to the west, as well as the tellers'-screen.
65. See n. 28 above.
66. Reynolds had advised the Catskill Savings Bank against choosing a corner lot because of the added expense of a side facade. He estimated a stone facade to cost about $300 a running foot in a report quoted in the *Catskill Recorder*, Feb. 7, 1908.
67. "The Tanners Bank at Home," *Catskill Recorder*, Nov. 25, 1911 (clipping in Scrapbook 8, Vedder Memorial Library, Greene County Historical Society, Coxsackie).
68. The colors recorded by the *Catskill Recorder* were not the first Reynolds had tried. According to Diary, July 7, 1910, the first color scheme had to be changed because it was "too effiminate." Unfortunately, he did not record what the first colors were.
69. *AA* 97 (1784, March 2, 1910) published Reynolds's competition drawings.
70. Deposits in the Hudson bank had almost doubled between 1895 and 1905, from $2,251,107 to $4,308,032 (*N. Y. Vol.*, 96-8). The president of the bank was Charles Van Deusen, for whom Reynolds had designed the Colonial Revival house at 441 Allen Street in 1904. See Ch. 3.
71. Published by Reynolds, *AA* 98 (1819, November 2, 1910).
72. A history of Greenfield's economy and the Savings Institution's role therein is contained in Gerald F. Reid, *150 Years, Heritage Bank, 1834-1984* (Northampton, Mass.: Benjamin Co., 1984).
73. The interior, now occupied by an insurance company, is in fairly good condition.
74. *AA* 102 (1913, August 21, 1912).
75. Published by Reynolds, *AA* 106 (2030, November 18, 1914).
76. Published by Reynolds, *AA* 107 (2062, June 30, 1915).
77. As a result of the extensive urban renewal program, including a new arterial system, that Amsterdam undertook in 1974, the bank was considerably enlarged. See Hugh P. Donlon, *Amsterdam, New York, Annals of a Mill Town in the Mohawk Valley* (Amsterdam: Donlon Assocs., 1980), 230.
78. *Fiftieth Anniversary of the Amsterdam Savings Bank, 1887-1937* (Amsterdam, New York: privately printed, n.d., unpaginated). The growth was particularly rapid between the $766,633 due depositors in 1895 and the $3,631,306 due depositors in 1905 (*N. Y. Vol.*, 158).
79. Reynolds admired this building enough to take his whole office to study it some years later. Diary, May 2, 1928.
80. *N. Y. Vol.*, 157, and *Fiftieth Anniversary of the Amsterdam Savings Bank*. In Amsterdam Reynolds was asked in May, 1914, two months after the bank was completed, to remodel an enormous Victorian house for John Sanford, president of the carpet company that dominated the city's economy, into a classical villa. Not one of Reynolds's greatest moments, the house was given by Sanford in 1932 to Amsterdam to use as the city hall, a function it still serves.
81. Eugene Nelson White, *The Regulation of the American Banking System 1900-1929* (Princeton, N.J.: Princeton University Press, 1983), 38-42. According to table 1.6, the number of trust companies in the United States doubled between 1890 and 1900, and tripled between 1900 and 1910.
82. *Retrospective-Prospective Vol.*, 235.
83. Shultz and Caine, 315-8, 418-19, 446-48, 468-74.
84. *Retrospective-Prospective Vol.*, 3.
85. Ibid.
86. Ibid., 77.
87. Ibid., iv.
88. At Greenfield, the irregularities of the cramped site probably precluded a vault, and the remarkably busy array of coffers obscured the fact that the side walls were not parallel.

89. "Recent Bank Buildings," 4.

90. See *Retrospective-Prospective Vol.*, 238-43.

91. Bank advertisements in the Albany City Directory for 1902 give a clear idea of how some men served as officers or directors of several banks simultaneously. Those men were frequently Reynolds's clients, relatives and/or friends. At the Albany Savings Bank, W. B. Van Rensselaer was pres. and Marcus T. Hun was first vice pres. Both were Reynolds's relatives. Ledyard Cogswell was secretary, and the trustees included Grange Sard, a stove manufacturer with a house on State Street by H. H. Richardson; Learned Hand, Hun's law partner; and G. Y. Lansing, Reynolds's classmate and client. At the New York State National Bank we find Cogswell as pres. and Van Rensselaer as vice pres., while the directors included Hun and Henry Sage, Cogswell's son-in-law and a Reynolds client. The Union Trust, set up to compete with the Albany Trust, had Grange Sard as pres. and Van Rensselaer as vice pres. Directors included Cogswell, Simon W. Rosendale, Robert C. Pruyn and Martin Glynn. All four were or would become Reynolds's clients. At the National Savings Bank, Rosendale was pres. and James H. Manning was vice pres. The National Commercial Bank had Pruyn as pres., Sard as vice pres., and Rosendale, Manning and Lansing as directors. The Albany City Savings Institution was out of this loop, but two trustees were Dr. Willis MacDonald, probably a Reynolds client, and Albert Hessberg, brother of a Reynolds client. The treasurer, William S. Hackett, would become Reynolds's major backer in the 20s. The Albany Trust Co. was also out of the loop, but its pres., John D. Parson, Jr., and its first vice pres., George P. Hilton, would both end up in Albany Rural Cemetery with monuments by Reynolds .

92. There is a survey of bank architecture in Nikolaus Pevsner, *A History of Building Types* (London: Thames and Hudson, 1976), and the history of bank architecture in the United States and Canada is given by means of a few outstanding examples in *Money Matters*. There is also the group of banks pictured and discussed in "Recent Bank Buildings." I am preparing a study of 19th and 20th century classical bank buildings in the United States.

93. "Recent Bank Buildings," 3.

94. Ibid.

95. The author failed, however, to recognize the existence of earlier American prototypes such as Benjamin Henry Latrobe's porticoed and domed Bank of Pennsylvania (1798-1800), torn down in the 1860s; William Strickland's Second Bank of the United States (1819-24), also in Philadelphia, with its Doric porticoes and barrel vaulted banking room; or James Dakin's Bank of Louisville (1835-37) in Kentucky; see *Money Matters*, 24-9. Dakin had faced the same problem that Reynolds faced in the mid-block site in Catskill, and he had solved it in a similar way. Two Ionic columns *in antis* dominate an aedicular facade, behind which opens a banking room lit by a skylight set in an oval dome. Certainly Reynolds had direct exposure to at least one early classical bank, Hooker's New York State National Bank. And he must have known about the curiously domed, early 19th century Mechanics' National Bank in Albany, sometimes attributed to Hooker. Rhoads, 744, n.14, notes the relationship between Cass Gilbert's Suffolk Savings Bank and the Boston Custom House of 1837 by Ammi B. Young and in n. 15, 755, provides a list of other Colonial Revival banks published after 1910. Philip Sawyer [of York & Sawyer], "The Planning of Bank Buildings," *Architectural Review* 12 (1905): 24-31, illustrates an article largely devoted to technical issues of layout with photographs the First Bank of the United States, Philadelphia (1795-97), and of two Greek Revival banks in Stonington, Conn. The relationship between the classical banks of the early 19th century and the late 19th and early 20th centuries needs further exploration.

96. For Sullivan's banks, the earlier of which are contemporary with Reynolds's, see Lauren S. Weingarden, *Louis H. Sullivan: The Banks* (Cambridge, Mass.: MIT Press, 1987).

97. How this community of expectation had come into being, however, we are unable to say at this point.

98. Even Sullivan's banks have elements of the classical in them, both in plan and in elevation. His Beaux Arts training in France persisted, even while his ornament moved off in inventive directions.

99. "Recent Bank Buildings," 4.

100. In the earliest of his banks, in Owatonna, there is a vestige of the island plan in the clock-bedecked polygonal screen placed on the main axis, but it hardly acts to exclude the customer from most of the central space of the building (Weingarden, 48-58).

101. The notion of the bank as temple and the banker as priest goes back well into the 19th century. See Lois Severini, *The Architecture of Finance: Early Wall Street* (Ann Arbor: UMI Research Press, 1983), 83.

102. Manning in *Retrospective-Prospective Vol.*, 148, marvelled at the amount of light admitted to the Albany Savings Bank by Cobb's dome, which acted "as a lantern during the night, for it is fitted with a large number of electric lights so arranged that a perfect flood of light can be thrown into the banking room, producing the effect of sunlight."

CHAPTER 3

1. Roth (1983), 100.

2. "Examples of Recent Architecture at Home and Abroad," *AR* 7 (1897): 177-9.

The Reynolds houses were the only American buildings included in the piece.

3. Reynolds, "Colonial Buildings," illustrates the staircase door, 428, and door frames, 427.

4. The early 19th century furniture in the dining room also came from the manor house.

5. *Hudson-Mohawk Memoirs*, 74.

6. Reynolds and Lansing remained lifelong friends. On July 8, 1914, Reynolds produced a tantalizing design for Lansing for a Tango Palace, whatever that may have been. On Oct. 18, 1909, he designed a sleeping porch for the rear of the house, and he also did some work on Lansing's country place.

7. Hills, 238.

8. Reynolds had already designed for his cousin Howard Van Rensselaer a lower-cost apartment house at the corner of Madison and Lark. The first schemes for this building date from Feb. 6,1901, but the plans were not issued until April 28, 1904.

9. Diary, July 16, 1903: "Ryder in about apt. house."

10. Elizabeth Collins Cromley, *Alone Together, A History of New York's Early Apartments* (Ithaca and London: Cornell Univ. Press, 1990).

11. Diary, Jan. 28, 1904: "Ryder accepted apt. dwngs"; Feb. 8, 1904: "E.N. Huyck first appeared and wanted to build a house for $12000." On Dec. 7, 1904, he "met Mrs. Huyck at the new house."

12. Diary, March 20, 1899: Senator Curtis Douglas "in for first time."

13. Diary, Feb. 1, 1908: "Met Judge Wallace for third time & he commissioned me to design new facade."

14. Diary, March 18, 1915: "Went over 7 Elk St. for first time with Mrs. Read."

15. The death of Harmon Pumpelly Read caused Reynolds a gastronomic inconvenience. He noted on Dec. 20, 1925, "Harmon P. Read at 11 a.m. had a convulsion & probably a stroke — their large dinner party abandoned. (died next day)." Reynolds's design for Read's tombstone is one of his lesser achievements.

16. Diary, July 22, 1904: "I went to Hudson & presented sketches to Van Deusen for picturesque house. they decided on square house with servants and billiard room in attic"; July 25, 1904: "revising van Deusen house Colonial design."

17. "Remarks of F. G. Bascom on Addison B. Colvin, Glens Falls Rotary Club, July 2, 1970," photocopy of typescript, Crandall Library, Glens Falls.

18. The biographical information on Colvin comes from a talk, without a title, delivered Oct. 18, 1950, to the Glens Falls Historical Meeting by James R. Cronkhite; *ms.* at Crandall Library.

19. Harvester Hiram [Addison Beecher Colvin], *Lumberman "Lew" A Story of Fact, Fancy and Fiction* (Glens Falls: Glens Falls Publishing Co., n.d. [1914]). The other novel, *Stray Steps*, appeared in 1920.

20. *Trip to Europe, "Dad" Mother and the Girls, Observations for Private Circulation Only, With the Compliments and Holiday Greetings of Yours Sincerely, Addison B. Colvin, Glens Falls, December 22, 1906*, 69; copies at Crandall Library.

21. Reynolds did not, however, design a bad bank for Colvin.

22. The pavement and chandelier are modern additions

23. On Oct. 22, 1903, Jones, his mother and his sister accepted Reynolds revised plans for the house. In 1905 Reynolds designed the stable, and a gate and a fountain in 1906.

24. Diary, July 7, 1903, and July 8, 1903.

25. Diary, Feb. 8, 1904 and June 8, 1904.

26. George E. De Mille, *Christ Church in the City of Hudson, 1802-1952* (Hudson: Rector, Wardens and Vestry of Christ Church in the City of Hudson, 1952), 50, n. 1. On her death in 1915, Jones's sister left $25,000 to the church. That and additional money contributed by Jones's mother financed a new parish house designed by Reynolds in 1916.

27. Frank Presbrey, *The History and Development of Advertising* (Garden City, N. Y.: Doubleday, Doran & Co., Inc., 1929), 377.

28. *Senior Class book Nineteen Hundred and Four, Williams College* (Williamstown: 1904).

29. The 1905 Hudson City Directory carried an ad for Race & Jones Insurance. The 1906 directory lists that partnership as well as Jones & Hardy, Mill Supplies. Jones became a director of the bank in 1911, and he served as vice president from 1915 to 1922 — that is, even after he had moved to New York.

30. *1904 Stork* 1 (Dec., 1915), copy in Williamsiana Collection, Williams College.

31. His various addresses in New York are preserved in alumni office records kept in the Williamsiana Collection.

32. Hewitt, 140-42.

33. Barr Feree, *American Estates and Gardens* (New York: Munn, 1904), 124.

34. Roth (1978), #813.

35. Material about the Lyon property at Selkirk has been made available through the kindness of Mary E. VanOostenbrugge, the granddaughter of J. B. Lyon, who lives in the MacDonald chalet. In 1890 Lyon made a second gift of land to another friend, Martin Glynn, the owner of the *Albany Times Union*. The Glynns erected a house designed by Reynolds in 1907 on this site. Elected Lt. Gov. of N. Y. in 1912, Glynn succeeded to the governorship for a little over a year when William Selzer was impeached. A Democrat, Glynn used his newspaper to fight the Republican machine of William Barnes, Jr., one of Reynolds's closest friends. The Italianate Glynn House,

now an Elks Club, had a U-shaped plan, with the arms facing north to embrace an entrance court; the Elks have seriously compromised the house by enclosing the entire court. Mrs. Glynn seems to have been the moving force behind the house. Frequently J. B. Lyon acted as a go-between for her with the architect. Why she chose an Italianate style is not, at this point, clear. The history of the Lyon property and the Glynn House is surveyed in a typescript (author's name not given) in Mrs. VanOostenbrugge's possession.

36. The Huyck House does not appear in Reynolds's diaries, which begin in 1899, but the drawings for the house are preserved in Reynolds's office files.

37. Francis Brown, *Edmund Niles Huyck, The Story of a Liberal* (New York: Dodd, Mead & Co., 1935), a book commissioned by Huyck's widow.

38. Roth (1983), 168.

39. Both porches probably have a common source in early Dutch houses of the Hudson Valley. See also Reynolds's use of this kind of porch in the Hees House at Sacandaga Park, 56-59.

40. It is also in keeping with what Mariana Van Rensselaer, "The Development of American Homes," *The Forum* 12 (Jan., 1892): 673, found a strength in American architecture: "Many of our new country homes, if we look at their outside only, seem to be built in no style at all, being quite devoid of ornament, dependent for their effect on mass and outline only, and differing in mass and outline from any Old-World models." She found (672) American country houses, as a group, the best of contemporary American architecture: "Here we are most successful because at once most rational and most individual, least conventional and imitative, least beset by the desire for mere display.... Here we have most frequently asked for just what we wanted and wanted things of a sensible kind."

41. Diary, Jan. 14, 1901.

42. Diary, Oct. 15, 1900: "to Williamstown Dr. Clarke's alteration ... bay window."

43. In 1898 Reynolds also designed a half-timbered "country residence" for the Albany Country Club (*Albany Chronicles*, 741), and in 1908 Reynolds designed a large half-timbered house in Troy for Elmer Cluett. That house, completed in 1910, is now part of the Emma Willard School.

44. For the persistence of the Shingle Style well into the 20th century, see Vincent Scully, *The Architecture of the American Summer: The Flowering of the Shingle Style* (New York: Rizzoli, 1989).

45. There is some correspondence between the plan of the Clarke House and that of the Charles Cook House, Elberon, N. J., of 1885 by McKim, Mead & White (Scully, *Shingle Style* , figs. 140-41), but the Reynolds plan opens itself much more to nature.

46. *Samuel Fessenden Clarke, As Revealed in Some of his Writings* , compiled by C.B.S. [Mrs. Harold Stimpson] (New York: Marchbanks Press, 1932), 20. I am grateful to William H. Pierson, who lives in Clarke's Williamstown house, for bringing this book to my attention.

47. Ibid., 86-7.

48. Ann Rockefeller Roberts, *Mr. Rockefeller's Roads, The Untold Story of Acadia's Carriage Roads & Their Creator* (Camden: Down East Books, 1990), 45, with a photograph of "The Eyrie" in its original condition.

49. Earle G. Shettleworth, Jr., Director, Maine Historic Preservation Commission, to author, May 27, 1992.

50. Ibid.

51. Diary, Jan. 18, 1899: "Hees house begun". The house has been destroyed by fire.

52. Illustrated in Harold Donaldson Eberlein, *The Architecture of Colonial America* (Boston: Little, Brown and Co., 1915), opp. 24.

53. See, for instance, the description of the house of Petrus Douw, "Wolven Hoek," of 1724 in *Hudson-Mohawk Memoirs*, 385-86.

54. Diary, March 20, 1909: "Hees laundry."

55. Nicholas King, "Living with Codman," in *Ogden Codman and the Decoration of Houses*, Pauline C. Metcalf, ed., (Boston: David R. Godine, 1988), 41-47, discusses the burden of laundry in country-house life.

56. Diary, April 30, 1912: "spent morning at Sacandaga Park with J. Ledlee Hees looking over his house Alteration nearly completed."

57. Interview with Rebecca Evans, whose parents had been friends of the Heeses, June, 1992.

58. *Landmarks of Albany County, New York*, Amasa J. Parker, ed. (Syracuse, New York: D. Mason & Co., 1897), Part 3, 50.

59. Examples of Hudson River houses with two-storied porticos include Edgewater, Barrytown (1820), and The Hill, Hudson (c. 1800). See Harold Donaldson Eberlein, *Historic Houses of the Hudson Valley* (New York: Architectural Book Publishing Co., 1942), Pls. 82, 100, 101.

60. The house was built on land her father, Judge William Law Learned, had purchased in 1870. Reynolds was related to the Learneds through his Hun cousins. The Patterson House has a two-story, four-columned Ionic portico that faces south, and a one-story porch that faces east toward the Hudson River. This may have been Reynolds's first Colonial Revival house.

61. Hewitt, 168-70; Keith N. Morgan, *Charles A. Platt, The Artist as Architect* (Cambridge: MIT Press, 1985), 96. The porch at Sylvania, however, does not face south, as do the porches at Selkirk, but west, simultaneously toward the gardens and the Hudson River. On the south side of the house a more intimate, one-story porch

opened off the library onto a garden.

62. *Architectural Review* 15 (Jan., 1908): 10. "The House of Mr. John J. Chapman at Barrytown, N. Y.," *AR* 24 (Sept., 1908): 207-17.

63. Interview with Albert Hessberg, June 11, 1992.

64. For ways in which the Colonial Revival could be used for purposes of assimilation into the dominant WASP culture, see William B. Rhoads, "The Colonial Revival and the Americanization of Immigrants," in *The Colonial Revival in America*, Alan Axelrod, ed., (New York and London: W. W. Norton & Co., 1985), 341-61.

65. The literature on the bungalow is vast and growing. Particularly interesting is Anthony King, *The Bungalow: Production of a Global Culture* (London and Boston: Routledge and Kegan Paul, 1984).

66. Diary, Jan. 22, 1909, through July 25, 1909 .

67. C.P. Connally, "Mr. Barnes of Albany," *Collier's* 49 (1912): 10, states: "There is a brick street pavement, built at the expense of the taxpayers of Albany, from the heart of the city out to the country club and to Barnes country bungalow. Two hundred and twenty five feet of this...extends beyond the city limits.... Forty thousand dollars of bonds were authorized by the city council for this Boulevard de Triomphe, dedicated to the convenience of Barnes and his friends."

68. An addition of 1912 consisted mainly of a bedroom for Barnes on the ground floor, west of the library. This architectural adjustment to the house may signal the development of the problems in the Barnes's marriage that led to their eventual divorce.

69. Norman S. Rice, "Living with Antiques, the Hudson Valley Home of Mrs. Henry Sage," *Antiques* (Dec., 1965): 806-11. The article is illustrated with views of the house as it was in Mrs. Sage's lifetime.

70. Edward W. Root, *Philip Hooker, A Contribution to the Study of the Renaissance in America* (New York: Charles Scribner's Sons, 1929).

71. Diary, Oct. 6, 1921: "Henry Sage stated his house had cost $150.000."

72. Diary, April 15, 1921.

73. Diary, Feb. 21, 1920 "All day trying scheme to move Sage big room to get entrance on axis. N.G." There had also been an earlier scheme for an oval entrance hall.

74. Rice, 810.

75. Ibid., 806.

76. Alwyn T. Covell, "Old Chatham and Neighboring Dwellings South of the Berkshires," *The White Pine Series of Architectural Monographs* 5, (5, Oct., 1919): 2-5. The article provides neither a name nor a date for the house.

77. For instance, the curious ornamental band under the cornice of the Palladian window, which looks something like a series of tic-tac-toe boards, appears on the great room side of the doorway that connects the great room and the music room.

78. Reynolds, "Colonial Buildings."

79. At first the house was to be of brick, but in July, 1919 the Sages opted for stone. Diary, Aug. 21, 1919: "Henry Sage & Mrs. S. with MTR went to Schoharie & examined Mix's quarry."

80. The Cooper House, by Frank P. Whiting, was published in "'Fynmere' The House of James Fenimore Cooper," *AR* 30 (1911): 361-67. I am grateful to Gilbert Vincent for bringing this house to my attention.

CHAPTER 4

1. There is no evidence that Reynolds had anything to do with the design of this headstone or with the design of the five more elaborate and matching headstones that flank it.

2. Diary, March 29, 1902: "Brines was settled with Hamilton & approved the finished cross." Brines had made the bronze statue of Dr. Edward Austin Sheldon, "Father of the Moral School System," that was placed in the Senate stairway of the New York State Capitol in 1900: *Albany Chronicles*, 750. He also carved the heads of all the governors of New York up to 1900 in the capitol, as well as much of the ornament. He worked at the capitol for eight years and supervised a number of stone carvers who had come from Westerley, R. I. In 1905 Reynolds designed Brines's own monument, a cross which reportedly is in the cemetery at Westerley. E. S. Van Olinda, "Best Collection of Stone Work Found in Capitol," an undated newspaper clipping from the *Albany Times Union* generously provided by James Gwynne. Brines also carved the figures that flanked the clock over the door of Reynolds's National Savings Bank in Albany. Diary, Dec. 20, 1902.

3. The iconographic analysis here depends on James Hall, *Dictionary of Subjects & Symbols in Art*, rev. ed. (New York: Harper & Row, 1979).

4. *Albany Evening Journal*, March 2, 1908, 8.

5. Ibid.

6. *New York Times*, Oct. 4, 1912, 2.

7. Diary, Jan. 31, 1905: "Mrs. Parsons 1st time monument (cross)."

8. The scene is based on the account of the resurrection in Matthew, who records a single winged figure addressing two women, who may be represented as the two kneeling women in the accompanying frieze.

9. *American Art Annual* (1913): 78. Presumably this was the second Diana, made to replace the first version that both St. Gaudens and Stanford White found too large for the building beneath it. See Roth (1983), 162 and 393, n. 97.

10. Maybelle Mann, *Walter Launt Palmer, Poetic Reality* (Exton, Pa.: Schiffer Publishing Ltd., 1984), 64.

11. Palmer actually gave his wife both laurel and oak branches.

12. J. Carson Webster, *Erastus Dow Palmer* (Newark: Univ. of Delaware Press, 1983), 161, lists twelve versions of Morning and, 143, thirteen of Evening.

13. Ibid., 161. Webster quotes Palmer's remarks on this image in a letter of 1850: "a torch (emblem of light) without a handle, it being so hackneyed and in my mind always associated with a turning lathe or manufacture, and would have distracted from the spirituality of my composition." Presumably Walter Launt Palmer could have communicated his father's concept of the torch to Reynolds.

14. On Dec. 30, 1907, Walter Palmer called on Reynolds to discuss a new gate for Albany Rural Cemetery, which was built in 1909. Constructed of yellow field stone and buff sandstone, Reynolds's gate, which marks the long, straight road that leads from Broadway to both St. Agnes Cemetery and the adjacent Albany Rural, is the last gate before the pearly ones for many Albanians.

15. The relief is signed "Oscar L. Lenz. Sc. c Roman Bronze Works New York."

16. Hills, 144.

17. *AEJ*, Dec. 19, 1904, 16.

18. The house Reynolds designed for Dalton in 1910 still stands in Scotia. It seems to have been based on Charles Platt's Woodston, the house for Marshall Slade at Mt. Kisco, N. Y., of 1904-8. In particular, the two-story porticos at each end of the rectangular block of the house must have come from the Platt design. See "The House of Mr. Marshall Slade at Mt. Kisco, New York," *AR* 22 (1907): 260-71, and Morgan, 97-101.

19. Building the cinerarium was occasioned by the death of Dalton's first wife earlier in the year.

20. Diary, Dec. 12, 1928.

21. It is probably misleading, and certainly naughty, to read the cylinder of the cinerarium as the vertically set boiler of a great locomotive.

22. See, for instance, Reynolds's house for Henry Reist, discussed in Ch. 6, n. 26.

CHAPTER 5

1. The building has received very little attention in architectural writings since its publication in MTR, "Office Building for the Delaware & Hudson Company," *AA* 107 (1915): 383-86, and MTR, "The Plaza at Albany, N.Y." *Architecture* 37 (1918): 164-67 and Pl. XCIV-XCVIII. Local literature is an exception, particularly "A Civic Monument," *Commercial Courier*, March, 1972, 16-30, and Lavinia Finin, "State University Plaza," *Chronica* 12 (May-June 1978): 1-7. The building was the subject of a paper presented by the author in 1990 at the annual meeting of the Society of Architectural Historians in Boston.

2. In his diaries Reynolds took note of his annual poker winnings for several years. In 1906, for instance, he played poker with Barnes 20 times. In 1907 Barnes won $110.70 from Reynolds, and Reynolds won $91.18 from Barnes. In 1908 Barnes won $55, while Reynolds made off with $122.40 from Barnes, who one assumes was as tough a poker player as he was a politician.

3. Dwight Macdonald, "Profiles: Neanderthal," *New Yorker*, June 3, 1933, 18-21. See also Jim Shaughnessy, *Delaware and Hudson* (Berkeley, Cal.: Howell-North Books, 1967) and *A Century of Progress: History of the Delaware and Hudson Company 1823-1923* (Albany: J. B. Lyon Co., 1925).

4. For the Evening Journal Building and the addition to the D & H Building the seam face granite was supplied by Plymouth Quarries, Inc. of Boston. Cast stone was ordered from Onondaga Litholite Co., Syracuse, and Emerson-Norris Co., New York. The molds for the cast stone were carved by John Evans & Co., Boston. Reynolds insisted on using Evans because of the company's experience in doing Gothic work for St. Thomas and St. John the Divine, New York, and in doing the porch of Trinity Church, Boston. Terra cotta was ordered from Atlantic Terra Cotta Co., New York, the firm that had supplied terra cotta for the Woolworth Building. Emerson-Norris made the cast stone for the first part of the D & H. See correspondence, dating from 1916 to 1919, between MTR and these companies in McKinney Library, Albany Institute of History and Art.

5. Thomas Finnegan, *Saving Union Station, Albany, New York: An Inside Look at Historic Preservation* (Albany: Washington Park Press, 1988), 15.

6. Robert E. O'Connor, "William Barnes, Jr.,: A Conservative Encounters the Progressive Era" (Ph. D. diss., State Univ. of N. Y., Albany, 1971), to which the account of Barnes given here is much indebted.

7. *AEJ*, Aug. 29, 1900, 2.

8. *AEJ*, Sept. 2, 1903, 9.

9. *AEJ*, Nov. 23, 1906, 1.

10. *AEJ*, June 8, 1907, 1; June 10, 1907, 1; and June 11, 1907, 10, with four photographs that vividly detailed the squalid conditions of the waterfront. For the complex politics of the situation, see the stories of March 1, 1907, 1, and the editorial of March 5, 1907, 4. Fear that the D & H was taking advantage of the city continued into 1910 (*AEJ*, June 20, 1910, 3).

11. *AEJ*, June 11, 1910, 1. On Feb. 4, 1902, Reynolds mentioned a waterfront project in his diaries, and so it would seem that his involvement in the project went back at least that far. The drawing of 1910 was the result of several months of work in

Reynolds's office, and of a rooftop conversation, overlooking the site, between Reynolds and Barnes. See Diary, Feb. 7, 9, 11, 1910; May 14, 17, 1910; June 7, 8, 11, 1910.

12. Information generously supplied to the author by Diana Waite.

13. *AEJ*, June 7, 1910, 4, stated the hope that the pier would be completed by fall.

14. On April 6, 1910, Reynolds showed Barnes plans for the boat house, and on April 12 he sent plans for it to Nantucket. Reynolds visited Barnes in Nantucket a number of times.

15. Marion H. Reynolds, 368.

16. *AEJ*, June 25, 1910, 1.

17. O'Connor, 83, notes the controversy between Barnes and Hughes over direct primaries. Barnes worried that Hughes wanted to substitute democratic government for the representative government Barnes favored (!). See also Burton J. Hendrick, "Governor Hughes and the Albany Gang: A Study of the Degradation of the Republican Party in New York State," *McClure's Magazine* 35 (1910): 495-512.

18. *AEJ*, Feb. 28, 1912, 1.

19. The role of Huyck in the river front project is discussed in Brown, 165-75.

20. Ibid., 169.

21. According to Brown, 170-71, the report also included recommendations to improve the trackage of the railroads and to give them better freight houses. State Street was to be straightened, Broadway widened, and the Reynolds park was to become a plaza in which trolleys would turn around. Brown may, however, be arguing after the fact here.

22. *AEJ*, Feb. 3, 1912, 2.

23. Arnold W. Brunner, "Studies for the City of Albany, New York, Arnold W. Brunner, A.I.A., Architect; Charles Downing Lay, Landscape Architect," *AA* 106 (1914): 113-26. The same material, expanded, appeared as Arnold W. Brunner, *Studies for Albany*, 1914. See also Rawson W. Haddon, "City Planning Studies for Albany," *AR* 36 (1914): 170-74.

24. Brunner, *Studies for Albany*, 18, and *AA* 106, 115.

25. Holly M. Rarick, *Progressive Vision: The Planning of Downtown Cleveland 1903-1930* (Cleveland: Cleveland Museum of Art, 1986), 18-26. Eric Johannesen, *Cleveland Architecture 1876-1976* (Cleveland: Western Reserve Historical Society, 1979),71-76. I am grateful to Walter and Sally Gibson for a copy of Rarick's book.

26. Brunner, *Studies for Albany*, 17.

27. Ibid., 27-8.

28. Rarick, *Progressive Vision*, and Johannesen, *Cleveland Architecture*.

29. Brunner, *AA* 106, 117 and 118.

30. Brown, 174.

31. Macdonald, 18.

32. Ibid.

33. Shaughnessy, 281.

34. Ibid., 283.

35. Ibid., 275.

36. Ibid., 281. Illustrated in *A Century of Progress*, 366.

37. Paul R. Baker, *Richard Morris Hunt* (Cambridge: MIT Press, 1980), 217-19. See also the slightly different account in *A Century of Progress*, 232-34.

38. The North Pearl Street building, which still stands, is illustrated in *A Century of Progress*, 300.

39. Shaughnessy, 283.

40. Robert A. Jones, *Cass Gilbert, Midwestern Architect in New York* (New York: Arno Press, 1982), 120. MTR to Atlantic Terra Cotta Co., Feb. 8, 1916 (McKinney Library), noted that "the Woolworth Building...is in somewhat similar style" to the D & H.

41. Marion H. Reynolds, 368.

42. The statement by a local resident that Reynolds went to Belgium in 1912 to study the Cloth Hall and consult a Belgian architect (Finin, 4-5) is not confirmed by Reynolds's diaries, which record no trip to Belgium in 1912 or 1913, the years the building was under design.

43. Montgomery Schuyler, "Last Words about the World's Fair," *AR* 3 (1893-94): 293 and 298, singled out the impressiveness of the use of repetitive bays in the 440' long facade of the Cloth Hall, "perhaps the most striking [example] that medieval architecture supplies." Reynolds is likely to have read Schuyler's essay.

44. MTR, "Office Building," 383. Montgomery Schuyler, "A Picturesque Skyscraper," *AR* 5 (1895-96): 299-302, had already made a similar equation between ethnic origin, irregular plan and choice of architectural style. He praised Henry J. Hardenbergh's Wolfe Building, William St. and Maiden Lane, New York, a 12-story skyscraper in a picturesque Dutch style that had a "special and local appropriateness to a building erected within the precincts of the ancient Dutch settlement...the very irregularity of which is a consequence of the Dutch street-plan."

45. For the Pruyn Library and the firehouse, see Ch. 6.

46. For an influential book on beavers in America, see Lewis Henry Morgan, *The American Beaver and His Works* (Philadelphia: J. B. Lippincott, 1868). I am grateful to Peter Just for pointing this volume out to me.

47. *AEJ*, Oct. 7, 1909, 1.

48. MTR to Onondaga Litholite Co., May 8, 1917, McKinney Library. The inscription went through several variations. The pedantic use of the Dutch word

"füyck," separated only by an umlaut and a "y" from an Anglo-Saxon indecency, gave Reynolds a puckish delight. He corrected a subordinate who had mistakenly written "beavers' Füyck." "If you drank beer you would know better," wrote Reynolds. (MTR to Henry Granger, n.d., but probably Aug. 12, 1917, McKinney Library.)

49. In addition to Hendrick Cuyler, the following appear, with dates of arrival and coat of arms: Kiliaen Van Rensselaer, 1630; Filyp Pietersen Schuyler, 1650; Jan Jansen Bleeker, 1658; Robert Livingston, 1674. The spelling is that given on the building, which is not always the same as that on the drawings produced in Reynolds's office for these reliefs. Reynolds was extremely fussy about the detailing of the coats of arms, insisting on the diagonal lines from upper left to lower right that represent the color green on the Schuyler and Cuyler arms, and horizontal lines indicating blue on the Bleeker arms. MTR to John Evans Co., Aug. 31, 1916, McKinney Library.

50. The Cuylers, nonetheless, had produced three mayors of Albany prior to the Revolution.

51. The Journal company had very lucrative printing contracts with the city, county and state. See Connolly, 32-35. In this muckraking article, Connolly noted that Barnes had cut the rival Argus printing company, controlled by Democrats, in on these contracts.

52. Drawings for the marks of the following printers, with dates, were made in Reynolds's office: Christophe Plantin, 1556; Fust & Schoeffer, 1457; Francoys Regnault, 1481; Jehan Petit, 1520; Lucantonio Guinta, 1495; Aldus Manutius, 1502; William Caxton, 1487; Valentin Fernandez, 1501; Johann Grüninger, 1494; Louis Elzevir, 1595; Sanctus Albanus, 1480; Juan Rosenbach, 1493. The spelling of the names is that which appears on the drawings.

53. O'Connor, 10.

54. August Claessens and William Morris Feigenbaum, *The Socialists in the New York Assembly; The Work of Ten Socialist Members During the Legislative Session of 1918* (New York: Rand School of Social Science, 1918).

55. O'Connor, 13.

56. *AEJ*, March 15, 1917, stated: "It seemed appropriate to use the emblems of earlier printing houses of distinguished reputation in the ornamentation of the new printing house of the Journal company."

57. Published by MTR in *Architecture*, 1918, Pl. XCIV.

58. *Albany Times Union*, June 26, 1930, 1. Also "Barnes against Roosevelt," *American Review of Reviews* 51 (1915): 533-34.

59. "Barnes, A Political Bravo of the Twentieth Century," *Current Literature* 50 (1911): 268.

60. Ibid., 269.

61. Poignantly, and ironically, during the years the D & H Building was being constructed, the Germans levelled the Cloth Hall at Ypres. Barnes and Reynolds were aware of what was going on in Europe. Reynolds noted in his Diary, on April 22, 1915: "Poison gases first used in battle — by Germans —2nd battle of Ypres."

62. Barnes sold the Evening Journal in 1925.

63. *Albany Times Union*, June 28, 1930.

64. For example, no picturesque or medieval example of City Beautiful planning is cited in William H. Wilson, *The City Beautiful Movement* (Baltimore: Johns Hopkins Univ. Press, 1989). Reynolds's own taste in urban planning also ran to the classical, as we know from his proposal for developing the block to the west of the state capitol. (MTR, "Clear Space Needed Back of Capitol Site To Show Real Beauty of State Buildings," *Knickerbocker Press*, Sept. 28, 1919, 2). Reynolds suggested keeping the recently cleared block empty and flanking it to the south with a new state office building that would match the length and height of Palmer & Hornbostel's State Education Building to the north. Reynolds cited as his precedent the Court of Honor at the World's Columbian Exposition. On the west side of the block he proposed a memorial colonnade consisting of two rows of columns of the same height as those of the education building. The colonnade would end in two pavilions set on an axis established by the pavilions at the western ends of the education and proposed state office buildings. The terminal pavilions of Reynolds's colonnade would also have been in line with the corner towers of the capitol. For this colonnade Reynolds cited the gigantic Victor Emmanuel Monument in Rome, completed in 1911, as precedent. When Reynolds's final illness struck in March, 1937, he was about to depart for Rome to address a conference at the American Academy on urban planning.

65. For the Chicago Tribune Tower, see Walter H. Kilham, *Raymond Hood, architect: form through function in the American skyscraper* (New York: Architectural Book Publishing Co., 1973).

66. Reynolds's D & H Building, the headquarters for a railroad, seems to have exerted a strong influence on a structure similar in site and function: Warren & Wetmore's New York Central Building, completed in 1929, located north of Grand Central Terminal on the axis of Park Avenue. Both buildings form a monumental closure to a broad street. Warren and Wetmore also seem to have taken the broadening of the tower at the top floors in tourelles, the pyramidal roof and the vertical flèche, all essential to the ability of the tower to control the long space in front of it.

67. A.D.F. Hamlin, "The Battle of Styles," *AR* 1 (1891-92): 265-75, 405-14, and "Difficulties," 135-50.

68. Hamlin, "Battle of Styles," 412.

69. Despite its Gothic style, Reynolds's building would not have pleased Ralph Adams Cram, the most vocal American proponent of Gothic architecture in these years. For Cram, structure and style were indivisible; a Gothic building had to be made entirely of stone, with a wooden truss supporting the roof. (Or so his theory went. There is steel in his chapel at Princeton, as William Morgan kindly pointed out.) For Hamlin and Reynolds, on the other hand, structure was something quite separate from architectural rhetoric. Cram spoke in Albany on medieval church architecture on April 28, 1910 (*AEJ*, April 29, 1910, 11), to a small audience of enthusiasts. *AEJ* reported: "Mr. Cram's lecture was also instructive in showing how far short of the work of the mediaeval (*sic*) ages many of the most notable examples of modern church architecture fall. The contrast, for example, between the mother church of Christian Science, Boston, which was completed lately at a cost of over $2,000,000 and the marvelously beautiful cathedrals of France and England was so grotesque that everybody in the audience laughed when the pictures were compared." Reynolds may well have been in the audience, but if he was, we may wonder if he joined in the laughter at the classical architecture of the Mother Church.

70. Hamlin, "Battle of Styles," 275.

71. Edith Wharton, *The Customs of the Country* (New York, Charles Scribner's Sons, 1913), 73: "society was really just like the houses it lived in: a muddle of misapplied ornament over a thin steel shell of utility. The steel shell was built up in Wall Street, the social trimmings were hastily added in Fifth Avenue; and the union between them was as monstrous and factitious, as unlike the gradual homogenous growth which flowers into what other countries know as society, as that between the Blois gargoyles on Peter Van Degen's roof and the skeleton walls suporting them."

72. MTR to Atlantic Terra Cotta Co., July 13, 1916, McKinney Library.

73. MTR to John Evans Co., April 6, 1916, McKinney Library.

74. Edward A. Freeman, "Choice in Architectural Styles," *AR* 1 (1891-92) 391-400.

CHAPTER 6

1. Another instance is the addition to the physics building at Union College, 1926, where he continued the arcaded, stuccoed walls of the original Union buildings around his new structure.

2. Diary, Oct. 6, 1904: "Hampton in with Gibson plans of Commercial bank."

3. Diary, Oct. 29, 1906: "The Hampton opened at noon." There were also additions designed by Reynolds to the rear of the Gibson building, plus a barber shop (Nov. 13, 1909: "det. Mycenian [*sic*] columns in Hampton Barber shop"), a cafe on Green Street (March 18, 1910: "Blueprinted Hampton grille and dining room & also Green St. building [cafe]") and other parts of a very complicated complex.

4. Carving was done in New York. See Diary, March 15, 1906.

5. The same thing happens, one should add, at the rear of Louis Sullivan's Wainwright Building of 1890-91 in St. Louis. In both cases the architectural rhetoric was thriftily reserved for the side(s) easily seen.

6. *Albany Chronicles*, 746 and opp. 750.

7. Cuyler Reynolds, *Genealogical and Family History*, 149-50.

8. *Albany Chronicles*, xiv.

9. It would be nice to be able to state that he had visited Vicenza and looked directly at Palladian structures there during the summer, but he did not. He was in Venice, however, for several days, where he doubtless took in Palladio's churches.

10. The urns and tripods appear in an old photograph of the building in the possession of the Historic Albany Foundation. I am grateful to Diana Waite for bringing the photograph to my attention.

11. Reynolds was not the first to revive Dutch architectural forms. In 1885-86 McKim, Mead & White had built in New York offices for Robert and Ogden Goelet on West 17th Street and a group of row houses for David H. King, Jr., on West End Avenue (Roth (1978), #328 and #447). These may have been the first examples of the Dutch Revival. See Stern et al, 365-67. In 1892, while Reynolds was in New York, Robert W. Gibson's Collegiate Reformed Dutch Church on West End Ave. opened. This was illustrated by Montgomery Schuyler, "Colonial Architecture," in the issue of *AR* that preceded the one in which Reynolds's "Colonial Buildings" appeared. The Gibson church was featured in a full-page spread in "New New Amsterdam," *Harper's Weekly* 38 (April 21, 1894): 369-70, together with illustrations of other structures in the Dutch style: a row of townhouses on West End Ave. between 84th and 85th Streets by Frank Miles Day, the American Institute by Romeyn & Stever and the St. Nicholas Club by Wood, Cooke & Palmer. The *Harper's* article found the Dutch style particularly appropriate for houses because it was largely a domestic style, and particularly appropriate to New York because of the city's Dutch origins. In 1895 Henry J. Hardenbergh's Wolfe Building, a Dutch skyscraper lavishly praised by Schuyler, opened. Montgomery Schuyler found the use of the Dutch style appropriate to the irregular street pattern of the old part of the city, laid out by the Dutch, in which it stood (see Ch. 5, n. 44). Schuyler did not like the use of the Dutch style for William E. Stone's Princeton Bank of 1896, because Princeton, N.J., had no connection with the Dutch in America (*Money Matters*, 55-56). See also Longstreth, 74.

12. Diary, March 7, 1900: "1st time Pruyn Library". See *Albany Chronicles*, opp. 756.

13. Frank Walker Stevens, *The Beginning of the New York Central Railroad, A History* (New York: G. P. Putnam's Sons, 1926), 376-77, contains Pruyn's memo recalling

his activities in "perfecting the Consolidation of the Rail Roads." See also *Landmarks of Albany County New York*, 68 where Parker, Pruyn's law partner and father-in-law, states that the work "could not have been done by an ordinary man."

14. "Colonial Buildings," 415.

15. William Kennedy, *O Albany!* (New York: Viking Penguin Inc., 1983), 8-11.

16. Huybertie Pruyn Hamlin Papers, Albany Institute of History and Art, McKinney Library, Box 19, Folder 140.

17. *Knickerbocker News*, April 7, 1951.

18. Diary, May 23, 26 and 27, 1910. He began final designs on June 13, three days after the drawing of the waterfront scheme had appeared in the *AEJ*.

19. Rebecca Zurier, *The Firehouse: an Architectural and Social History* (New York: Abbeville Press, 1982), 135.

20. Dutch firehouses seem relatively rare, at least on the basis of Zurier's compilation. Engine 46, Philadelphia, 1895 (134), has stepped and scrolled gables. The Litchfield, Conn., Fire Station, 1891 (136), has certain vaguely Dutch characteristics, and the splendid Central Fire Station, Cortland, New York, 1914-5 (252-53), might have been influenced by Reynolds's design.

21. Diary, March 19, 1915: "Presented Cooperstown sketch to Sims who did not like the style of station and wanted it more Colonnial (*sic*)."

22. Diary, June 30, 1913: "awarded Industrial competition."

23. During June, 1913, Reynolds's office worked on the elevations of the D & H Building and the drawings for the Industrial Building simultaneously.

24. Diary, Feb. 9, 1914: "Industrial contract to Keeler"; June 30, 1915: "I settled up with Peter Keeler on Industrial."

25. Robert D. Kohn, "Architecture and Factories," *AR* 25 (1909): 131-36.

26. Diary, April 16, 1909: "Geo. Emmons first wrote concerning the proposed schemes of an entrance to the Gen'l Electric Co." Reynolds broke into the GE circle by designing a house for one of its engineers, Henry Reist, and his wife, in 1908. In that year Reist arranged for Reynolds to get the commission for the new office building of the Schenectady Illuminating Co., which was owned by GE. Reynolds was still working on these designs when he was approached by Emmons in April, 1909. The Schenectady Illuminating Co. Building, like much of downtown Schenectady, has been demolished.

The Reist House, in a rather delicately detailed Colonial Revival style, seems a tasteful reproach to its Queen Anne and Shingle Style neighbors in the so-called G.E. Realty Plot, a neighborhood developed for General Electric executives in Schenectady. See Bruce Maston, *An Enclave of Elegance, A Survey of the Architecture, Development and Personalities of the General Electric Realty Plot Historic District* (Schenectady: Schenectady Museum, 1983), Fig. 139.

27. Diary, May 29, 1909: "GE garage"; July 12, 1909: "G E Co Employment Bureau"; July 13, 1909: "G E general layout."

28. Reynolds also designed the Edison Club for GE. Diary, April 8, 1912: "presented GE Club (Edison Club) plans." Apparently the club, now demolished, stood in an area now occupied by a parking lot behind Blds. 27 and 33.

29. Leo Marx, *The Machine in the Garden* (New York: Oxford Univ. Press, 1964).

30. The history of the Schenectady Railway Co. is outlined by Larry Hart, *Schenectady's Golden Era 1880-1930* (Scotia, N.Y.: Old Dorp Books, 1974), 95-123. In 1912 Reynolds designed a waiting room and office building for the railway on State Street, Schenectady. See "Waiting Room and Office Building Schenectady Railway Company, Schenectady, New York," *AA* 107 (2061, June 23, 1915). Also Hart, 119-20. Unfortunately, most of the building is gone. On the exterior, only the Doric columns of the Lafayette Street facade remain. The grand interior of the waiting room, a small, vaulted version of the Forum of Nerva, has been demolished.

31. In 1910 Reynolds had completed a school building in a Jacobethan style for the Troy Orphan Asylum. "Competition for a Manual Training School for the Troy Orphan Asylum," *AA* 98 (1810, Aug. 31, 1910). The building, also known as the Peterson Memorial, no longer stands.

32. In March, when Hackett first consulted Reynolds about the new bank, only MTR and his nephew Kenneth were working in the office, but by September six employees had been added to take care of the simultaneous jobs of bank and school.

33. The original School 4 had been built in 1893, to serve the westward expansion of the city along Madison and Western Aves. Charles W. Blessing, *Albany Schools and Colleges Yesteday and Today, An Anniversary Volume, 1686-1936* (Albany: Fort Orange Press, 1936), 81, provides a list of new elementary schools built after 1866, as well as a list of replacements for older buildings.

34. The workings of the Corning-O'Connell machine are wonderfully detailed in Kennedy, *O Albany!* See also Frank S. Robinson, *Albany's O'Connell Machine, An American Political Relic* (Albany: The Washington Park Spirit, Inc., 1973). Eventually, Reynolds lost the patronage of Edwin Corning. MTR, Diary, Nov. 30, 1929: "KGR & MTR went down to see Edwin Corning about the new Junior High. [He] declared that he knew nothing but that I had never loosened up for the organization." Reynolds walked out of Corning's office, and the commission for the school went to another architect.

35. The excuse given for razing the school is said to have been that the building was unsafe because the contractor had weakened the structure by putting too much sand in the concrete. Many remain skeptical of this explanation. The school site is now occupied by a playground.

36. Diary, July 6, 1922: "Joint meeting of Board of Contract & Supply & Board of Education at 2.30 to which I presented plans for School 4. Strongly opposed by Dyer on the ground of economy. Instructed to prepare new facade of packing box design to satisfy Dyer and then decision will be reached between the two." (William S. Dyer, a lawyer with offices at 100 State St., was president of the Board of Education and a director of the Albany City Savings Institution. He was also on the building committee for that bank.) Diary, July 11, 1922: "Found Edwin Corning in office. We discussed School 4 until 11.15. Decided against Dyer scheme"; and July 12, 1922: "Gave Mayor Hackett alternate of School #4 according to Dyer. They liked it no better than I."

37. *Education in Albany, An Opportunity and a Business* (Albany: Chamber of Commerce, n.d. [c.1923-4]), 13. Credit for the expansion for the school system should also go to its superintendent from 1912 to 1932, C. Edward Jones, under whose administration seven new grammar schools and the two junior high schools were constructed. Blessing, 94-96.

38. Kennedy, 283.

39. Diary, March 8, 1926: "wrote obituary of Hackett for City Planning Commission".

40. *In Loving Memory*, 25.

41. Rhoads, *Colonial Revival*, 687-88, n. 196, lists several schools in the Colonial Revival mode.

42. Kennedy, 121.

43. See Ch. 3, n. 64.

44. Hackett died while vacationing in Cuba of injuries sustained when he was thrown from an open automobile.

45. Blessing, 72.

46. Ibid., 71.

47. *In Loving Memory*, 12.

48. Blessing, 73, was left breathless by the school, which he described as "a masterpiece of pure architectural beauty both inside and out...the finest of its time in plan and equipment."

49. Diary, Jan. 31, 1922: "Taking down the sturgeon & pumpkin weathervane from 2nd Presbyterian Church to place on Boys Academy." From the old Academy the weathervane was moved to the new.

50. Diary, Nov. 20, 1929: "Gave copy of Roots book on Philip Hooker for box."

51. Diary, Dec. 17, 1934: "bids opened for remodelling of Albany Academy $121,850."

52. On Oct. 22, 1929, the *Knickerbocker Press* stated that a fund drive for $1,071,000 would begin in January, with occupancy of the new school planned for the fall of 1931. October, 1929, turned out not to be a good month to contemplate a fund drive.

53. A key example of the diminishing quality of the output of the Reynolds office is the Gideon Putman Hotel at Saratoga Springs. For an account of the Saratoga Spa State Park, in which the hotel stands, see James K. Kettlewell, *Saratoga Springs: An Architectural History* (Saratoga Springs, N.Y.: Lyrical Ballad Book Store, 1991), 117-26. Reynolds was given the contract to design the hotel on Aug. 10, 1933, after Al Smith had intervened on his behalf. The design went through many schemes, some fairly sizeable, during Aug. and Sept. On Oct. 10 Reynolds was told to limit the cost of the hotel to $250,000. On the basis of this restricted budget, his office began a new scheme, which Reynolds, in anger, deprecated with an anti-Semitic phrase, "Kike boarding house." As work on the hotel drew to a close in 1935, Reynolds came into conflict with Dorothy Draper, the well known interior decorator. On June 7 he had "a good old fight with her all day" over her proposed color schemes for the buildng. A compromise was reached the next day.

54. Diary, May 8, 1923: "Paid Westcott Burlingame $2929 for Pieter Schuyler portrait by Sir Geofry (*sic*) Kneller."

55. Diary, March 29, 1923: "Wrote Hackett offering the portrait of Peter Schuyler to the City." The text of the letter is recorded in Cuyler Reynolds, "Pieter Schuyler, Albany's First Mayor. Historical Narrative of his life, his family relations, residence, career, and his many public acts...," typescript, Albany Public Library. I am grateful to Norman Rice for unearthing this document.

56. Ibid., 39.

57. Diary, Sept. 19, 1923 "KGR started Schuyler mantel for Mayor's office."

58. Diary, May 22, 1924: "Mercury weathervane raised on City Savings Bank Frame of Pieter Schuyler raised in Mayors Office."

59, C. Reynolds, "Pieter Schuyler," Presentation 3.

60. The plain Richardsonian interior of the mayor's office had already vanished underneath a classicizing redecoration of 1917.

61. Cuyler Reynolds, "Pieter Schuyler," Presentation 6.

BIBLIOGRAPHY

Albany Architects, The Present Looks at the Past. Albany: Historic Albany Foundation, 1978.

Albany's Historic Street. Albany: National Savings Bank, 1918.

Bacon, Mardges. "Toward a National Style of Architecture: The Beaux-Arts Interpretation of the Colonial Revival," in *The Colonial Revival in America,* Alan Axelrod, ed., 91-121. New York and London: W. W. Norton & Co., 1985.

Baker, Paul R. *Richard Morris Hunt.* Cambridge, Mass.: MIT Press, 1980.

Baltzell, E. Digby. *The Protestant Establishment.* New York: Random House, 1964.

Banks, Talcott M. *First Report of the Class of 'Ninety.* Williamstown, Mass.:1892.

"Barnes, A Political Bravo of the Twentieth Century." *Current Literature* (1911): 268.

Bennett, Allison. *More Times Remembered, Chronicles of the Towns of Bethlehem and New Scotland, New York.* Delmar, N.Y.: Newsgraphics of Delmar, Inc., 1987.

Bennett, Allison. *Times Remembered, Chronicles of the Towns of Bethlehem and New Scotland, New York.* Delmar, N.Y.: Newsgraphics of Delmar, Inc., 1984.

Blessing, Charles W. *Albany Schools and Colleges Yesterday and Today, An Anniversary Volume.* Albany: Fort Orange Press, 1936.

Boyer, M. Christine. *Manhattan Manners: Architecture and Style 1850-1900.* New York: Rizzoli, 1985.

Brooklyn Museum. *The American Renaissance, 1876-1917.* New York: Pantheon Books, 1979.

Brown, Francis. *Edmund Niles Huyck, The Story of a Liberal.* New York: Dodd, Mead & Co., 1935.

Brunner, Arnold W. *Studies for Albany, Arnold W. Brunner, Architect; Charles Downing Lay, Landscape Architect.* New York: Bartlett-Orr Press, 1914.

Brunner, Arnold W. "Studies for the City of Albany, New York, Arnold W. Brunner, A.I.A., Architect; Charles Downing Lay, Landscape Architect." *The American Architect* 106 (1914): 113-26.

Butler, William. "Another City upon a Hill: Litchfield, Connecticut, and the Colonial Revival" in *The Colonial Revival in America,* Alan Axelrod, ed., 15-51. New York and London: W. W. Norton & Co., 1985.

Caine, M. R., and William Shultz. *Financial Development of the United States.* New York: Prentice Hall, 1937.

A Century of Progress: History of the Delaware and Hudson Company 1823-1923. Albany: J.B. Lyon Co., 1925.

"A Civic Monument." *Commercial Courier* (March, 1972):16-30.

Claessens, August and William Morris Feigenbaum. *The Socialists in the New York Assembly; the Work of Ten Socialist Members During the Legislative Session of 1918.* New York: Rand School of Social Science, 1918.

The Colonial Revival in America, Alan Axelrod, ed. New York and London: W. W. Norton & Co., 1985.

"Competition for a Manual Training School for the Troy Orphan Asylum." *The American Architect* 98 (1810, August 31, 1910).

Connally, C.P. "Mr. Barnes of Albany." *Collier's* 49 (1912): 10-11, 30-32.

Constitution, By-Laws and Resolutions of the American Economic Association, With List of Officers and Members. Supplement: American Economic Association Publication (July, 1889): 3.

Covell, Alwyn T. "Old Chatham and Neighbouring Dwellings South of the Berkshires." *The White Pine Series of Architectural Monographs* 5 (5, Oct., 1919): 1-14.

Cromley, Elizabeth Collins. *Alone Together, A History of New York's Early Apartments.* Ithaca and London: Cornell Univ. Press, 1990.

Crook, J. Mordaunt. *The Dilemma of Style: Architectural Ideas from the Picturesque to the Post-Modern.* Chicago: Univ. of Chicago Press, 1987.

Davidson, Marshall B., and Elizabeth Stillinger. *The American Wing at the Metropolitan Museum of Art.* New York: Alfred A. Knopf, 1985, 52-55.

De Mille, George E. *Christ Church in the City of Hudson, 1802-1952.* Hudson, N.Y.: The Rector, Wardens and Vestry of Christ Church in the City of Hudson, 1952.

Donlon, Hugh P. *Amsterdam, New York, Annals of a Mill Town in the Mohawk Valley.* Amsterdam: Donlon Associates, 1980.

Eberlein, Harold Donaldson. *The Architecture of Colonial America.* Boston: Little, Brown, and Co., 1915.

Education in Albany, An Opportunity and a Business. Albany: Chamber of Commerce, [c.1923-24].

Ely, Richard T. "Report of the Organization of the American Economic Association." *Publication of the American Economic Association* 1 (1, March, 1886).

"Examples of Architecture at Home and Abroad." *Architectural Record* 7 (1897): 177-79.

Feree, Barr. *American Estates and Gardens.* New York: Munn, 1904.

Fiftieth Anniversary of the Amsterdam Savings Bank, 1887-1937. Amsterdam, N.Y.: privately printed, 1937.

Finin, Lavinia. "State University Plaza." *Chronica* 12 (May-June 1978) :1-7.

Finnegan, Thomas. *Saving Union Station, Albany, New York: An Inside Look at Historic Preservation.* Albany: Washington Park Press, 1988.

The Fort Orange Club, 1880-1980. Albany: The Fort Orange Club, 1980.

"'Fynmere' The House of James Fenimore Cooper." *Architectural Record* 30 (1911): 361-67.

Gaines, Edith. "Paintings and Antiques in the Loudonville, New York, Home of Mrs. Ledyard Cogswell, Jr." *Antiques* (November, 1959): 430-33.

Gerber, Morris. *Old Albany.* Vol. 1. Albany: privately printed, 1961.

Haddon, Rawson W. "City Planning Studies for Albany." *Architectural Record* 36 (1914): 170-4.

Hall, James. *Dictionary of Subjects & Symbols in Art.* Rev. ed. New York: Harper & Row, 1979.

Hamlin, A. D. F. "The Battle of Styles." *Architectural Record* 1 (1891-92): 265-75, 405-14.

Hamlin, A. D. F. "The Difficulties of Modern Architecture." *Architectural Record* 1 (1891-92): 137-150.

Hamlin, A. D. F. *A History of Ornament Ancient and Medieval.* New York: The Century Co., 1916.

Hamlin, A. D. F. *A History of Ornament Renaissance and Modern.* New York: The Century Co., 1923.

Hamlin, A. D. F. *A Textbook of the History of Architecture.* New York: Longmans, Green and Co., 1895.

Handbook of the American Economic Association, Together with Report of the Sixth Annual Meeting, January, 1894.

Hart, Larry. *Schenectady's Golden Era 1880-1930.* Scotia, N. Y.: Old Dorp Books, 1974.

Harvester, Hiram (pseudonym for Addison Beecher Colvin). *Lumberman "Lew," A Story of Fact, Fancy and Fiction.* Glens Fall, N.Y.: Glens Falls Publishing Co., *s. d.* [1914].

Hayden, Dolores. *The Grand Domestic Revolution.* Cambridge: MIT Press, 1981.

Hendrick, Burton J. "Governor Hughes and the Albany Gang: A Study of the Degredation of the Republican Party in New York State." *McClure's Magazine* 35 (1910): 495-512.

Hewitt, Mark Alan. *The Architect and the American Country House, 1890-1940 .* New Haven: Yale Univ. Press, 1990.

Hills, Frederick S. *New York State Men, Biographic Studies and Character Portraits.* Albany: The Argus Co., 1910.

Hines, Thomas. *Burnham of Chicago.* New York: Oxford Univ. Press, 1974.

History and Descendants of John and Sarah Reynolds [1630?-1923], Marion H. Reynolds, ed. Brooklyn: The Reynold Family Association, 1924.

Hopkins, Alfred. *The Fundamentals of Good Bank Building.* New York: The Bankers Publishing Co., 1929.

"The House of Mr. John J. Chapman at Barrytown, N.Y." *Architectural Record* 24 (1908): 207-17.

In Loving Memory of William Stormont Hackett, Sixty-Seventh Mayor of Albany, compiled by David M. Kinnear. Albany: The Argus Co., 1926.

Johanesen, Eric. *Cleveland Architecture 1876-1976*. Cleveland: Case Western Reserve Historical Society, 1979.

Jones, Robert. *Cass Gilbert, Midwestern Architect in New York*. New York: Arno Press, 1982.

Jordy, William. *American Buildings and Their Architects, Progressive and Academic Ideals at the Turn of the Century*. Garden City, N.Y.: Doubleday, 1972.

Kennedy, William. *O Albany!*. New York: Viking Penguin Inc., 1983.

Kettlewell, James K.. *Saratoga Springs: An Architectural History*. Saratoga Springs, N.Y.: Lyrical Ballad Book Store, 1991.

Kidney, Walter C. *The Architecture of Choice: Eclecticism in America 1880-1930*. New York: George Braziller, 1974.

Kilham, Walter H. *Raymond Hood, Architect: Form through Function in the American Skyscraper*. New York: Architectural Book Publishing Co., 1973.

King, Nicholas. "Living with Codman," in *Ogden Codman and the Decoration of Houses*, Pauline C. Metcalf, ed., 41-47. Boston: David R. Godine, 1988.

King, Anthony. *The Bungalow: Production of a Global Culture*. London and Boston: Routledge and Kegan Paul, 1984.

Klebaner, Benjamin J. *Commercial Banking in the United States: A History*. Hinsdale, Ill.: Dryden Press, 1974.

Kohn, Robert D. "Architecture and Factories." *Architectural Record* 25 (1909): 131-36.

Landmarks of Albany County, New York. Amasa J. Parker, ed. Syracuse, New York: D. Mason & Co., 1897.

Lazzaro, Claudia *The Italian Renaissance Garden, from the Convention of Planning, Design, and Ornament to the Grand Gardens of Sixteenth-century Central Italy*. New Haven: Yale Univ. Press, 1990.

Lears, T. J. Jackson. *No Place of Grace: Antimodernism and the Transformation of American Culture, 1880-1920*. New York: Pantheon, 1981.

Lewis, R.W.B. *Edith Wharton, A Biography*. New York: Harper & Row, 1975.

Longstreth, Richard W. "Academic Eclecticism in American Architecture." *Winterthur Portfolio* 17 (1982): 55-82.

Longstreth, Richard W. *On the Edge of the World: Four Architects in San Francisco*. Cambridge, Mass.: MIT Press and the Architectural History Foundation, 1984.

Macdonald, Dwight. "Profiles: Neanderthal." *The New Yorker* (June 3, 1933): 18-21.

Mann, Maybelle. *Walter Launt Palmer, Poetic Reality,*. Exton, Penn.: Schiffer Publishing Ltd., 1984.

Manning, James H. *Century of American Savings Banks, New York Volume*. New York: B. F. Buck & Co., 1917.

Manning, James H. *Century of American Savings Banks, Retrospective-Prospective Volume*. New York: B. F. Buck & Co., 1917.

Marx, Leo. *The Machine in the Garden*. New York: Oxford Univ. Press, 1964.

Maston, Bruce. *An Enclave of Elegance, A Survey of the Architecture, Development and Personalities of the General Electric Realty Plot Historic District*. Schenectady, N.Y.: Schenectady Museum, 1983.

Meeks, Carroll L. V. "Wright's Eastern Seaboard Contemoraries: Creative Eclecticism in the United States around 1900," in Acts of the Twentieth International Congress of the History of Art, *Studies in Western Art: Problems of the 19th and 20th Centuries*, vol. 4, 64-77. Princeton: Princeton Univ. Press, 1963.

Monkhouse, Christopher. "The Making of a Colonial Revival Architect," in *Ogden Codman and the Decoration of Houses*, Pauline C. Metcalf, ed., 49-64. Boston: David R. Godine, 1988.

Morgan, Keith N. *Charles A. Platt, The Artist as Architect*. Cambridge: Mass.: MIT Press, 1985.

Morgan, Lewis Henry. *The American Beaver and His Works*. Philadelphia: J.B. Lippincott, 1868.

Morgan, William.. *The Almighty Wall: The Architecture of Henry Vaughan*. Cambridge, Mass.: MIT Press and the Architectural History Foundation, 1983.

Museum of Fine Arts, Houston, and Parnassus Foundation, *Money Matters, A Critical Look at Bank Architecture*. New York: McGraw-Hill Publishing Co., 1990.

A Neat Plain Modern Style, Philip Hooker and his Contemporaries, 1790-1814. Mary Raddant Tomlan, ed. Amherst: Univ. of Massachusetts Press, 1993.

1904 Stork 1 (No.2, December, 1915).

O'Connor, Robert E. *William Barnes, Jr.: A Conservative Encounters the Progressive Era*. Ph. D. Dissertation, State University of New York, Albany, 1971.

Ogden Codman and the Decoration of Houses. Pauline C. Metcalf, ed. Boston: David R. Godine, 1988.

O'Gorman, James F. *Three American Architects: Richardson, Sullivan and Wright, 1865-1915*. Chicago: University of Chicago Press, 1991.

Peltz, William Law Learned. *The Banks and Savings Banks of Albany, New York*. New York: The American Historical Co., 1955.

Peltz, William Law Learned. *The Top Flight at Number One Lafayette Street*. Albany: privately printed, 1939.

Pevsner, Nikolaus *A History of Building Types*. London: Thames and Hudson, 1976.

Platt, Charles A. "Italian Gardens." *Harper's New Monthly Magazine* 87 (July, 1893): 165-80 and (August, 1893): 393-406.

Platt, Charles A. *Italian Gardens*. New York: Harper & Brothers, 1894.

Presby, Frank. *The History and Development of Advertising*. Garden City, N. Y.: Doubleday, Doran & Co., Inc., 1929.

Pratt, Edward K. "Marcus T. Reynolds: Albany's Elegant Eclectic Architect." *Alumni Horae* (alumni magazine of St. Paul's School, Concord, N.H.) (autumn, 1991): 160-62.

Putnam, J. Pickering. "The Apartment House." *American Architect and Building News* 27 (1890): 5.

Putnam, J. Pickering. *Architecture Under Nationalism*. Boston: Nationalist Education Association, 1890.

Rarick, Holly M. *Progressive Vision: The Planning of Downtown Cleveland 1903-1930*. Cleveland: Cleveland Museum of Art, 1986.

"Recent Bank Buildings of the United States." *Architectural Record* 25 (1909): 3-66.

Reid, Gerald, F. *150 Years, Heritage Bank, 1834-1984*. Northampton, Mass.: The Benjamin Co., 1984.

Remarks of F. G. Bascom on Addison B. Colvin, Glens Falls Rotary Club, July 2, 1970. Photocopy of typescript at Glens Falls, N.Y., Crandall Library.

Reynolds, Cuyler. *Albany Chronicles, A History of the City Arranged Chronologically*. Albany: J.B. Lyon Co., 1906.

Reynolds, Cuyler *Genealogical and Family History of Southern New York and the Hudson River Valley*. 3 vol. New York: Lewis Historical Publishing Co., 1914.

Reynolds, Cuyler. *Hudson-Mohawk Genealogical and Family Memoirs*. 4 vol. New York: Lewis Historical Publishing Co., 1911.

Reynolds, Helen Wilkinson. *Dutch Houses in the Hudson Valley Before 1776*, introduction by Franklin D. Roosevelt. 1929. Reprint. New York: Dover Publications, 1965.

Reynolds, Kenneth G., Jr. "Marcus T. Reynolds (1869-1937)," in *Albany Architects Look at the Past*, 19-21. Albany: Historic Albany Foundation, 1978.

Reynolds, Marion H. *The History and Descendancy of John & Sarah Reynolds*. Brooklyn: Reynolds Family Association, 1924.

Reynolds, Marcus T. "The Housing of the Poor in American Cities." Prize Essay of the American Economic Association for 1892, *Publication of the American Economic Association* 8 (2 & 3) (1893): 135-262.

Reynolds, Marcus T. "The Colonial Buildings of Rensselaerwyck." *Architectural Record* 4 (1894-95): 415-38.

Reynolds, Marcus T. "The Villas of Rome." *Architectural Record* 6 (1896-97): 256-88.

Reynolds, Marcus T. "The Villas of Rome, Part II." *Architectural Record* 7 (1897-98): 1-32.

Reynolds, Marcus T. Diaries, 1899-1937. McKinney Library, Albany Institute of History and Art.

Reynolds, Marcus T. "Office Building for the Delaware & Hudson Company." *The American Architect* 107 (1915): 383-6.

Reynolds, Marcus T. "The Plaza at Albany, N.Y." *Architecture* 37 (1918): 164-67.

Reynolds, Marcus T. "Clear Space Needed Back of Capitol Site to Show Real Beauty of State Buildings." *Knickerbocker Press*, Sept. 28, 1919, 2.

Reynolds, Marcus T. Letter to W.S.B. Hopkins, June 20, 1934.

Rhoads, William B. *The Colonial Revival*. 2 vols. New York and London: Garland Publishing, Inc., 1977)

Rhoads, William B. "The Colonial Revival and the Americanization of Immigrants" in *The Colonial Revival in America*, Alan Axelrod, ed., 341-61. New York and London: W. W. Norton & Co., 1985.

Riis, Jacob A. *How the Other Half Lives, Studies among the Tenements of New York.* New York: Scribners, 1890.

Rice, Norman S. "Living with Antiques, the Hudson Valley Home of Mrs. Henry Sage." *Antiques* (December, 1965): 806-11.

Roberts, Ann Rockefeller. *Mr. Rockefeller's Roads, The Untold Story of Acadia's Carriage Roads & Their Creator.* Camden, Maine: Down East Books, 1990.

Robinson, Frank S. *Albany's O'Connell Machine, An American Political Relic.* Albany: The Washington Park Spirit, Inc., 1973.

Rohdenburg, Theodore K. *A History of the School of Architecture, Columbia University.* New York: Columbia Univ. Press, 1954.

Root, Edward W. *Philip Hooker, A Contribution to the Study of the Renaissance in America.* New York: Charles Scribner's Sons, 1929.

Roth, Leland M. *The Architecture of McKim, Mead & White, A Building List* . New York: Garland Publishing, Inc., 1978.

Roth, Leland M. *McKim, Mead & White, Architects.* New York: Harper & Row, 1983.

Samuel Fessenden Clarke, As Revealed in Some of his Writings , compiled by C.B.S. [Mrs. Harold Stimpson]. New York: The Marchbanks Press, 1932.

Sawyer, Philip. "The Planning of Bank Buildings." *The Architectural Review* 12 (1905): 24-31.

Schoelwer, Susan Prendergast. "Curious Relics and Quaint Scenes: The Colonial Revival at Chicago's Great Fair," in *The Colonial Revival in America*, Alan Axelrod, ed., 184-216. New York and London: W. W. Norton & Co., 1985.

Schultz, Stanley K. *Constructing Urban Culture, American Cities and City Planning, 1800-1920.* Philadelphia: Temple Univ. Press, 1989.

Schuyler, Montgomery. *American Architecture and Other Writings.* Cambridge: Belknap Press of Harvard University Press, 1961.

Schuyler, Montgomery "A History of Old Colonial Architecture." *Architectural Record* 4 (1894): 95, 312-66.

Schuyler, Montgomery "Last Words About the World's Fair." *Architectural Record* 3, 1893-94, 293 and 298.

Schuyler, Montgomery. "A Picturesque Sky-scraper." *Architectural Record* 5 (1895-1896): 299-302.

Schuyler, Montgomery. "Russell Sturgis." *Architectural Record* 25 (1909): 146, 220.

Schuyler, Montgomery "Russell Sturgis's Architecture." *Architectural Record* 25 (1909): 404-10.

Schuyler, Montgomery "The Sky-scraper up to Date." *Architectural Record* 8 (1899): 231-57.

Schuyler, Montgomery. "State Buildings at the World's Fair." *The American Architect* (Jan. 2, 1892): 10.

Scully, Vincent. *The Architecture of the American Summer, The Flowering of the Shingle Style* . New York: Rizzoli, 1989.

Scully, Vincent. *The Shingle Style.* New Haven: Yale Univ. Press, 1955.

Severini, Lois. *The Architecture of Finance: Early Wall Street.* Ann Arbor: UMI Research Press, 1983.

Shaughnessy, Jim.. *Delaware and Hudson.* Berkeley, Cal.: Howell-North Books, 1967.

Shultz, William J., and M. R. Caine. *Financial Development of the United State.* New York: Prentice-Hall, Inc., 1937.

Stern, Robert A. M., Gregory Gilmartin and John Montague Massengale. *New York 1900: Metropolitan Architecture and Urbanism 1890-1915.* New York: Rizzoli, 1983.

Stevens, Frank Walker. *The Beginning of the New York Central Railroad, A History.* New York: G. P. Putnam's Sons, 1926.

Stevens, Frederic B. *History of the Savngs Banks Association of the State of New York, 1894-1914* . Garden City and New York: Doubleday, Page & Co., 1915.

"The Tanners Bank at Home." [Catskill] *Recorder*, November 25, 1911.

Tarn, John Nelson. *Five Per Cent Philanthropy, An Account of Housing in Urban Areas between 1840 and 1914.* Cambridge: Cambridge Univ. Press, 1973.

Trip to Europe, "Dad" Mother and the Girls, Observations for Private Circulation Only, With the Compliments and Holiday Greetings of Yours Sincerely, Addison B. Colvin, Glens Falls, December 22, 1906. Copies at Glens Falls, N.Y., Crandall Library.

Van Rensselaer, Mrs. John King. *The Social Ladder.* New York: Henry Holt and Co., 1924.

Van Rensselaer, Mariana. "Recent Architecture in America. Public Buildings. I." *The Century Magazine* 28 (May, 1884): 48-67.

Van Rensselaer, Mariana. "Recent Architecture in America. II. Public Buildings." *The Century Magazine* 28 (July, 1884): 323-34.

Van Rensselaer, Mariana "Recent Architecture in America. III. Commercial Buildings." *The Century Magazine* 28 (August, 1884): 511-23.

Van Rensselaer, Mariana. "Recent Architecture in America. IV. Churches." *The Century Magazine* 29 (January, 1885): 323-38.

Van Rensselaer, Mariana. "Recent Architecture in America. V. City Dwellings. I." *The Century Magazine* 31 (February, 1886): 548-58.

Van Rensselaer, Mariana. "Recent Architecture in America. VI. City Dwellings. II." *The Century Magazine* 31 (March, 1886): 677-87.

Van Rensselaer, Mariana. "American Country Dwellings. I." *The Century Magazine* 32 (May, 1886): 3-20.

Van Rensselaer, Mariana. "American Country Dwellings. II." *The Century Magazine* 32 (June, 1886): 206-20.

Van Rensselaer, Mariana. "American Country Dwellings. III." *The Century Magazine* 32 (July, 1886): 421-34.

Van Rensselaer, Mariana. "The Development of American Homes." *The Forum* 12 (January, 1892): 667-76.

Van Rensselaer, Mariana *Handbook of English Cathedrals.* New York: The Century Co., 1893.

Van Santvoord, Seymour. *The House of Caesar and the Imperial Disease.* Troy, N.Y.: Pafraets Book Company, 1902.

Van Santvoord, Seymour. *Octavia, A Tale of Ancient Rome.* New York: E.P. Dutton, 1923.

Van Santvoord, Seymour. *Random Addresses.* New York: E.P. Dutton, 1930.

Waite, Diana S. *Ornmanental Ironwork, Two Centuries of Craftsmanship in Albany and Troy, New York.* Albany: Mount Ida Press, 1990.

Ward, David. *Poverty, Ethnicity, and the American City, 1840-1925.* Cambridge and New York: Cambridge University Press, 1989.

Ware, William R. *The American Vignola, The Five Orders.* Scranton: International Texbook Co., 1902.

Webster, J. Carson. *Erastus Dow Palmer.* Newark: Univ. of Delaware Press, 1983.

Weingarden, Lauren S. *Louis H. Sullivan: The Banks.* Cambridge, Mass.: MIT Press, 1987.

Welfling, Weldon. *Savings Banking in New York State.* Durham, N.C.: Duke University Press, 1939.

Wharton, Edit., *The Age of Innocence.* New York: D. Appleton & Co., 1920.

Wharton, Edith. *The Customs of the Country.* New York: Charles Scribner's Sons, 1913.

Wharton, Edith. *Italian Villas and Their Gardens.* New York: The Century Co., 1904.

White, Eugene Nelson. *The Regulation of the American Banking System, 1900-1929.* Princeton, N.J.: Princeton University Press, 1983.

Wilson, Richard Guy. *McKim, Mead & White, Architects.* New York: Rizzoli, 1983.

Wilson, Richard Guy. "Edith and Ogden: Writing, Decoration, and Architecture," in *Ogden Codman and the Decoration of Houses*, 133-84. Boston: David R. Godine, 1988.

Wilson, Richard Guy. "Architecture, Landscape, and City Planning," in Brooklyn Museum, *The American Renaissance, 1876-1917*, 75-109. New York: Pantheon Books, 1979.

Wilson, Richard Guy. "The Great Civilization," in Brooklyn Museum, *The American Renaissance, 1876-1917*, 11-70. New York: Pantheon Books, 1979.

Wilson, William H.. *The City Beautiful Movement.* Baltimore: The Johns Hopkins Univ. Press, 1989.

Wright, Frank Lloyd. "In the Cause of Architecture." *Architectural Record* 23 (March, 1908): 155-221.

Zurier, Rebecca. *The Firehouse: An Architectural and Social History.* New York: Abbeville Press, 1982.

INDEX